Silent Dilemmas of Project Managers

Solving the Existential Puzzle

Matija Radomir Djolic

berghahn
NEW YORK • OXFORD
www.berghahnbooks.com

First published in 2025 by
Berghahn Books
www.berghahnbooks.com

Library of Congress Cataloging-in-Publication Data
A C.I.P. cataloging record is available from the Library of Congress
Library of Congress Cataloging in Publication Control Number: 2024045433

British Library Cataloguing in Publication Data
A catalogue record for this book is available from the British Library

ISBN 978-1-80539-804-2 hardback
ISBN 978-1-80539-805-9 epub
ISBN 978-1-80539-806-6 web pdf

https://doi.org/10.3167/9781805398042

To my daughter ***Katarina*** and my son ***Petar***

my guardian angels

Contents

FIGURES

Introduction

The Philosophical Context

The multidisciplinary fascination with identity parallels the movement from the 'scientific management' tradition to modern post-bureaucratic practices that treat the individual as an irreducible 'building block' of any given system of organizing. This ontological emphasis on the individual is a direct outcome of the intellectual migration from positivist doctrines to a constructivist understanding of societal dynamics. At the heart of this transition lies the pre-eminence of 'meaning' as a cornerstone for deciphering social reality. Grounded in the viewpoint that social realities are *constructed* rather than intrinsic, the concept of 'meaning' thus becomes integral to identity research. This implies that in the absence of meaning, facets of the self and social phenomena become obscured because both individual understanding and collective acknowledgement rely on meaning – thus emphasizing the deep interplay between the creation of meaning and the formation of identity, as discussed by Peterson (1999).

However, the 'liberation' of self-identity from the deterministic 'confines' of positivistic epistemology also introduces new challenges. Highlighting meaning as the central aspect to interpreting sociality shifts the focus away from the plausibility of enduring and permanent aspects of the social world (and inadvertently the self) towards the situated and emergent nature of social phenomena. The impermanent nature of meaning therefore serves to instantiate an inconclusive ontology in matters of (social) discernment and interpretation. Consider, for instance, that the significance attributed to events and experiences is inherently mutable, frequently assuming diverse guises and altering its essence over a lifetime. Consequently, the identity that arises from such a pliable basis is itself transient and malleable: a divorce, initially experienced as a calamitous event, may with time be reinterpreted as a rite of passage, instrumental in forging a renewed self-conception. The shifting nature of meaning inscribed in the multiple contexts of self, the other(s) and discourses has therefore rendered futile various analytical attempts at highlighting a distinctive and enduring self: 'coherence' in matters of identity becomes an oxymoron when the meaning of things is largely dependent on 'where we sit' (Clegg 1975).

The ramifications of this fragmentary ontological perspective manifest most acutely in a diminished sense of personal agency. Given the ephemeral nature of the self-knowledge from which the meaning of individual identity claims is derived, the nexus between daily agency and an ostensibly constant 'pre-existing' self increasingly eludes clear reference. This raises a pivotal question: on what grounds do we assert any claim to 'knowledge'? Conversely, while one might argue for the enduring and impermeable character of self-knowledge, the fluidity of personal experience and the capricious dynamics of interpersonal interactions cast doubt on the validity of such assertions. Thus, in the absence of a discernible, unique self mirrored by self-expression, we turn to discourse as the final adjudicator in ascribing meaning to our being and experiences. In this context, identity is construed as an outcome of social interaction, effectively dismissing the individual's active role in the process of forming their own identity.

At this juncture, we encounter a theoretical impasse: without appealing to the notion of 'fixed' and 'permanent' characteristics within objects, entities and concepts, the inherently relative nature of the social sphere casts all precursors of self-expression into a realm that is either analytically impenetrable or ontologically ambiguous. The current identity literature therefore fails in its dissociation between the fluid nature of identity and one's choice to assume and adopt different versions of oneself. In a post-bureaucratic world, everything is subject to scrutiny and as such even our intention and willingness to take action can be rationalized simply as automatic or unselfconscious normative behaviour. Alienation of the self therefore becomes inevitable in scenarios where the individual's autonomy in attributing meaning to their experiences is diminished or removed.

The decoupling of intent from self-knowledge, or rather, the elision of the subjective precursors to daily agency, engenders an impersonal character of contextual experiences. If we accept that meaning is interwoven with discourse, then assertions of identity are, in Wittgenstein's articulation, merely a reflection of a meticulously orchestrated language game. In the context of these arguments, the meaning of things emerges from the presupposed nature of structured role relationships (such as being a father, a friend, a coworker):

I am anxious because of the onerous work arrangements, not because I perceive the work arrangements as onerous in the first instance. Extending these arguments would also suggest that everyone within the same 'onerous' work arrangements would be anxious in the same way. This decouples the objective experience from the subjective lens through which we interpret the world.

The issue inherent in this stance lies in the unwarranted dissociation between the management of adverse repercussions of burdensome work arrangements and an individual's ability to undertake actions that can both exacerbate and mitigate such consequences. In this instance, depression and anxiety become emotional states that can only be changed by way of removing oneself from the context of particular interaction, or by restructuring the arrangements in question. While this perspective may be practical in certain situations, it ultimately endorses only the reactionary aspects of agency. In this context, the concepts of self-regulation and self-management paradoxically conflict with their intended meanings. This myopic perspective holds particular relevance – and presents significant issues – within the high-pressure context of professional realms like project management, where foresight and strategic self-awareness are critical.

In light of the preceding arguments, this book is an attempt to make the subjective antecedents of situated identity positions visible. It is an attempt at illuminating the highly personal, and in turn distinctive, nature of self-identity. It will do so by considering situated experiences as intended circumstances of *internal* soliloquy without obviating the need to recognize the effects social arrangements have on delimiting and shaping the thought tendencies that precede self-expression. The book will attend to the situated implications of internal soliloquy by way of a phenomenological analysis of experiences of anxiety in project-based work arrangements. The focus on the *experiences* of anxiety is influenced by Archer (2000), who considers negative emotional experiences as a 'window' into the perceived world of the subject. In attending to the 'outliers' of everyday interaction, such as the experience of anxiety, the book therefore seeks to 'peek' into the contents of one's subjectivity to assess how such artefacts shape perception, speech and the experiences of the 'external' world.

By underscoring self-identity as a 'distinctive entity' that guides self-expression, I aim not only to illuminate the 'self-fulfilling prophecy' of established self-definitions but also to draw attention to the limiting tendencies inherent in self-referential modalities of perception. By demonstrating how adopted identities 'create problems' on the empirical level, the book develops a *critical inquiry* into identity and in doing so foregrounds the *problematic*, in addition to the precarious, nature of the phenomenon. Most importantly, however, the book highlights a way to return the responsibility for how we experience the surrounding world to the individual. Echoing the philosophy of solipsism, the arguments presented in the book offer a way out of existential dilemmas, and one that is not solely dependent on discriminating the particularity of structural arrangements, objects and processes that affect how we act and behave. In a way, the arguments presented in the book seek to empower project managers to assume responsibility for the professional worlds they *co-create*.

It is worth recognizing that identity encompasses not just the outward portrayal of self, but also the introspective narrative through which individuals conceive their existence. Suggesting that identity encompasses both who we are and how we reflect upon ourselves acknowledges that unravelling its intricacies is tantamount to solving the existential puzzle – answering the question of 'who am I?' becomes a profound journey of understanding one's place within and contribution to the tapestry of personal beliefs, societal roles and the continuous construction of self-meaning. Thus, from a theoretical standpoint, my intention with this book is to present a philosophy that transcends dualistic inclinations to conflate the self with society (or the reverse), thereby proposing an alternative to the predominantly non-humanist portrayals of the self found in postmodern discourse. Pragmatically speaking, however, the aim of the book is to delineate an *object* of existential anxiety and in doing so provide the possibility for a more self-guided process of personal development. By advocating for individuals to assume ownership of their experiences, this book provides a pathway for project managers to construct their professional environment in a manner that reinforces their self-identity. Thought-provoking to say the least, the arguments presented in the book should nonetheless come as a welcomed change to a practice (that of project management) 'consumed' by institutional isomorphism.

Chapter 1

The Becoming of Self

The Creation and Perpetuity of Identity

My Life as a Project Manager: A Reflexive Tale

> If I am I because you are you, and if you are you because I am I, then I am not I and you are not you.
>
> —Alan Watts, cited in D. Knights and C. A. Clarke, 'Pushing the Boundaries of Amnesia and Myopia'

My interest has always been captivated by the ways in which our subjective constitution both shapes and confines our day-to-day encounters and perceptions of events, of ourselves and of others. By 'experience', I refer to our conceptual and emotional 'reaction' to our interactions with the world – a highly intimate and subjective discernment of circumstances, the self and the other. 'Subjective constitution', as I use the term, denotes our personally crafted perspective of ourselves and the external milieu, the mental repository we draw upon to interpret reality and our existence within the social sphere. This repository incorporates our accumulated experiences, the knowledge derived therefrom and our self-awareness, and extends to include our aspirations that we aim to realize through our pursuits: ambitions, longings and intentions. Within the scope of this exploration, 'subjective constitution' is effectively synonymous with self-identity because any conceptualization of self-identity must necessarily encompass our past experiences, our future aspirations and our present motivations and interests (as Watson 2008 suggests). Peterson (1999: 28) concurs that the synthesis of past, present and anticipated experiences is essential in constructing a self-concept that grounds our capacity to act:

> The maps that configure our motivated behaviour have a certain comprehensible structure. They contain two fundamental and mutually interdependent poles, one *present*, the other *future*. The present is sensory experience as it is currently manifested to us – as we currently understand it – granted motivational significance according to our current knowledge and desires. The future is an image or partial image of perfection, to which we compare the present, insofar as we understand its significance.

The relationship between this subjective world and everyday experiences came to be particularly relevant in the project management organizational settings where I spent the last fifteen years of my professional career. Project managers grapple daily with stress and anxiety as they strive to meet the diverse and numerous expectations of project stakeholders. Stakeholders internal to the organization (such as colleagues, immediate supervisors and executives) expect the project manager to deliver a high-quality product, analogous to the 'image' of the organization, all the while maximizing the project's profitability, which maintains the organization's stability and competitive edge. As such, the 'destiny' of the organization and its employees is in the hands of the project manager, whose 'success' is assimilated with the success of the project. On the other hand, project managers are also required to manage expectations of clients and other project stakeholders (for example, the design team and public and council representatives) external to the organization. They are supposed to mitigate the trade-offs between design, cost and time and ensure the materialization of a concept in unpredictable live environments. To add insult to injury, no two projects are ever the same. On that note, and as suggested by Clegg and Courpasson (2004), project managers have to face the harsh reality of being only 'as good as their last project'.

The professional standing of a project manager is intricately linked to their skill in navigating a multitude of 'external factors'. For project managers, 'gatekeepers' exist on either flank of the project control group[1] – senior management representing organizational interests on one side and clients along with stakeholders shaping the design on the other. While it is ostensibly a singular project, the interests it serves are diverse; structural engineers may dismiss concerns over ergonomics or aesthetics, typically the purview of architects, who in turn might overlook the financial strain of their designs, often the predominant concern of clients. Thus, project management is not merely about adhering to deadlines and the specific requirements of a design brief. It also involves alignment with the varying visions and interests – and consequently the emotional stakes – of all parties involved in the project's life cycle. This implies that the criteria of a project manager's professional (self-)worth are far from universal, as they mirror the diverse and sometimes conflicting interests of those implicated in the project's progression.

In this regard, it could be posited that the project manager's subjective constitution is predicated upon the external perception of their ability to fulfil the complex array of 'requirements' essential for the realization of a 'successful' project. Nevertheless, given that the evaluation of an individual's skills and capabilities is contingent upon the particular needs and desires of the professional making the judgement,[2] concepts like 'success' and 'quality', as well as 'time' and 'project manager', warrant quotation marks to underscore the highly subjective nature of the definitions proffered by various project participants. Accordingly, as the constructs of skill, excellence and achievement are 'relational and activity dependent' (Archer 2003), shaped by the expectations and desires of diverse project stakeholders, it is evident that my professional journey as a project manager, alongside my professional identity and self-esteem, are considerably moulded by the interest-driven assessments of those I interact with during the entire project process. My self-perception in the professional sphere is therefore reliant on these stakeholders' experiences and evaluations of my performance, particularly when I concede to their position as the ultimate 'gatekeepers' of my 'capacity to execute'. Considering the implicit consensus that a successful project equates to a content project control group, the relinquishment of self-defined standards of success is not an unlikely dilemma in the competitive arena of professional life.

Recognizing this is akin to accepting that others' experience and perception of my performance are substantially influenced by their own personal and professional objectives, goals and desires. Following this line of argument further, it stands to reason that my self-experience as a project manager ought to be similarly moulded, at least to some degree, by my own ambitions, necessities and aspirations. This is not to say that there are no normative representations of quality and success, such as those encapsulated in the Australia's Building Code, for example. The point I am making is that interest-based decision-making also persists in the context of normative descriptions of reality such as the one reflected in the contractual arrangements between parties to a building contract. The subjective realm is our primary – and possibly sole – arena of engagement. Consequently, the stakeholders' assessments and observations of my 'performance' carry weight only if I elect to regard them as significant, justified and credible. My decision thus 'binds' me to their evaluations as long as it stems from a purpose of professional ambition, embedded within a defined normative framework dominated by a hierarchy that tends to marginalize my personal subjectivity – performance reviews being a tangible expression of this relative imposition.

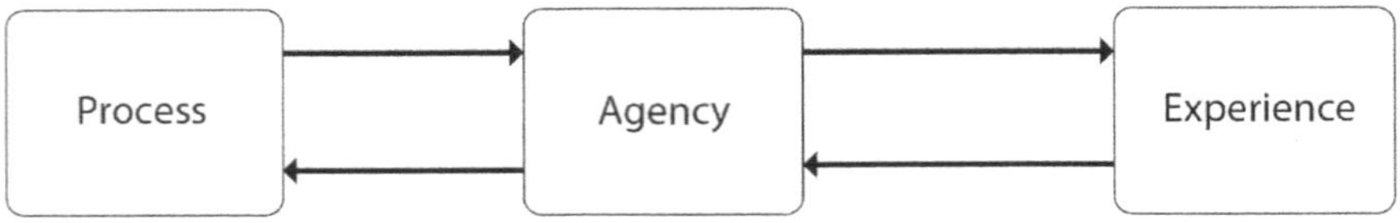

Figure 1.1. This figure highlights the relationship between our subjective constitution and our situated experiences. It suggests that our view of the world shapes how we act and what we say and in doing so affects what we experience in our interaction with others. © Matija Radomir Djolic.

It appears that my evaluation of myself, my assessment of others, and their judgements of me are all products of relative perception. These views arise in accordance with the intentions, objectives, needs and desires of the individuals doing the perceiving, rather than deriving from any intrinsic qualities of the entity being observed. In the context of these arguments, a discussion of anxiety and stress in project-based organizational settings must not exclusively be a discussion of 'onerous' working arrangements and 'unreasonable' demands of project stakeholders (see Bateson 2002). Rather, it should also be a discussion of our subjective constitution and the effect it has on providing the possibility for particular forms of perception, speech and agency[3] (see Figure 1.1 for a flow chart representation).

However, this relationship cannot be presupposed. Therefore, before we accept self-identity as a subject of interpersonal interaction, this book will first need to discern how one's subjective constitution[4] is shaped within the context of specific normative arrangements. The best way to do this would be to task ourselves with the process of identity formation and determine the extent to which the individual exercises choice in the appropriation of self-definitions. This will provide an appropriate philosophical pretext to scrutinize the relationship between one's subjective constitution, everyday speech and agency. Furthermore, it equips us to tackle the adverse repercussions arising from 'institutional isomorphism' within project-oriented environments (Baker and French 2018), doing so through a lens that is decidedly personal.

Identity Formation: An Ontological Inquiry into the Onset of Identity Formation

Delving into the nature of our personal identity demands an examination of how we come to understand ourselves within the web of social interactions. Scholarly discourse on the genesis of self-identity diverges along two distinct

philosophical trajectories: the first accentuates the individual's intrinsic capacity to craft their identity autonomously, whereas the second posits that broader social and structural contexts play a determinative role in its articulation. As noted by Brown (2018: 14):

> A range of work either implicitly or explicitly assumes that individuals have considerable agency in matters of identity … Other studies take a contrary stance and emphasise the extent to which identities are the effects of relations of power which operate variously to seduce, insinuate, insist, restrict or even coerce both people's identity options and their choices.

These divergent ontological stances on the process of identity formation have, predictably, engendered a plethora of theoretical complexities within the realm of scholarly debate. For example, on account of one's *inconsiderable* agency in matters of identity, self-identity becomes regarded as a *predicate* of social interaction, or what Brown (2018) terms 'the effect of relations of power'. In this scenario, the locus of responsibility for the emergence of individual identities is attributed to predefined role relationships, as the normative substance embedded within these contexts supplies the essential cognitive and expressive resources necessary for the development of the self. Given this framework, where the scaffolding of role relationships imparts the foundational materials for self-construction, a self-characterization could be elegantly rendered thus: 'As a project manager, my professional persona is fundamentally interwoven with my capacity for lateral thought processes and my approachable demeanour.' The same is enunciated in every project manager's job description.

The 'role identity theory' (Snow and Anderson 1987) therefore suggests that even if one recognizes one's predispositions for active choice making in the identity formation process, the attributes of the self thus appropriated are predetermined by the limiting number of possibilities provided by the normative notions of right and wrong, plausible or otherwise. As noted by Snow and Anderson (ibid.: 1366), '[this] conceptualises identity as internalised positional designations that constitute the self and that exist insofar as the person is a participant in structured role relationships' (emphasis mine). In the instance of such 'outsourced' (self-)volition, the notion of 'identity formation' becomes more sensible as identity *regulation* since 'meaning, culture or ideology are articulated by and implicated in structural configuration of control' (Alvesson and Willmott 2002: 620).

Role identity theory (Snow and Anderson 1987) thus limits the possibility of enduring aspects of self-identity and does so on account of circumscribed boundaries of various normative orders. In doing so, however, it imparts upon self-identity a fragmentary and precarious quality (Beyer and Hannah 2002;

Collinson 2003; Ibarra 1999; Kaufman and Johnson 2004). Fragmentary, since there exist innumerable 'structured role relationships' within which the individual participates (for instance, being a father, a friend, a Manchester United supporter or a tax agent). Precarious, in that what is formed in a particular context is rendered as 'obsolete' and irrelevant in other domains of life. As recognized by Knights and Clarke (2017: 341), 'history cannot be "read off" independently of current concerns, as Wittgenstein made clear in speaking about indexicality, for the meaning of any concept is tied to the context of its use, and thus to our present anxieties and preoccupations.'

The consequence of the fragmentary and precarious view of self-identity (Becker2010, 2011; Watts 1951) is that it severs the relationship between the many context-specific identities. In this instance, the identity of 'being a good father' is independent of one's professional identity. The unrelated nature of the many adopted self-notions is founded on the heterogeneity of norms 'offered' by structural arrangements within which the individual participates (for example, that of family and that of work). As such, given that self-identity is *produced* by disparate 'rules of engagement', different context-specific selves are siloed away by virtue of normative *dissociation* (Pratt et al. 2006). As recognized by Becker et al. (1961: 420) '*students do not take on a professional role while they are students*' (emphasis mine).

Normative determinists such as Parsons and Turner (1991), however, disagree with the notion of 'unrelated context-specific selves', suggesting instead that the link is one of socialization into a 'central value system'; in its Marxist mirror image, this is interpellation by a dominant ideology. Nevertheless, this perspective renders it challenging to conceive of a scenario in which individuals possess significant agency in shaping their self-identity, as emphasized by Brown (2018: 14). Within the discourse on social identity, the importance of such claims notwithstanding, both adherents of normative determinism and proponents of a fragmented epistemology tend to downplay the role of the individual's agency (Archer 2000, 2003). This is substantiated by the proposition that our self-conceptions are sculpted by manifestations of power, which categorize us within particularized identities (Knights and Clarke 2017: 338). From this perspective, self-identity is conceptualized as an epiphenomenon of prevailing structural and cultural dynamics (Knights and Clarke 2017). Yet this approach falls short of accounting for the striking heterogeneity observed among individuals within comparable spheres of life.

In light of these arguments, the complexity of understanding the relationship between being a 'socially inept, number crunching' tax agent and a ferocious 'Red Devil'[5] supporter, for example, thus becomes a case of developing an 'independent criterion of knowledge' (McHugh 1971). One could contend that the independent criterion of knowledge is mirrored in the endeavour to synthesize disparate moments and events into a coherent

continuum, thereby encapsulating the life of the subject as a whole. As affirmed by Ibarra and Barbulescu (2010: 137), 'stories are uniquely suited for making sense of ambiguous or equivocal situations because they selectively distil fragmented or contradictory experiences and information into a coherent portrait.' In this instance, identity becomes a phenomenon that is *formed* from a 'retrospective gaze' (Schutz 1945, 1967) or an organized narrative woven from the fabric of one's *life history* (Down and Reveley 2009; Ibarra and Barbulescu 2010; Watson 2008).

The 'self-portrait' is, however, highly selective and *narrow* since 'our mind *singles out certain features from the perception filed* [emphasis mine], conceiving them as well delineated things which stand out over against a more or less inarticulate background or horizon' (Schutz 1945: 535). The *narrated identity* is, as such, an 'abstraction' that can be said to invoke the self arbitrarily, for the sake of 'stabilising meaning and reality' (Knights and Clarke 2017: 338). Delving into the post-structuralist perspective (see Driver 2013; Knights and Clarke 2017), one could suggest that self-identity, once invoked, is essentially a mirage, predicated on the initial need for a referential assignment of veracity (Driver 2013) that legitimizes its abstracted form. Correspondingly, as noted previously, the evaluation of 'good project manager' status is subject to a plurality of criteria, each shaped by particular interests that discern and legitimize varying levels of performance.

We can therefore argue that the connection among distinct selves tailored to particular contexts can only be comprehensively explained through the notion of a fundamental self. As posited by Müller et al. (2022: 20), 'individuals cannot be reduced to these specific roles but must be treated as complete human beings'. Consequently, routine conduct should be perceived as an array of actions that reflects the persistent parameters of our 'intrinsic core' (Harnad and Skinner 1988). Therefore, certain contentions supporting the existence of a core self (Ashforth and Mael 1989) suggest that daily actions are preordained – an assertion that has been critiqued as untenable by numerous post-structuralist scholars (see Alvesson et al. 2008; Burr 2003; Driver 2013; Knights and Clarke 2017). The essentialist viewpoint consequently renders the notion of social transformation challenging to envision, as it constrains every action to a predetermined spectrum of potential outcomes.

Conversely, identity may be viewed as a layered construct, implying a distinction between the fundamental self and 'the identity of the I that perseveres amid its diverse experiences' (Heidegger 1953: 126). Nevertheless, this distinction becomes operative exclusively through the subject's volitional acts of decision-making. Within this framework, concepts like discretion, tact and artifice gain plausibility, as the subject opts to deploy communicative strategies that safeguard their core identity while simultaneously facilitating smooth social navigation. The faculty of 'active choice-making'

(Archer 2000, 2003, 2010) intimates that individuals, in response to the circumstances they perceive, deliberately exhibit select aspects of their identity while concurrently reserving others for private contemplation. Here, reactions to environmental stimuli are intentional rather than reflexive, resulting in the potential for innovation (and unforeseen outcomes) within the arena of social interchange.

In contradistinction to 'role identity theory', the proposition of a 'sovereign self' arises from the 'processual perspective', which accords greater weight to the agency of the self in the fabricating and affirming of identities. This view is in harmony with contemporary theoretical movements in both moral philosophy and psychology (see Snow and Anderson 1987). The 'processual perspective', therefore, imbues the identity construction process with an attribute of personal agency. As Cerulo (1997: 393) elucidates, 'identities emerge and movements ensue because … group members consciously develop offences and defences, consciously insulate, differentiate, and mark, cooperate and compete, persuade and coerce'. Acknowledging these insights, any discourse on the genesis of identity must recognize the role of individual volition (Brown 2018) in the 'adoption' of self-concepts. Within this framework, self-concepts are evaluated based on their congruity with one's self-identity. Consequently, for identity formation to be viewed as a deliberate and discerning enterprise, the existence of an observant and deliberative agent is imperative.

However, although the proponents of the processual perspective do (attempt to) celebrate the subject's capacity for active choice-making, they fail to explain how notions of social and personal change fit their arguments. For example, advocates (see Cerulo 1997; Harnad and Skinner 1988; Jung 1966) of the processual perspective suggest that '*subjective definitions imprison individuals in spheres of prescribed action and expectation*' (emphasis mine) (Cerulo 1997: 388). These observations provide little avenue for understanding how the plethora of 'subjective definitions' come to pass as 'formative forces' that delimit agency in the first instance. We can recognize that some aspect of everyday behaviour is attributed to habit. But we also must not explain away habit by suggesting that behaviour that led to its constitution came from nowhere, or that it was always present in the 'finite repository' of the self. Therefore, assigning immutable qualities to aspects of the self inadvertently reifies 'modernity' given that situated action remains contingent upon prescribed and predetermined action. On that note, arguments put forward by proponents of the processual perspective of identity formation are open to accusations of narcissism (Knights and Clarke 2017) since they leave unexplained, or deliberately ignore, the influence that 'liquid modernity' (Bauman 2000) has on *(re)formulations* of one's 'subjectivity' (Boussebaa and Brown 2017; Kuhn 2006).

The provisional character of theoretical frameworks thus sharply divides the discourse that seeks to account for the processes by which self-identity is constructed and sustained. For instance, if the concept of sovereign agency is brought into question, the individual aspect of identity is then perceived as nothing but a phantom attribute within the arena of interpersonal relations. Conversely, should identity be envisaged as cast within a definitive schema of subjective interpretations, the outcomes of interpersonal encounters are inexorably scripted through 'prescribed actions and expectations'. In a milieu where predictability prevails, social and individual transformation withers. Thus, such lines of reasoning sidestep the 'reality' that fails to reflect the immediacy of daily experience, wherein one understands oneself to be both the 'author' and 'guardian' of one's 'fate', yet simultaneously a 'participant' within the more extensive demands of societal institutions. The consequence of diminishment of the subject to normative ideals, or the ossification of the social aspect by an immutable core self, is that it positions identity either as a subject of, or as a predicate to, interpersonal interactions (Bourdieu 1990). Thus, the essence of the challenge lies in our collective challenge to suitably conceptualize the relationship between the conscious agent and systematic norms and rules without one overshadowing the other.

The Sovereign Aspect of Agency: An Ontological Inquiry into the Temporality of Identity Work

To navigate the dichotomous terrain carved by the rationale of 'identity formation', it is imperative that we further grapple with the notion of personal agency – or its absence – in sculpting one's self-identity. Advocates of identity politics, for instance, elucidate decision-making by elevating the significance of 'psychological' factors (Archer 2000, 2003). By acknowledging the interplay between 'psychic modalities' and self-articulation, they propose that our daily agency unfolds through a distinct array of cognitive (Ashforth and Mael 1989; Tajfel and Turner 1986) faculties inherent to us as individuals (Grotevant 1987). Therefore, the psychoanalytic tradition's endorsement of the 'sovereign self' has predominantly zeroed in on the mental orientations that individuals apply throughout the process of forming their identity (ibid.: 204–5) (see also Berzonsky 1989; Berman et al. 2001). Within this context, our capacity for 'personal agency' transpires through innate psychological mechanisms of 'categorization, depersonalization, and social comparison' (Brown 2017: 297).

The psychoanalytic tradition (proponents of which are Carl Jung and Jordan Peterson, among many others) is thus firm in suggesting that individuals must 'have considerable agency in matters of identity' (Brown 2018: 14).

Extending the normative determinist's arguments (Parsons and Turner 1991), psychoanalysts assert that socialization into a central values system is not a mere 'reaction' to normalizing forces of social orders. They rather argue for one's capacity to choose to act *in light of one's own personal qualities* (Giorgi and Palmisano 2017). This inadvertently limits propositions that couple social identity with 'renounced sovereignty' on the grounds of 'group-think', which presupposes a collective of ostensibly 'like-minded' individuals. As noted by Ashforth and Mael (1989: 21), 'to identify, an individual need not expend effort towards the group's goals; rather, an individual need only perceive him- or herself as psychologically intertwined with the fate of the group.' Consequently, discerning both the differences and similarities between the self and our affiliations indicates that the subject is cognizant of their own characteristics and those of the group as unique (Bateson 2002), whereby the act of (group) 'identification' emerges as a deliberate mode of self-expression. The essence of these discussions is captured poignantly in a remark attributed to Mark Twain: 'If everyone is thinking alike, then nobody is thinking.'

Counterarguments have emerged, however, contending that the plethora of cognitive processes at play tend to operate autonomously (Brown and Starkey 2000; Brown and Toyoki 2013; Gabriel 2000; Hoyer and Steyaert 2015). Within this framework, consciousness is postulated to arise as an emergent attribute of intricate chemical reactions transpiring within the cerebral realm. Consequently, the concept of the 'mind' is constrained within the confines of the cerebral domain. In such a deterministic paradigm, my capability to wield agency regarding self-identity is not intrinsically 'conscious' or consequently deliberate, but rather a result of ingrained 'habituation' (Bourdieu 1990). Here, habit denotes 'what William James termed "sequences of behaviour that have become virtually automatic" or what Giddens designated as actions that are "relatively unmotivated"' (Archer 2010: 279). Nevertheless, the habitual paradigm tends to diminish the scope for deviations, inadvertently conceding scant regard to the reality that identity routinely relies on the unpredictable and sometimes capricious 'others' for affirmation of its asserted legitimacy (Knights and Clarke 2017: 338; see also Boussebaa and Brown 2017; Kuhn 2006). The issue of unique 'conceptual content' hence persists unresolved when the premise of active choice-making is anchored in a suite of cognitive processes that yield homogeneous conclusions from various individuals.

To address the importance of distinction in the conceptual content and the supposed ability such information has in endowing the subject with power to choose, we therefore must not preclude the effect of language on the structuration of our thoughts. Theorization of self-identity and agency from without, therefore, cannot obviate the recognition of discourse in encapsulating and influencing the phenomena under examination (for instance, self-identity).

Before moving on to highlighting the implications of such a position, it is important to note that 'the use of the term "discourse" … incorporates not just language but practice too' (Burr 2002: 63). Discourse, in the context of these arguments, frames how the 'language available to us sets limits upon, or at least strongly channels, not only what we can think and say, but also what we can do or what can be done to us' (ibid.). The notion of discourse is thus taken to signify macro-social constructivism in that it extends beyond the immediate context of language use (Burr 2002). Subsequently, locating the sovereign agency argument in the domain of symbols and language cannot sidestep an attempt to scrutinize the effect that larger domains of social, cultural and institutional symbols have on subjectivity. In the context of project management, for example, statements such as 'I am a perfectionist' must not obviate consideration of norms of the 'structured role relationship' that *reward* high attention to detail. Judging by the job adverts and job descriptions, one cannot sidestep that calling oneself a 'good project manager' *must* coincide with inquisitive self-qualities. Therefore, considering that how we define ourselves can be 'borrowed' from 'contextually sanctioned normativity' (Archer 2000) suggests that arguments for 'personal power in forming one's own self-identity' are contentious, since nothing about the self can be conceived in complete isolation from the demands upon our practical accomplishments (Bateson 2002; Heidegger 1953; Sartre 2018).

The inescapability of discourse thus emerges as a principal contention against the autonomy of the individual in shaping their identity (Knights and Clarke 2017). Should every action be attributed to external influences, if our intimate aspirations and motives are subordinate to the imperatives of social assimilation, then the discernment of a clear divide between the self and the other becomes challenging to substantiate (Butler 2011; Thomas and Davies 2005; Trethewey 1999; Weedon 1987). As confirmed by Karreman and Alvesson (2001: 63):

> Rather than following from biology, early childhood, life history and/or a set of sociological standard-sheet categories, identity is partly a temporary outcome of the powers and regulations that the subject encounters.

Given the foregoing discussion, we find ourselves imprisoned by a specific theoretical impasse: contending that everything about ourselves is reflective of personal scripts 'borrowed' from the world that surrounds us from birth does not furnish one with the understanding of how and by whom the 'external world' of discourse was thus created. Furthermore, do we play a role in the re-creation and co-creation of discourse? In the same way, unless one is to adopt a Freudian perspective that sees agency dominated by uncontrollable (biological) urges (Jung 1933), conceptualizing everyday behaviour as a mere reflection of habit says little about the origin of involuntary 'programmes' and memorized behaviour(s). More importantly, once these are created, what (or who) is it that makes them so entrenched and enduring? Confronted with these predicaments, envisioning discretionary and autonomous agency becomes challenging within an analytical framework that, on one side, underscores the foundational role of discourse (Alvesson and Willmott 2002; Burr 2002) yet, on the other side, implies that 95 per cent of daily activity is driven by the unreflective regularity of habit (Dispenza 2012). Regardless, a meaningful exploration of self-identity seems to be in vain, as both stances estrange the individual – one through unreflective automaticity and the other by relinquishing the self to the dominion of discourse (Cerulo 1997). Thus, these enduring theoretical conflicts condense into a singular philosophical debate: one struggling to account for a self-aware actor without confining them to 'spheres of prescribed action and expectation' (ibid.: 388). This is also recognized by Down and Reveley (2009: 382), who note that 'a pivotal point of contention has been the extent to which human agency shapes self-identity in the context of wider discourses and other social structures'.

A different path through the deadlock of these conflicting arguments might involve examining the 'retentive' and 'protentive' facets of situated agency (Dostal 1993).[6] The notion of *identity work* attempts to communicate how such epistemologically varied content influences the construction of identity. Identity work, for example, 'refers to *people being engaged in* [emphasis mine] forming, repairing, maintaining, strengthening or revising the constructions that are productive of a sense of coherence [and distinctiveness]' (Sveningsson and Alvesson 2003: 1165). Identity work portrays agency as an arrangement of 'situational stratagems' (Down and Reveley 2009) aimed at reducing inconsistencies in the (perceived) unity of the self. The definition of identity work thus suggests that action is a purposeful enactment aimed at self-realization. Subsequently, the notion of identity work does not exclusively promote the 'internal self-focused process' (ibid.: 384) of identity formation, but also seeks to address the 'ongoing cyclical interaction between [self] narration *and action*' (emphasis mine) (Ezzy 1998: 251). As such, notwithstanding that 'objectivity' of self-identity might be difficult to sustain with the inconclusive and impermanent nature of language, the identity work arguments do not discount the *foresight* of positioning ourselves in the 'world of discourse' *in accord with our self-perception*. As aptly asserted by Down and Reveley (2009: 383), 'the concept of identity work accommodates the agential powers of *identity seeking* [emphasis mine] individuals'.

On that note, it can be argued that agency is a phenomenally different form of self-expression to speech. Contrary to Foucault's (1980) claims that nothing exists outside of discourse, we could suggest that there is a distinction between the process of *self-narration*, or what is regularly referred to as narrative self-identity, and that of *dramaturgical* identity work, that is, identity work performed in face-to-face interactions (Down and Reveley 2009). On the one hand, narrated self-identity cannot avoid being 'translated into academic universes of discourse' (Archer 2010: 291) given that it must draw on context-specific language games to permit sense-making to take place. Conversely, given that daily enactments of identity are suffused with personal stakes – which inherently relate to competitive conduct – the self as manifested in actions maintains a nuanced correspondence with the context-dependent language games. This is because the ontology of situated action may be rooted in motivations that surpass the norms of the immediate context. The very presence of 'irrational behaviour' corroborates the credibility of these assertions. For example, one can choose to act in a particular way to be better positioned for a 'promotion', while another's reason for action can be underpinned by the desire to be a 'good father'.[7] As noted by Heidegger (1953: 46), 'every idea of a "subject" – unless refined by a previous ontological determination of its basic character – still posits the subjectum ontologically along with it, no matter how energetic are one's ontic protestations against the "substantial soul" or the "reifications of consciousness"'.

On this matter, although the concepts of 'promotion' and 'good father' may be understood through discourse, and acknowledging that work and family contexts are not distinctly separable, it is imperative to recognize that the idea of dramaturgical identity work posits action as a deliberate performance, initiated by a defined and premeditated concept of the desired outcome held by the 'identity-seeking individual'. Venturing further into this discourse, one might assert a similar stance regarding self-narration, as it too must stem from intention – a need to thoroughly engage with the 'who am I?' inquiry, whether posed internally or by external parties. To that extent, everything brought into existence must have an originator, else every word spoken or deed undertaken carries undertones of the miraculous. This perspective suggests that certain dimensions of agency are deeply personal, analogous to epiphanies, contemplations or bursts of inspiration. The dramaturgical model illuminates that actions are born from subjective considerations that envelop the unique conception of the self, encompassing what the 'self' desires and the particular impression of others with whom this self interacts. These conceptions shape our behaviours; or to rephrase, they are mirrored in how we conduct ourselves.

Nevertheless, the subjective content encapsulating the retentive and protentive elements of agency distinguishes itself not merely by targeting a personal, pragmatic outcome. Asserting that agency is intentional does not by itself carve out a clear and autonomous subject, for, as Porpora (1989: 197) suggests, 'the causal forces of interests are likewise entrenched in structured role relationships'. Take, for instance, project management: the commitment to finish a project on time and within budget might reflect an individual's ambition yet simultaneously represent an organizational mandate, which then calls into question the autonomy and uniqueness of an agency geared towards achieving such goals. Thus, intentional agency could denote a conscious and independent actor only as far as it operates because of a perceived divergence between one's own needs and those of others, between personal aspirations and the (perceived) demands of the prevailing normative framework. This distinction can only emerge if two project managers harbour divergent overarching ambitions. Consider a scenario wherein the pursuit of meeting (project management) KPIs (key performance indicators) is fuelled by a desire to dispel others' doubts for one person, while for another, the motivation lies in the promise of a salary increase or promotion. In both scenarios, their intentionality is tethered to the regulations encompassing their professional roles within the organization; yet their foundational ontologies are notably particular, as they envelop the unique 'life histories' (Watson 2008) of the individuals. On one side, an individual attributes value to personal advancement through competitive interactions, and on the other, the focus is on financial security and professional stature.

Pursuing this train of thought, it becomes necessary to contemplate not solely the purpose behind executing a task, but further, the rationale for performing it in a particular manner. It is within the dialectic of what is 'mandated' by structured role expectations and what, in light of such mandates, is nonetheless aspired to and actualized by the individual that one can begin to discern the unique subject. The theoretical import of this stance lies in affirming the existence of a subject whose situated identity manifestations – though they may appear disparate – deliberately strive towards crafting a 'coherent and distinctive notion of personal self-identity' (Watson 2008: 129). Even if this concept seems nebulous, it exerts a tangible influence as it shapes the parameters of agency through its envisioned objectives. Consequently, it stands to reason that it characterizes a conscious entity capable of exercising (a sovereign) choice – that is, capable of recognizing and interpreting itself and others, and of making decisions informed by such discernment.

Moreover, the unique nature of everyday actions, alongside their intricate prior rationalizations, implies the presence of a continual interchange between a singular subject and the structuring influence of established norms. This dialogue not only affords the potential for distinct subjective content but also indicates that only through a dialectical interplay between subjects, or between a subject and an object, can the evolving epistemology of 'before' and 'after' (Fairclough 1993, 2013; Silverman 2013; see also Berger and Luckmann 1991) manifest, thus leading to alterations in our sense-making and modes of self-expression. As acknowledged by Burr (2003: 185), 'humans continually construct the social world, which then becomes a reality to which they must respond'. The import of the 'before' and 'after' in the context of situated identity positions thus hints at the mutability of social phenomena, given that agency could not possess retentive and protentive characteristics if the content exchanged or internalized were to remain eternally unchanged. Crucially, this perspective acknowledges that alterations in an individual's subjective framework do not exclude concurrent shifts within dominant discourses, thereby suggesting that the dynamic between self and society (or self and the other) should be comprehended without resorting to a causality that results in the estrangement of either the self or society.

The constant flux or the trade of (pre-established) subjective content during interpersonal interactions therefore indicates that temporality is an essential quality intrinsic to the process of identity formation. A typical example of the contrary is reflected in claims made by Alvesson et al. (2008: 15), who suggest that people can be seen to engage in practical accomplishment of identity when the *routinized* reproduction of a self-identity is *discontinued* at times of pressures and uncertainty. While it may appear trivial upon initial observation, within this context normative expectations are instrumental in shaping self-identity. However, adopting this argument inherently places the normative structure as ontologically preceding the individual, thereby transforming their interaction into a relationship dictated by causation rather than dialogue. Such a viewpoint undervalues the importance of the retentive components of agency, thereby inadvertently negating the feasibility of continuous and deliberate 'strategizing'. As a result of being attributed to unforeseen shifts in structural contexts, this outlook effectively denies the individual the ability to develop foresight and intentionality – a proficiency typically garnered through learning and experience. As aptly described by Archer (2010: 274), 'what is missed inter alia by such co-determinism is the double morphogenesis in which actors themselves change in the very process of actively pursuing changes in the social order'.

Consequently, if our inquiry narrowly fixates on the results of situated interactions to affirm the existence of a coherent and distinctive self, we inadvertently undervalue the foundation of the antecedent subject. The predicament inherent in this analytic orientation is that it engenders a propensity towards reductionism in social theory. Particularly, an emphasis on the constructive aspects of situated engagements (Ahuja et al. 2018; Beech et al. 2016) overlooks the critical need to consider how 'tensions' and normative imperatives initially emerge as significant to the subject. Within such a narrowly tailored perspective, structures keep acting upon agents irrespective of agents' perception of structures. As a result, the retentive and protentive aspects of agency become merely conceptual constructs, as the absence of a conscious agent at the core of a situated decision renders the ideas of 'before' and 'after' epistemologically untenable.

The ontological polarization that emerges from such subject/object binary thinking fosters theoretical schisms concerning concepts of self and agency. Among its various consequences, the pertinence of this ontological split in light of our preceding discussion is that the subject is transfigured into a mere predicate – tenuous at best – while identity work is reduced to an intermittent, thus ostensibly atemporal, conundrum. The 'existential puzzle' concerning the nature of the self remains unresolved, as the mystery of events occurring in the gaps of episodic identity work continues to evade ontological clarity. As noted by Brown (2015: 25):

> One focal area of contention is the importance of the identity work that occurs more-or-less continuously in the course of organizational life, triggered by run-of-the-mill events … Researchers play-down the significance of this 'mundane' identity work, referring to it as automatic and instinctual, effortless and unselfconscious and as involving only minor tweaks and edits.

By failing to capture the continuous nature of 'social communication, negotiation, entrepreneurial behaviour, leading and following, decision-making, and strategizing' (Brown 2018: 11), we also capitulate to conceiving of self-identity as a phenomenon imbued within the everyday of organizational life. To avoid this, we need to appropriately address the implications of *subjective antecedents* on everyday agency, simply because the subjective world of objects and norms is, in an ontological sense, the one *first* encountered by the subject (Peterson 1999). Pushing the boundaries of these scholarly confines will, thus, enable a more nuanced comprehension of the interplay between an individual's subjective constitution, daily agency and contextual experiences amid the rigorous exigencies of project management.

Synopsis

The arguments presented thus far unveil the intricate conundrum of self-identity. Although it is employed as a means to decipher the dynamics of organization (Alvesson et al. 2008; Corlett et al. 2017; Miscenko and Day 2016; Ybema et al. 2009), both in professional realms and beyond, an absence of ontological agreement within research on self-identity calls into question the validity of the positions discussed to date. The main point of contention upon which any subsequent disagreements are ventured revolves around the credibility of the theoretical and empirical notions of the 'distinctive self-identity' (or the conscious agent) and 'intentional agency'.

On the one hand, the psychology-oriented management literature contends that the 'self is a repertoire of behaviour appropriate to a given set of contingencies' (Harnad and Skinner 1988). Such a position reifies the self in such a way that everyday agency becomes treated as an empirical manifestation of a fixed number of traits pertaining to the individual in question. The implications of such a view are that the individual retains the power of decision-making. This means that at every juncture of structural or social change there is a distinctive and sovereign individual as a 'subjectum' (of change) (Heidegger 1953). Processes such as identity formation and identity work are at the discretion of the individual who proactively shapes themselves and the surrounding environment.

There are, however, numerous shortcomings in the arguments ventured by supporters of this 'entitative' epistemology. First, by emphasizing the reified nature of one's 'psychology' by way of a fixed repertoire of behaviour, essentialists downplay the inherent malleability of self-identity that results from the unpredictable nature of social interaction(s). In this instance, the entitative epistemology does not permit *intentional agency*, since abstract deliberations have been reduced to being an epiphenomenon of a reified psyche. It is because of this that the subjective antecedents of everyday agency (Archer 2000, 2003) remain largely unexplained in the context of self-identity. The self-identity thus formed cannot be said to be in one's 'possession' since it is more of an inborn attribute than an intentionally acquired prospect.

The social constructivist and post-structuralist literature, on the other hand, goes further in explaining the complexity of everyday behaviour and the implications that shifting meaning structures have on the formation of self-identity. Much of the literature in recent years has highlighted the importance of considering the general and specific other (Brown 2017, 2018; Knights and Clarke 2017) – also represented in socially sanctioned normativity – in shaping our self-perceptions. Although a rather commanding position at one level of analysis, such a view can be considered narrow simply because it imprisons the 'search for identity' within the domain of norms, symbols and language. This realization is also supported by Brown (2017), who highlights that much of the work produced in the *Organization Studies* journal focuses primarily on discourse, drawings on contributions of Foucault, as the dominant position for analysing self-identity.[8] It is an inevitable consequence of this perspective that dissecting identity through the lenses of discourse or social norms does not negate its inherent ephemerality and dispersed character. Consequently, it challenges the coherence of identity as an enduring subject of social structures except in passing moments.

In doing so, the postmodern arguments have put into question one's sovereignty in decision-making and have subsequently placed doubt on one's level of personal causal efficacy in the identity formation process. As such, challenging the notion of *intentional agency* 'through exercises of power that constitute us' (Knights and Clarke 2017), much of the literature highlights attempts to theorize distinctive self-identity as self-defeating. Within the scope of these discussions, the self grows intensely fractionalized as agency – lacking unique self-defined measures – arises in response to the pressures of social conformity. Although such a position might explain the 'power' of modernity, it is inconceivable to dispel intentional agency simply because what we say is not plausible unless reflected in some form of 'objective' and consensual reality, whatever that might be.

Reversing the premise to avoid starting with discourse or societal norms and instead addressing the issue from the standpoint of individual subjectivity, there arises the possibility to identify 'conceptual drivers' that underpin daily agency and experience, positioning self-identity centrally within the realm of social interaction. When probing the complex terrain of self-identity, it is vital to comprehensively engage with the subject's 'interpretive repertoires', without bias towards affirming or refuting a unique self. Emphasis ought to be placed on identifying a reflective agent equipped to drive meaningful change, thereby rendering both reactive and proactive behaviours as integral facets of decision-making. Absent this critical aspect, the risk emerges that the concept of self-identity could be diminished to nothing more than a heuristic device, an abstraction relegated to expounding upon individualized repositories of meaning (Clegg 1975; Driver 2013; Knights and Clarke 2017). As a result, the forthcoming arguments will concentrate on investigating the impact of subjective precursors on routine decision-making and actions.

Notes

1. The project control group (PCG) represents the individuals and their respective organizations that are involved in the design, development and construction of the project. They include the builder, the client, the design team (architects and engineers, for example) and public representatives, among many others.
2. The executives of the organization have different interests to the client and other project stakeholders. More importantly, these interests are often contradictory in nature. For example, the organization's executives want the project to make as much money as possible while the client wants to get the highest value for money ratio. This means that if any of them were to render judgement about the project manager's professional capability, they would do so from the vantage point of their interests, needs and objectives.
3. This is recognized in the literature as non-Cartesian split thinking. Cartesian split thinking is indicative of phenomenology of reduction through which one places the subject or the world in 'brackets'. It originates from Descartes but was however further developed in Husserl's phenomenology and it supports a binary relationship between the subject and the object or the subject and the world (Cohn 2002). When such thinking is considered in the context of interpersonal relations, either the self or the general or specific other assumes a dominant role in which case either the subject or the object becomes phenomenally inconsequential.

4. The terms 'subjective constitution', 'personal identity' and 'self-identity' will be used interchangeably since all are indicative of the contents of one's mind with respect to the perception of the self and the surrounding world (of others).
5. Red Devil supporters are football enthusiasts supporting the team from the English Premier League called Manchester United.
6. Any moment is what it is in virtue of what it retains from the past (retention) and what it anticipates from the future (protention) (Dostal 1993: 146).
7. In this instance, the subject equates work performance with their ability to provide for their family.
8. The study will use the term 'self-identity' because it contends that the notions of the self and identity cannot be ontologically separated by understanding the boundaries of one as different to those of the other. For this reason, the notion of self-identity encapsulates both the notion of self and the notion of identity, which are used interchangeably in the previous and following pages.

Chapter 2

The Purposefulness of the Autonomous Subject

Self-Critical Identity Work

In light of previous discussions, an alternative approach to understanding the interplay between self-identity, everyday agency and situated experience – without rendering the external environment as fixed – would be to examine agency and the daily construction of identity through the lens of their subjective origins. To refine this further, by shifting the nexus of structure and agency to the realm of inner dialogue, one is afforded the chance to assess how normative pressures shape self-perception, all the while preserving the reflexive prerequisite of autonomy (Archer 2000, 2003). For instance, an introspective analysis of our thoughts, responses and motivations before, during and after actions enables us to recognize potential differences between our rationales for actions and those attributed to others. By integrating situated identity claims with our interpretative frameworks, we inadvertently merge the psychological with the discursive in the pursuit of self-understanding, acknowledging that the reflexive experience of being-in-the-world necessarily encompasses both subjective and intersubjective dynamics (Archer 2000, 2003). It is crucial, however, to start by comprehending one's subjective make-up to grasp the effect that intersubjective interactions have on shaping one's self-perception. Ultimately, discerning the existence and nature of a unique and self-determining subject requires an incisive exploration into the intricacies of individual subjectivity to distinguish between the authenticity of our own thoughts and the degree to which they are shaped or echoed from the wider spectrum of societal thoughts and ideas. This inquiry leads to a pivotal question: if the self does indeed exist, at what juncture can we pinpoint its inception?

I maintain that a fruitful approach to this inquiry involves immersing oneself in the emotional undercurrents of the subject's experience. The clearest manifestations of these 'concealed' (subjective) processes often emerge during episodes of self-critique in the context of observation and dialogue (Brown 2015, 2017, 2018; Ellis and Ybema 2010; Marks and O'Mahoney 2014). Within this framework, we can acknowledge negative emotions like fear and anxiety as pivotal to the formulation of conscious intent, influencing alterations in our self-identity, daily behaviours or discourse. The act of regarding emotions as 'inputs' for self-expression is crucial as it suggests the presence of underlying determinants that precede and shape situated action (Panksepp 2005). These poignant (Ahuja et al. 2018) facets of agency reinvigorate the potential for intentional decision-making within the framework of everyday life, and they do so by illuminating the individual who makes choices, possibly to their own detriment, in the name of an aspirational self (see Figure 2.1).

However, in positing that an emotional response is an antecedent to action, it is critical not to overlook the catalysts of such emotional states. For instance, can one's agency be considered truly autonomous, or emerging spontaneously, if the 'psychological reflections' that lay the groundwork for everyday actions are instigated by the individual's emotional responses to external stimuli? More pointedly, what does it mean for our understanding of agency if emotions are merely seen as reactions to external triggers? These probing inquiries call for an in-depth examination of the intricate relationship between individuality and sociality, with the objective of identifying the roots of origination – be it related to cognition, behaviour or the self in its fullness. Consequently, a more sophisticated explanation is needed, particularly since existing scholarly discussions often presuppose external influences as a priori determinants.

For example, Ahuja et al. (2018: 1002) underline how 'cynical and self-depreciating emotional talk of CAD monkeys[1] constituted a pejorative identity that expressed feelings of frustration, isolation and disillusionment'. Conversely, Gill (2013: 309) contends that the forces of foresight and anticipation act as catalysts for behaviour, positing that the potential of 'losing a valued status in the social hierarchy' provokes an emotional reaction, which in turn fuels the (re)shaping of an individual's self-identity to avert an existential 'loss of self'. In both cases, the surfacing of emotions signifies a reaction to either the 'unreasonable' expectations of norms or the 'esteemed' ranks within a professional context. It implies that feelings of 'frustration, isolation and disillusionment' are common responses to rigid and enduring organizational

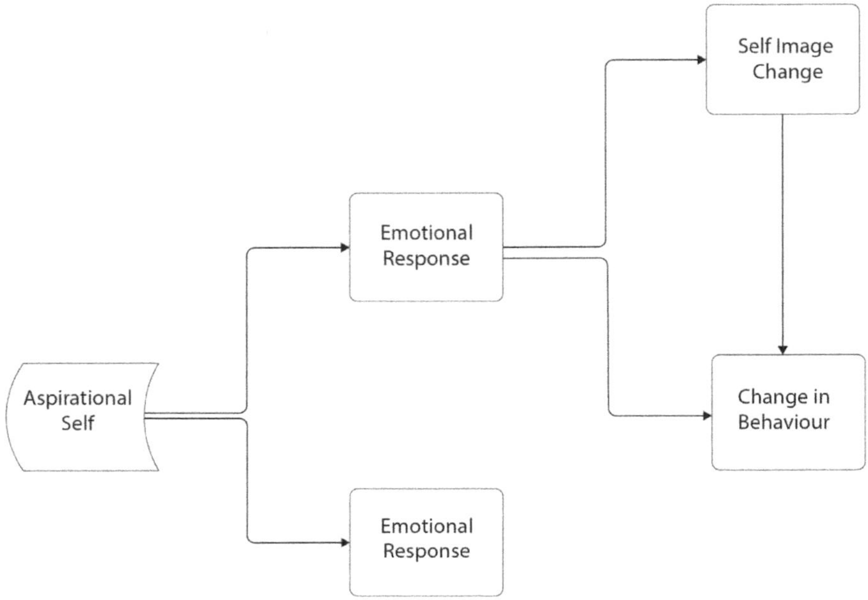

Figure 2.1. This figure demonstrates that our emotional responses to interactions with others in the world serve as markers that our aspirational self is under threat. For example, the experience of anxiety is a signal that our view of the world and views of the self are being challenged. Such experiences allow us to thereafter adjust our behaviour so that our desired self-image is also reflected in our daily actions. © Matija Radomir Djolic.

structures, just as a specific status within social hierarchy might universally hold value. Consequently, these analyses direct focus to the innate aspirations or perceived risks inherent in professional roles, inadvertently obscuring the interpretative schemas that shape the individual's perception of 'purpose' and 'threats'. This is evident in the following observation made by Ahuja et al. (2018: 993):

> We conceptualise emotions as discursive *resources* [emphasis mine] for junior professionals' identity work, as they seek to navigate discrepancies between idealised notions of professional identity and their situated experiences of work.

Thus, the inquiry persists – can we assert that the normative expectations of a specific professional milieu are universally 'unreasonable' based on the perception of a single person, or are such expectations perceived uniquely by each individual subject to their own interpretive lens? Further elaboration on this topic is forthcoming, but at this juncture, it is important to acknowledge that while some theories support a layered ontology of context-bound self-expression – by mapping a sequence from norms to emotions to psychological contemplations to speech – they do so by ascribing a primary ontological status to the normative framework, or intersubjectivity, over an individual's *perception* of 'norms' and 'order' (Bardon and Josserand 2010; Bardon et al. 2012; Winkler 2018). Moving beyond this deadlock, we must therefore acknowledge that our perception of the external realm does not provide 'a veridical representation of its structure' (Fields et al. 2017: 187), but is instead a projection of our most deeply held concerns. By extension, just as a tree falling in an uninhabited forest makes no sound, normative imperatives attain anthropomorphic qualities simply because the individual assigns value to what they represent (Archer 2000, 2003; Marks and O'Mahoney 2014). As suggested by Archer (2000: 230–31):

> The emotions stand neither in the role of the Freudian Superego nor of the Id: *they retain their part as commentaries upon something other than themselves* [emphasis mine] … And this is how it must be, for the whole purpose of the [internal] dialogue is to *define what we care about most and to* which we believe we can dedicate ourselves [emphasis mine].

Neglecting the ontological importance of personal concerns, as Archer (2000) puts it – what the individual holds as important – tends to demote nuanced self-expression to an overemphasized domain of unreflective response (Alvesson and Willmott 2002; Snow and Anderson 1987; Sveningsson and Alvesson 2003; Watson 2008). The most grievous implication of this is that it diminishes the *emergent*, and therefore personal, nature of decision-making (Archer 2003). Take, for instance, the investigation into the perspectives of junior architects (Ahuja et al. 2018), which starts primarily with the examination of 'emotional narratives'. This sets up the framework of 'disheartening' and 'devaluing' work conditions as a presupposed starting point. In such a scenario, any adverse emotional impacts stemming from these pre-established conditions are likewise treated as given, leaving no room for individuals within the field to navigate and ameliorate their emotional experiences. As aptly argued by Archer (2003: 94), '*the personal cause efficacy* (emphasis mine) of our deliberations cannot be taken over by the forces of 'socialisation': this would be to replace the power of the person by the power of the society.' This one-directional interplay between the self and the structural framework objectivizes the existing work conditions by 'bracketing' (Husserl 1982) anything that precedes 'emotional discourse', effectively rendering it as indeterminate or beyond ontological reach.

Considering the foregoing discussion, it is possible to propose an alternative perspective: the ideas of 'dejected selves' (Ahuja et al. 2018) or 'self-questioning selves' (Beech et al. 2016) can be interpreted as strategies of superimposed self-validation, designed to protect individuals' preferred conceptions of themselves. This line of reasoning indicates that an instance of speech can serve dual purposes: it can be an exercise in self-inquiry as well as an occasion for self-confirmation. Take, for instance, the situation of 'dejected selves' (Ahuja et al. 2018), in which the disparaging dialogue regarding junior architects as 'CAD monkeys' might be interpreted as an effort to differentiate oneself from peers. In this act of 'recognition', the individual effectively elevates themselves above the collective typified by this notion of professional denigration. Such an interpretation would thus position the newly introduced 'CAD monkeys' discourse as a strategy for aligning, as opposed to distancing, the person entertaining such observations with the *ideal* of becoming a 'starchitect'. Challenging this view, the acts of self-questioning and self-critique in which junior architects (Ahuja et al. 2018) or independent musicians (Beech et al. 2016) partake could be characterized as 'non-dialogical'. This is because the articulated word would not arise from a 'subjective platform' that describes the specific social conditions of their existence from a unique perspective (Caetano 2014, 2016). As a result, engaging in self-criticism (Ahuja et al. 2018; Beech et al. 2016) entails a kind of meta-reflexivity (Archer 2003), demanding a reflexive examination of one's internal dialogues. Authentic self-reflection prompts questions such as: 'Do I critique existing work setups to assert my own superiority? Am I motivated by a sense of greater competence compared to my peers? Do I genuinely fit the label of "junior"?' (ibid.). The one-dimensionality of the 'discursive focus' thus cannot but position the 'starchitect' identity as an a priori property of any context populated by architects, for example. However, in truth, individual aspirations are never uniform.

Furthermore, the inherent dialogue central to introspective criticism is not considered by Beech et al. (2016), leaving unexplored whether the identity 'demanded' in the indie music scene propels an acceptance of instability in pursuit of the esteemed (Heidegger 1953) ideal of creativity. If this perspective holds merit, it suggests that the 'challenges' faced by indie musicians, as described by Beech et al. (2016), might be self-imposed in the service of creative expression more than as a method of distancing themselves from the rigorous demands of the music industry, often expressed through acts of 'rebellion' to 'shield the fragile self' (Ahuja et al. 2018: 1003). This interpretation reframes episodes of self-questioning not as manifestations of conflict or a reflection of a disheartened self (Ahuja et al. 2018), but rather as exercises in self-inquiry aimed at self-actualization – a demonstration of reflexive agency set against the backdrop of 'the particular social conditions of existence'.

Although only a side note to their contribution, these arguments are implicit in the following statement made by Beech et al. (2016: 509):

> The indie musicians in our study invest so much of their sense of self into their work … They fall into self-doubt and deliberately step into self-critique in these processes. However unpleasant, frustrating and infuriating at times, for their sense of who they are, the struggle is essential, not the outcome.

The prior discussions lead to the conclusion that verbal utterances should not be relegated to a uniform 'consensual interpretation' of reality, a conflation that would oversimplify the rich complexity of knowledge (epistemology) by equating it with the nature of being (ontology). Rather, the spoken word should be acknowledged as a 'multidimensional' construct, where the expressed sentiments may carry one significance for the listener and another, potentially divergent, for the speaker. The acknowledgement of the potential for duplicity – as humans are indeed capable of deceit – enables a nuanced interpretation of agency. It recognizes that outward conformity expressed through speech might be a tactical choice, one that belies the speaker's true thoughts and demonstrates a discerning engagement with the surrounding norms. As noted by Archer (2003: 95), 'the problem here is to retrieve a strong enough person (who is also a social self) such that she can conceive of projects within society and also deliberate about the conditions of their relations, without society orchestrating the discussion from within'. Therefore, the argument maintains that in order to explore agency in light of its subjective origins and to understand the dynamic between self-identity, everyday agency and situated experience, it is imperative to engage with the issue of reflexivity and its influence on daily conduct. By addressing this dimension, we are granted the possibility of identifying a unique subject, a consideration that is indispensable for any meaningful discourse on an individual's existential quandaries.

The Problematic of Reflexivity in Self-Identity

The foregoing arguments challenge the binary view of self-expression, such as speech being either self-affirming or self-questioning. This oversimplified dichotomy, while it might appear trivial, effectively diminishes individual agency by not recognizing speech as a product of interpretive repertoires that allow a person to articulate one thing while intending something entirely different. Ignoring the role of reflexivity leads to two significant repercussions: it frees individuals from the burden of internal 'dialogue', and instead situates society as the substitute, internal interlocutor (Archer 2003).

'This undoubtedly gives us a dialogical partner within the inner conversation, but at the high price that it ceases to be ourselves to whom we are talking' (ibid.: 95). Outsourcing the dialogical 'axis' effectively transforms individuals into 'monological' subjects, limited to basic reflexivity. An individual functioning under such a constraint might resolutely declare: thus, I am certain of what I know, and equally certain that I am aware of this knowledge (ibid.: 97), with the added conviction that this knowledge is universally applicable. Crucially, situating society as the internal conversational partner subjects the process of self-development and self-critique to the authoritative approval of the 'generalized other' (Archer 2003; Heidegger 1953). Consequently, the significance of personal agency in the growth of 'self-knowledge' is diminished, as the notion of individual causality gives way to the primacy of social determinants (Archer 2003). This shift replaces the 'uncritical' self with an externally critical 'other'. In this instance, 'we become the *trager* [bearer or carrier] of society rather than active and deliberative agents who are ultimately the makers of society' (ibid.: 94). From a theoretical standpoint, this implies that variations in meaning are attributed solely to linguistic misconceptions and miscommunication, rather than being considered the result of accurately or inaccurately representing one's patterns of thought (Archer 2003). As noted by Marks and O'Mahoney (2014: 67):

> as a strong discursive approach dissolves all notions of the individual into language games, it generates an anti-humanism which is impotent in explaining how resistance is possible in the face of discourses generated by organisations, professions, or governments.

The problematic of the monological subject is therefore rooted in the inadequate formulation of *reflexivity*, which began with Immanuel Kant (Kant and Meiklejohn 2018) and Auguste Comte (1830). Both Kant and Comte argue for the impossibility of one simultaneously being an observing subject and the object of observation. As noted by Kant (Smith 2008: 73):

> That I am conscious of myself is a thought that already contains a twofold self, the I as a subject and the I as object. How it might be possible for the I that I think to be an object (of intuition) for me, one that enables me to distinguish me from myself, is absolutely impossible to explain, even though it is an indubitable fact.

In support of these claims, Comte (1830: 34–38) further notes:

> The thinker cannot divide himself into two, of whom one reasons while the other observes him reason. The organ observed and the organ observing being, in this case, identical, how could observation take place?

Acknowledging the insight of these scholars, it must be recognized that self-development is fundamentally predicated on reflexive self-scrutiny, with the goal of diminishing the occurrence and severity of 'strains', 'tensions' and 'surprises' (Brown 2015) that define the volatile character of social interactions (Archer 2003). This argument is aptly supported by Archer (ibid.: 95–96), who states:

> In a nutshell, if I am to have any self-knowledge, I have to be both the one who knows something, but also the one who knows that she knows that – and can thus report it to herself ... If we could not fulfil both roles, then we would be self-blind like Sydney Shoemaker's George, who believed and desired certain things but was incapable of knowing that he did so. This makes him non-functioning because he cannot shape the thought 'I want X' to himself – he can only produce such a sentence by imitating others. Without the capacity to be both subject and object to himself, he becomes his own worst enemy, since he cannot know his own wants and thus pursue them.

Therefore, Archer (2003) offers a resolution to the dilemma of reflexivity (and the sovereignty of the subject) by proposing that the multilayered ontology of situated action hinges fundamentally on the importance of internal dialogue. This posits that the intersection of agency and structure originates within our minds, or more precisely, that the singular realm where agency interacts with structure is within the cognitive landscape of our thoughts. More specifically, as explained by Archer (ibid.), (1) situated agency is 'tied' to the (2) ongoing nature of the internal commentary whose purpose is to assess the (3) surrounding environment in light of the need to preserve one's most (4) valued *concerns* (see also Archer 2010; Archer et al. 2015) (see Figure 2.2 for a procedural representation).

Thus, these arguments propose that the external environment is perceived through a filter of one's personal preoccupations, the substance of which frames the immediate context that the individual experiences. Furthermore, within this framework, the emotional impetus for action is derived from perceptions that endeavour to safeguard one's established 'hierarchy of values'. In this manner, the external world continues to exist but with a specificity and relevance tailored to the perceiving subject, without disregarding the subject's capacity to act in ways not readily explicable by the norms and regulations of the immediate situation. Here, the interaction between the world and the mind is more accurately characterized as a dialogical exchange. As further noted by Archer (2000: 94):

> The 'internal conversation' is a personal emergent property (PEP) rather than a psychological 'faculty' of people, meaning some intrinsic human disposition. This is because; inner conversations are *relational properties* [emphasis in the

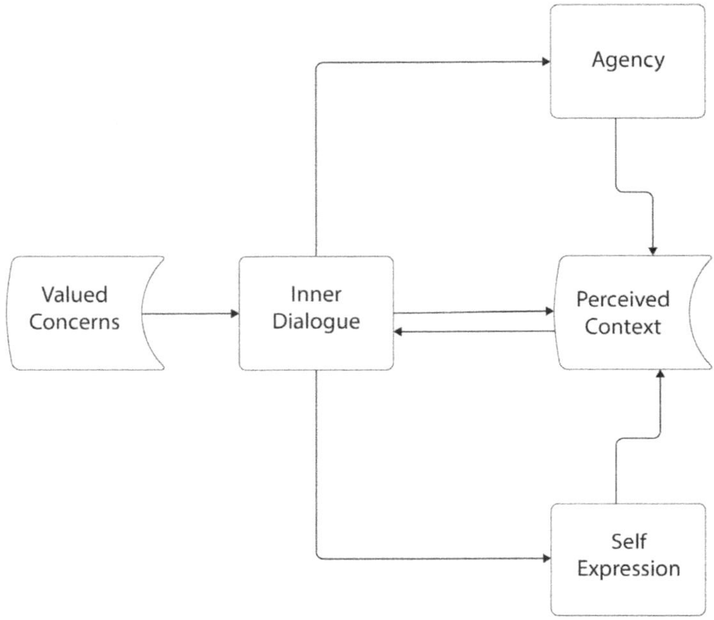

Figure 2.2. This figure demonstrates that the inner dialogue mediates the relationship between our most valued concerns and the external world. Our most valued concerns act as resources for our perception and behaviour. What we see in the external world acts as input into our reflexive assessment of the world. If the external environment is perceived as threatening our most valued concerns, we adjust our behaviour to preserve that which we care about the most. © Matija Radomir Djolic.

> original], and the relations in question are those which obtain between the mind and the world. As emergents, our 'reflexive deliberations' belong to the personal domain of activities, *especially our continuous sense of self* [emphasis mine]. Without our individual minds they would not exist, just as there could be no culture without ideas and no structure without resources.

This suggests that a particular set of subjective beliefs and preferences underpins the reflexive enactment of their principles (Archer 2000, 2003). It proposes that rather than being a passive backdrop, the external world is actually a construct of an interpretive feedback loop that shuttles between perception and action. Crucially, this loop springs from a pre-established interpretive schema, which begins with our self-concept. Despite the apparent solipsism, this perspective underscores that our engagement with the world is highly individualized. While this concept may seem self-evident, it is frequently overlooked in discourses on anxiety and depression, as attributing the genesis of such negative emotional states to the individual seems to unjustly add to their burden. Yet, despite potential initial misgivings, such insights offer a pathway to transforming the subjective framework that shapes emotional experiences. By reassigning responsibility to the individual, we also re-empower them with the autonomy to mould their own experiences.

On this account, we should comprehend situated agency by recognizing that the subject's perception of their environment is simply a reflection of their internal world, a concept grounded in reflexivity (Jung 1957). Jung (ibid.: 48) poignantly states that 'consciousness is a precondition of being', and he elaborates that 'the preference for certain psychological functions leads us to select or avoid specific situations, culminating in experiences that are unique to us and distinct from the experiences of others' (Jung 1933: 88). Consequently, any exploration of situated experiences, including within project management, ought to consider the subjectively constituted 'social conditions of existence' that give rise to particular experiences. This approach acknowledges that what appears to be the inherent structure of the outside world is in fact a mirror of the subject's endeavour to sustain and prioritize what holds personal significance.

Self-Identity and the Crises of Project Management

In relation to the aforementioned discussions, how have project management practitioners and academics conceived of the relationship between situated experiences and self-identity? The reflexive tale outlined at the beginning of Chapter 2 would suggest that the context of project management provides many challenges that shape the formation of one's professional self-image and self-worth (Baker and French 2018; Clegg and Courpasson 2004; Clegg et al. 2020). This is also supported by the extant project management literature, which foregrounds the largely onerous demands placed upon project managers in fulfilling their day-to-day professional duties (Gale and Cartwright 1995; Buckle and Thomas 2003; Lindgren and Packendorff 2006; Chasserio and Legault 2009, 2010; French et al. 2013). The 'time pressure, expectations from many stakeholders, project assignments combined with tasks employees have in their regular position in their base organisation' (Clegg et al. 2020: 462) come to be positioned as factors that induce high levels of role ambiguity and uncertainty. As previously asserted by Clegg and Courpasson (2004), project managers are only as good as their last project. Given the endemic pressure and uncertainty inherent in the role, it can be argued that 'being' a project manager predisposes one to a state of continuous self-reflection and self-questioning (Love and Edwards 2005; Clegg et al. 2020):

> Lack of structure, unclear goals and high levels of uncertainty can put a lot of strain on the project manager in a difficult situation with regards to the progress and coordination of tasks for the project team … The project manager may be exposed to a conflicting pressure from key stakeholders who wish to influence delivery or enforce clarifications and completion. (Clegg et al. 2020: 466)

Given these arguments, the project manager's situated experiences, notions of self-worth and self-image are largely shaped by the instrumental factors of the project management professional 'tradition' (Clegg 1975). For example, Baker and French (2018: 801) discuss how institutional project-based management tactics have 'been offered as an explanation for women's career challenges in project-based organisations'. By the same token, Clegg et al. (2020: 462) suggest that the systemic scarcity of resource allocation in project management 'often causes a burden on employees and can lead to negative feelings such as stress and burnout'. Lindgren and Packendorff (2006) go further by arguing that project management work practices serve to reproduce 'lived experiences' by instantiating 'devotion to work and commitment to the profession of project management' (cited in Baker and French 2018: 801). The arguments of Lindgren and Packendorff (2006) are also acknowledged and supported by Buckle and Thomas (2003) and Collinson and Hearn (1998). Subsequently, a critical analysis of these positions might suggest that the institutional practices of project management guide and potentially limit the expression of professional individualism.

Ontologically, however, these arguments place the 'social conditions of existence' in a dominant position to personal volition and choice. By assuming a primary position in the order of being, the arguments presented minimize the role of a project manager's individual ambitions, desires and aims in conferring unique characteristics upon the dominant normative structure. For example, Baker and French (2018) suggest that the masculinity of the project management profession has been institutionalized in such a way that it obstructs the ambitions and progress of female project managers. Although these claims might appear valid and sensible at first sight, they say little about the subjectively constituted view of enablement and constraints to (female) project managers' self-realization (Archer 2003). A woman must first become aware of, and give credence to, the prevailing societal belief that her gender places her at a disadvantage in professional settings. Only when she accepts this perspective as a defining reality can it begin to limit her, shaping her perception of her prospects and challenges in her career. As argued by Archer (ibid.), for something to be considered an enablement or a constraint, we first must care about it enough for it to matter. In my view, it is overly simplistic and unhelpful to entirely dismiss one's role in accepting a narrative that ultimately contributes to one's own sense of disconnection or alienation. Doing so is comparable to attributing one's struggles with alcohol solely to peer pressure experienced in high school. Archer (2000: 217) goes on to recognize this by saying that:

> Society holds out innumerable norms without these gaining universal take-up. It is perfectly possible to be wholly indifferent about school achievement, whilst dispassionately recognising the standards and expectations involved. Thus, in order to say something more precise about the emergence of social emotions, we need to go further into the nature of society's normative evaluations and into what individuals themselves bring to the relevant situations – which together account for the emergence of emotionality in the social order. After all, if no importance is attached to the subject's concerns we end up with yet another 'oversocialized view' of the social subject, and would not be talking about emergence but about unilateral causality.

In this regard, whether altering the attributed significance to normative structures would impact the advancement of women is a separate issue; what remains crucial, within the scope of the discourse this book engages in, is that if the meanings individuals assign to their immediate environment are neglected, experiences of stress and anxiety are externalized and consequently solidified within predetermining conditions of existence. This provides little recourse to those trying to manage and improve their emotional states. Philosophically speaking, referring to 'a priori conditions of existence' presents an inherent contradiction. On this note, embedding professional challenges within organizational structures and procedural practices fails to adequately consider the role of stakeholders' interests and objectives in defining what constitutes a challenge. For example, an everyday task such as sending an email can become a challenge when the subject is consumed by questioning the adequacy of every written word. Maybe the email is going to someone whom the subject perceives as important, which suddenly affects the subject's capacity to do something that they did yesterday with ease. As suggested by Clegg (1975: 28) elsewhere, 'the problem, however, is not that "what you see depends on where you sit", but rather that "nothing is more difficult than to know exactly just what we do see"'. Therefore, the concept of a 'challenge' is inherently situational and may vary from day to day based on the subject's perception of the significance of the circumstances they face. This is also confirmed by Van der Hoorn and Whitty (2019: 364), who, in their analysis of the extant project management literature, suggest that 'there is an inherent subject-object dualism with the soft-skills paradigm given its focus on skills that can be acquired and improved'. In this context, what is deemed 'competent' or 'well informed' hinges greatly upon the 'subject's concerns' (Archer 2000:

217), implying that such a stance cannot be regarded as an autonomous corpus of knowledge isolated from the individual's perspective. As noted by McHugh (1971: 332):

> a finding is true (or false or ambiguous) ... only after applying to it the analytic formulations of a method by which that finding could have been understood to have been produced ... *an event is transformed into the truth* [emphasis mine] only by the application of a canon that truth seekers use and analysts must formulate as providing the possibility of agreement.

By not adequately considering the (subjective) world as initially encountered by the individual, practitioners and scholars of project management thus offer a detached portrayal of situated experience. First, (1) this is problematic when considered in the context of arguments for identity formation. As examined in the preceding chapter, to prevent conflating the self entirely with societal constructs (and vice versa), the process of identity formation should be understood as a deliberate complexity rooted in a dialogical interplay between a distinct and self-determining individual and the fluid context of modernity. In this sense, 'liquid modernity' denotes the amalgam of concepts that exert influence upon and contour our self-perception. Put simply, this means that individuals enter social interactions with preconceived self-concepts, which have the potential to evolve or be reframed or reconstituted through such engagements. In this light, identity is simultaneously the agent and the outcome of social interactions. Nonetheless, discourses that emphasize the overriding importance of the social backdrop often fail to acknowledge institutional elements – such as scarcity of resources, the absence of structure, or role uncertainty – as factors contributing to self-direction, thereby overlooking, from an ontological perspective, the intrinsic agency of the individual in pursuit of identity. As advised by Van der Hoorn and Whitty (2019: 364):

> This 'lived experience' perspective focuses on appreciating the actuality (how it is experienced by the practitioner) of what occurs in project work rather than what should or is supposed to occur, and it recognises that project management is more than the contents of the bodies of knowledge. This 'lived experience' perspective is complemented by one focus of the critical perspective of project management agenda, which is to provide a socio-political critique of the instrumentalist project management guides.

Secondly, and more critically, (2) by prioritizing 'social conditions of existence' over individual agency, such research diminishes the capacity of individuals to mitigate the impacts of negative emotional states. While current literature expounds on the restrictive effects of institutional 'forces' on choice-making, it offers little guidance on coping with institutional isomorphism at a personal level. This oversight is significant, especially in discussions advocating for the 'conscious agent', as it suggests that the 'soft despotism' inherent in the project management tradition (Clegg and Courpasson 2004) privileges survival over self-fulfilment. This dichotomy between the individual's experience of anxiety and their capacity to manage such distress undermines the concept of self-development, leaving it largely unaddressed and enigmatic. As noted by Van der Hoorn and Whitty (2019: 364), 'more contemporary perspectives of project management recognise that such Cartesian thinking can limit our conceptualisations of project work and how it is managed'.

In light of the previous discussions, an alternative approach to exploring personal experiences in the realm of project management would entail starting with the experience itself, rather than the professional institutional norms, job specifications or key performance indicators (KPIs). Bearing this in mind, it is worth mentioning that this grassroots, phenomenological perspective has increasingly been embraced in recent project management research. For example, Drouin et al. (2021) adopt a phenomenological philosophical stance to develop the theory of 'balanced leadership in projects'. Sewchurran and Brown (2011) use phenomenological concepts to analyse information systems projects, while Van der Hoorn and Whitty (2019) draw on Heidegger's (1953) *Being and Time* to examine project work. Finally, Rolfe et al. (2017) promote the use of existential hermeneutic phenomenology (also known as EHP) to assist project managers in coping with experiences of the onerous demands of project work.

Outside of the project management discipline, but still within the domain of the focus on practice, there are numerous studies that have argued for a shift from the 'intellectualocentism of practice' (Van der Hoorn and Whitty 2019) as a way of accessing the tacit, that is, personal, aspect of situated professional performances. For example, Dreyfus and Dreyfus (1980), using Heidegger's (1953) being-in-the-world ontology, develop a skill acquisition model that stresses the importance of 'situational awareness' and the relationship between action and one's perception of circumstance. By the same token, Müller et al. (2015: 2) and Drouin et al. (2021) develop a 'socio-cognitive theory perspective to leadership' which 'affirms that personal … influences cause human behaviour'. These arguments are also echoed by Benner (1982), Cicmil (2006), Gibbs and McRoy (2006) and Lum (2003). Therefore, by facilitating conversations and scrutiny of aspects of practice that extend beyond the strictly rational or functional and may remain tacit (Van der Hoorn and Whitty 2019: 367), the significance of these arguments lies in their establishment of a connection between situated experiences, agency and the significance attributed by individuals to the specifics of their circumstances. As noted by Van der Hoorn and Whitty (ibid.: 366), 'what we *care* about frames our *world* and we are *solicited* … to behave in a certain way [emphasis in the original]'.

Enhancing the aforementioned 'bottom-up approach' further would therefore entail maintaining the connection between situated experiences and the subjectively constituted world where these experiences occur. This also suggests recognizing that the essence of 'praxis' is rooted in its subjective origination (Müller et al. 2022). The proposition here is that intentionality should not be perceived as merely 'in the mind', a viewpoint Van der Hoorn and Whitty (2019) critique; rather, it should be understood as an emergent characteristic of the reflexive interplay between an individual's mind, replete with concerns, and the personal significance they ascribe to the overarching normative context. More crucially, by positing the subjective realm as ontologically foundational relative to the intersubjective sphere, this perspective offers a personalized account of situated experiences, which is vital for developing methods to 'navigate the lived experience of project work' (Rolfe et al. 2017). As asserted by Rolfe et al. (ibid.: 742):

> Whereas phenomenology is the art of becoming attuned to the lived experience, part of hermeneutics, in Heideggerian terms, is the art of becoming aware of our pre-conceptual attunement which informs our lived experience. Existential anxiety is the basis of becoming attuned to lived experiences and is the basis of hermeneutic inquiry into *the pre-conceptual attunement which underpins lived experience* [emphasis mine].

Within the framework of these discussions, self-expression emerges as a phenomenon to be evaluated according to its effectiveness in mitigating the emotional weight of 'constant self-questioning and self-doubt'. A more 'accountable' depiction of situated agency would support efforts aimed at tackling institutional isomorphism within project management, doing so in a manner that is both personally resonant and pragmatically applicable.

Unanswered Questions

> While we may be upbeat about the prospects of increasingly engaged debates in principle, it is noteworthy that with the exception of some ethnographies and in-depth case studies, most scholars have as yet adopted a single, often somewhat narrow approach to the study of identities, in part at least because of entrenched ideological assumptions … [as such] theory development and constructive dialogue in the identities field is being hindered by a 'lack of construct clarity' and … it would be more

likely to benefit from synergies between different designs and theoretical perspectives. (Brown 2018: 14–15)

Consequently, the philosophical discourse posited here upholds the notion that rescuing the self-aware subject from a confinement within 'spheres of prescribed action and expectation' is fundamentally unattainable – a stance that highlights the opacity in the quest to formulate a holistic framework for theorizing the bond between self-identity and situated experience. By 'integrative', what is envisioned is a methodology that embraces the contextualizing influence without sacrificing the distinctiveness and autonomy of the self. To construct a more 'comprehensive' argument, it becomes necessary to rethink the concept of self-identity, positing it as both subject to, and an articulator of, social interaction. This necessitates addressing the ensuing persistent questions:

1. How does one's self-identity shape one's situated professional experiences? Responding to this question will aid in clarifying what holds value and significance for individuals in particular contexts. Such an exploration enables us to illuminate the interplay between elements of the world deemed 'objective' and those articulated by the individual as unique and personal constructs of reason. By shedding light on the meaningful connection between subjectivity and perceived objectivity, we pave the way for an understanding of 'encounters in the world' through the lens of subjective foundations that allow for their recognition and significance.
2. How do one's professional experiences (re)shape the process of (re)articulating (professional) self-identity?
   Considering how self-notions influence our understanding of circumstances, answering the second question would naturally link the uniqueness of one's experiences with the shaping of professional identity and agency.

The goal here is to direct our analytical focus towards the depths of our own minds, to explore the inner architecture that orchestrates our lived experiences – a concept touched upon by scholars such as Archer (2000, 2003), Brown (2015) and pivotal philosophers like Heidegger (1953) and Husserl (1982). This critical self-examination lays the groundwork for questioning the self-views we have taken for granted, recognizing how profoundly they can influence our daily behaviours. Yet, to avoid getting disoriented in this inward exploration, a necessary first step is to create a foundational ontology – a map of being, so to speak. This will allow us to understand self-identity in a more anchored way. Heidegger famously framed it as the 'subjectum', viewing it as both a participant and a recipient within the tapestry of situated experiences. By adopting such a framework, we can not only locate but also come to understand the role our sense of self plays amid the complexities of our interactions with the world around us.

Note

1. CAD (Autocad) is a software used by architects and the term 'CAD monkeys' highlights the administrative as opposed to creative aspects of the profession.

Chapter 3

STRATIFIED ONTOLOGY OF SELF-INDUCED REALITY

Ontological Position: The Claim for the Ontology of Self-Notions

While it is true that certain facets of the self remain beyond the reach of our conscious understanding – as highlighted by Schutz (1967) – we cannot ignore the profound impact of our personal inner worlds on our interactions with others (Brown 2015, 2018). This implies that there exists a unique 'I' within us, a core individuality that perceives and comprehends the world through a self-referential lens (Archer 2000, 2003; Peterson 1999). Thus, the standpoint I advocate interweaves the very notions of agency and experience. I see them as inherently bound together, not merely as a co-occurrence but as two sides of the same coin, both shaped by and through our individual subjectivity. These presuppositions are aptly echoed by Fields et al. (2018: 187) who state that:

> According to interface theory of perception (ITP), the perceived world, with its space-time structure, objects and causal relations, is a 2) virtual machine implemented by the coupled dynamics of an organism and its environment. Like any other virtual machine, the perceived world is merely an 1) interpretive and semantic construct; its structure and dynamics bear no law-like relation to the structure and dynamics of its implementation … . [Thus] *perceptual systems, in general, provide only an organism-specific 'user interface' [of] the world, not a veridical representation of its structure* [emphasis mine].

The task of unravelling the tapestry that weaves together self-identity and the experiences we encounter is, at its core, an ontological journey. It seeks to illuminate how we, as individuals, perceive and make sense of the world around us. It puzzles me to consider how any discourse on experience could possibly exclude the individual – unless, of course, we come to see all conceptions of 'self' as mere illusions. This warrants further discussion later on. But, to delve more deeply, what ontological perspective allows us to embrace both a dialogical interplay between the observer and the observed, and the foundational potential for conscious decision-making? This perspective would acknowledge our ability not only to perceive and understand ourselves and others but also to act with deliberate intent in light of this awareness. The key to navigating this philosophical territory lies within a nuanced, multilayered ontology. This framework integrates seminal contributions such as: Heidegger's (1953) exploration of 'being-in-the-world', Peterson's (1999) examination of goal-directed action, and Archer's (2000, 2003) discussion of the individual's capacity for personal causation in the realm of agency.

The World I Know is the World I See: Phenomenology of Stratified Ontology of Reality

> Our way of looking at things is conditioned by what we are.
>
> —C. G. Jung, *Modern Man in Search of a Soul*

In constructing his argument, Jung (1933) echoes a theme similar to Heidegger's powerful concept of 'being-in-the-world' (Heidegger 1953). Heidegger urges us to rethink our presence in the world, suggesting that it is not a matter of simply being located somewhere, like an object among others – for instance, the way a bench occupies space within a lecture hall. He insists on a more profound understanding of existence. To Heidegger, we are not merely 'in' the world in a physical sense; we existentially 'dwell' and meaningfully engage with the elements around us, and in this engagement, we find ourselves 'taking care'. This 'taking care' is not just an action; it is a fundamental aspect of our being, an 'existential' term in Heidegger's language, which points to the essence of what it means to be truly present and involved in our world (ibid.: 57). Allow me to elucidate further:

We can reach a consensus that the concept of 'taking care' reflects a deliberate, purposeful act. Such an intention-based perspective demands a world imbued with personally relevant entities. It is this very connection that transforms isolated objects into an interlinked web of meaningfulness. The value of this interconnectedness arises from the significant relationships among the elements within this network. For instance, the red light at a traffic signal is not just a coloured bulb; it takes on heightened importance when it stands between us and a timely arrival at a highly anticipated job interview. As noted by Heidegger (1953: 158):

> there always belongs to the being of a useful thing a totality of useful things in which this useful thing can be what it is ... [This] structure of 'in order to' contains a *reference* of something to something. In accordance with their character of utility, useful things always are *in terms* of belonging to other useful things. (Emphasis in the original)

The idea that significance or utility is subjective – shaped by an individual's needs and goals – holds profound implications. What stands out about this understanding is the parallel between the 'objective' arrangement of meaningful entities in the external world and our personal perception of that world. This convergence happens because our subjective self-concept informs and moulds our interactions with the objects, events and individuals around us. Our existence prompts a sense of necessity and desire; we engage with the world in ways that mirror our self-identity. Thus, thoughtful consideration arises from the principle of personal value, which animates the world around us based on their utility in achieving our aims. Heidegger (1953) offers an eloquent encapsulation of this relationship: the world is a network of interrelated 'in-order-tos', a fabric where every thread serves a purpose towards some eventual end. As further noted by Heidegger (ibid.: 79–82):

> the circumspect dealings in the surrounding world needs a useful thing at hand which, in its character of being a useful thing, takes over the 'work' of *letting* things at hand become *conspicuous* ... what is encountered within the world is freed in its being for heedful circumspection, for taking matters into account. (Emphasis in the original)

An individual's reality – or their subjective world – is fundamentally the world that surrounds them. This world is a collection of unique situations, which include objects, events and people, appearing as meaningfully immediate elements in their life (Heidegger 1953). Take, for instance, the simple action of opening a door. In this motion, we don't just interact with a doorknob; we engage with it as a means to an end – the doorknob exists 'for the sake of' enabling us to access a new space. This act itself draws the once-peripheral doorknob into our field of attention, highlighting its role within the broader context of the door, the rooms on each side and our journey through these spaces. This network of relationships – the doorknob, the door, the rooms they connect – becomes perceptible to us through the purposeful act of opening the door, all prompted by our intention to perform a specific task. In essence, our needs call particular aspects of the world into prominence from the backdrop of everyday life. Conversely, this observation implies that without need or purpose, we cannot attend to everything simultaneously; much of the world remains unseen, awaiting its turn to be noticed and made significant by our actions. As confirmed by Heidegger (ibid.: 82):

> Beings are discovered with regards to the fact that they are referred, as those being which they are, to something. They are relevant *together with* something else. The character of being of things at hand is *relevance*. To be relevant means to let something be together with something else. (Emphasis in the original)

The concept of 'subjective objectivity' speaks to the idea that our personal world of meaning – our web of interconnected relationships – precedes and shapes our immediate recognition of relevance as we interact with our environment (Heidegger 1953; Peterson 1999). This suggests that our understanding of the importance of any single item emerges from our existing knowledge and grasp of the broader system of connectedness to which it belongs. For instance, when I want to access a book that I need, which is on a shelf in another room, the door to that room becomes a significant point of engagement. To fully appreciate the weight of this notion, imagine a scenario in which performing a simple, usually mundane action – like opening a door – is not possible. In the absence of this basic capability, the mundane is suddenly cast into sharp relief and recognized for its true importance. As noted by Heidegger (1953: 82–83):

> *Which* relevance things at hand have is prefigured in terms of the total relevance. The total relevance which, for example, constitutes the things at hand in a workshop in their handiness is 'earlier' than any single useful thing, as is the farmstead with all its utensils and neighbouring land.

This brings to light the concept of an intrinsic, pre-existing purpose, which defines whether an object or entity is deemed 'useful'. It is this intrinsic purpose that weaves together seemingly disparate objects in the external world into a cohesive system of utility for an individual. Thus, it becomes apparent that we cannot strip away this foundational 'motivational factor' when contemplating the ontology of objects. In essence, the elements that hold significance for an individual imbue objects with their 'objectivity'. At the heart of Heidegger's existential philosophy is the idea that objects devoid of meaning remain beyond the scope of our immediate awareness. Therefore, the 'positive' or 'negative' attributes we perceive in the external world gain prominence due to their alignment with our own motives and needs. It is through their capacity to satisfy our pragmatic ends that useful and meaningful things come to be experienced as immediately relevant to us. Consequently, Heidegger (1953) posits that the entities that hold value for us generate unique, individual-specific ontological frameworks; these frameworks give form and substance to each person's world.

Building on the idea of motivational significance, Peterson (1999) expands our understanding to include the goal-oriented nature of everyday actions. This concept implies that our daily actions are not random or arbitrary; rather, they represent calculated steps towards achieving specific, individual goals. The power of this view lies in recognizing that our actions are embedded in time – they are expressions of the self that draw from past experiences while simultaneously reaching towards future possibilities. Thus, the import of this perspective hinges on its recognition of the self as a temporal entity, with actions that are not only shaped by our historical context but also by the prospects of what we aim to become. In other words, our present behaviour is a tapestry woven with threads of memory and strands of aspiration, each movement towards our objectives further defining who we are and who we might yet be. As noted by Peterson (1999: 29):

> We posit a goal, in image and word, and we compare present conditions to that goal. We evaluate the significance of ongoing events in light of their perceived relationship to the goal. We modify our behavioural outputs – our means – when necessary, to make the attainment of our goal ever more likely. We modify our actions within the game but accept the rules without question. *We move in a linear direction from present to future* [emphasis mine].

The matrix of meaning attributed to objects, events and individuals – essential to the construction of one's 'immediate' world – is shaped not only by an accumulation of personal knowledge but also by projections from our imagined realities (Peterson 1999: 28). This suggests that the significance we grant to the tangible 'objective' elements in our external world emerges from an intricate dialogue between our interpreted past, perceived present and anticipated future. This synthesis results in a unique framework, through which we are selectively attuned to particular aspects of our environment. It enables us to 'see', or rather, notice selectively, certain features of our surroundings – those objects, events and people that resonate with our carefully constructed ideas. As recognized by Dostal (1993: 146):

> Any present ... moment is what it is in virtue of what it retains from the past (retention) and what it anticipates from the future (protention). *Every present moment carries these two aspects as essential to its being what it is as present* [emphasis mine].

This reveals that the ontological bedrock of our everyday actions integrates a configuration of our present self-awareness, which itself is informed by a repository of past experiences, along with a projection of potential self-awareness drawn from our conceptions of future possibilities. This foundational structure aids in rendering meaningful aspects of the external world salient to the individual. Crucially, it implies that the 'properties' we discern in the world are inseparable from this underlying ontological framework. As asserted by Peterson (1999: 28):

> We compare our interpretations of the world as it unfolds in the present to *the desired world, in imagination*, not mere expectation; we compare what we have (in interpretation) to what we *want*, rather than to what we merely think *will be*. Our goal setting, and consequent striving, is motivated: we chase what we *desire*, in our constant attempts to optimise our affective states. (Emphasis in the original)

Thus, Heidegger posits that 'being-in' our environment cannot be fully comprehended through mere physical characteristics – for example, considering 'being-in' the world as a spiritual trait rooted in the physicality of being human, an attribute that somehow 'depends on' the body (Heidegger 1953: 56). Rather, it should be understood as an existential condition, a profound and intimate connection between the individual and their world – a connection that originates within the subject. As noted by Jung (1933: 88):

> The predominance of a function leads us to construct … certain situations while we avoid others, and therefore to have experiences that are peculiar to us and different from those of other people.

Heidegger's concept of being-in-the-world posits that our mindful navigation through daily life is inherently imbued with purpose – the things that hold significance for us. Expanding upon this, the concept of goal-directed behaviour delves into the temporal depth of our actions, revealing that our motivating significances are laced with both historical and future aspirations. These significances help carve out an ontological foundation for the self, setting the stage for authentic self-expression. Moreover, examining the core of rational choices, Heidegger (1953) and Peterson (1999) also shed light on the deeper, often subconscious, precedents of agency. With our anticipatory concerns guiding our actions to safeguard the potential for an ideal future, it becomes evident that the precursors of agency are propelled by our determination to maintain the essentials of self-actualization. Heidegger (1953: 33) asserts:

> Dasein[1] always understands itself in terms of its existence – in terms of a possibility of itself: to be itself or not itself. Dasein either has chosen these

> possibilities itself or got itself into them, or grown up in them already. Only the particular Dasein decides its existence, whether it does so by taking hold or by neglecting.

Furthering the discourse set forth by Heidegger (1953) and Peterson (1999), Archer (2000, 2003) proposes a nuanced view. She delineates being-in-the-world and goal-directed behaviour as deeply interwoven with a reflexive agency – a personal causality born of reflection. Archer posits that the individual infuses the objects of the external world with meaning by reflexively assessing how these objects enable or hinder their inherent drive towards self-fulfilment. It is through this introspective process that the subject 'refers back' to established 'depositories of meaning' – previously identified as the 'touchstones' of agency – which then inform situated judgements. Archer (2000: 195) solidifies this view by suggesting that 'problems' and 'challenges' are contextual, deriving their significance from the interplay with our personal concerns, which assign importance to various situations due to our subjective engagement. Thus, for significance to manifest within the external world, the existence of a discerning subject, with its own ontological framework, is essential in bestowing meaning upon situations that are perceived as 'problematic' or 'challenging'. This is confirmed by Heidegger (1953: 46) who recognizes that

> every idea of a 'subject' – unless refined by a previous ontological determination of its basic character – still posits the *subjectum ontologically* [emphasis in the original] along with it, no matter how energetic are one's ontic protestations against the 'substantial soul' or the 'reifications of consciousness'.

According to Archer (2000), reflexivity stands as a key property that cannot be overlooked – it forges a dynamic link between the social fabric that we navigate and our internal reservoirs of meaning. Archer (ibid.: 195) emphasizes the significance of this link by stating that 'irreducible properties of our human selves interact with our sociality, and this interaction is consequential because of the inner dialogue and the outcomes it generates'. This intimate conversation with ourselves is pivotal in shaping our engagement with the world. While Heidegger (1953) and Peterson (1999) lay down the ontological groundwork of our existence within the world, Archer (2000, 2003) builds on this foundation, highlighting the intricate selection process inherent in our agency. The profound insight offered by Archer's stance is that our lived experiences are in fact the tangible expressions of a deeply layered ontology. This layered ontology unfolds in the interplay between: (1) the established ontological foundations and diachronic nature of the self, (2) the process of internal dialogue or reflexivity and (3) the manifestation of agency and experience. Archer (2000: 195) explains this by saying:

> Different clusters of emotions represent commentaries upon our *concerns* [emphasis mine] and are emergent from our human relationships with the natural, practical and discursive orders of reality respectively. Matters do not finish here. Because of our reflexivity, we review these emotional commentaries, articulate them, monitor them, and transmute them; thus, elaborating further upon our emotionality itself. This occurs through the inner conversation which is a ceaseless discussion about satisfaction of our *ultimate concerns* [emphasis mine] and a monitoring of the self and its commitments in relation to the commentaries received.

Our experiences unfold in layers, mirroring the contours of our inner landscape – our needs, desires and the dreams that stir us into action. This personal tapestry weaves itself into society's broader fabric, creating a dialogue between our individual impulses and the societal structures that both confine and define us. As we navigate this interplay, every interaction etches new patterns into our consciousness, framing our cognition within the collective mould. Our grasp of the world's norms, therefore, cannot be extricated from the personal yearnings that fuel our journey. Amid this dance of influence, where each step informs the next, lies the crux of our self-understanding. Our ontological blueprint, the essence of who we are and could be, emerges as a living, breathing construct. It brings into question not just how we shape the world, but also how the world shapes us, insisting that the lines connecting the layers of our essence must point every which way, acknowledging a constant, mutual shaping. This duality of subjective reality – as both the core and the outer edge of experiential exploration – serves as our philosophical compass. It is an invitation to delve deeper into the nature of lived experiences, a trajectory we will pursue in the pages to come.

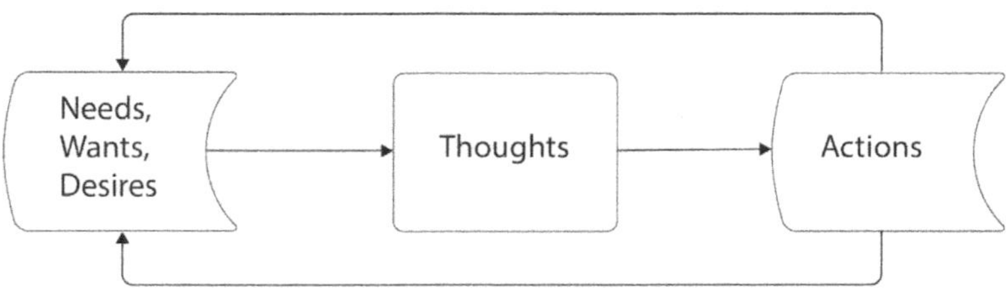

Figure 3.1. Our needs, wants and desires act as resources for thinking – what we want and desire affects how we think and act in the world. © Matija Radomir Djolic.

Paradigm: The Emergent Ontology of Critical Realism

Given that our insights into the subjective realm of an individual's world manifest primarily through their discourse and deeds, we must ask: which patterns crystallize in the moment due to the aforementioned layered ontology? The immediate consequence is acknowledging a reality teeming with distinct entities, each distinguished by their intrinsic characteristics – a view congruent with critical realism. In such a framework, society is perceived as an entity distinct from the individual, much like how an institution stands separate from the self. As noted by Archer (2010: 275):

> This is shown by the difference in their properties and powers, *despite* [emphasis in the original] the fact that they are crucial for one another's formation, continuation, and development … . As Bhaskar put it succinctly: 'People and society … Do not constitute two moments of the same process. Rather they refer to radically different things'. Thus, an educational system can be centralised, while a person cannot, and humans are emotional, which cannot be the case for structures.

Arguably, the most consequential aspect of Archer's line of thought is the recognition that the 'world' is a mosaic of things and entities, each with its own distinctiveness that resists being homogenized by deterministic links. Such deterministic connections assume fixed traits of subjects and objects, inadvertently imposing a perpetual uniformity on diverse phenomena. This kind of reasoning would blur lines between entities, rendering two items merely as variations of one, rather than as truly separate entities. Pushing back on this notion, Archer proposes a model of existence where things and entities are understood through their reciprocal engagements. It is precisely these distinctive properties that not only enable an exchange between two entities but also allow us to perceive that an exchange has occurred. These singular attributes of objects, events and individuals thus create a world teeming with variety, which inevitably opens up the ontological potential for transformation – a dynamism born out of the importance of 'before and after' discussed previously.

The intricacies of Archer's (2010) concept of 'double morphogenesis' lie in the recognition that as individuals actively engage in shaping social structures, they themselves are transformed in the process – a mutual evolution encapsulated when she notes that 'actors themselves change in the very process of actively pursuing changes in the social order' (ibid.: 274). The pivotal concept of 'before and after' not only accentuates the continual variation and the epistemology of distinctiveness inherent in this change but also establishes an ontology of interconnectivity that spans across time: intertwining past, present and future; bridging the self from one day to the next;

interlacing individual utterances that evolve from unique, fleeting thoughts, which sequentially appear and dissipate but always in relation to each other. This web of connections endows us with a profound experiential sense of 'why', embracing the full spectrum of our temporal and existential journey. As noted by Marks and O'Mahoney (2014: 75):

> The inclusion of reflexivity in the transformation cycle means that the tendencies generated by our psychology cannot be framed as determinants. The self is a product of emergent historical processes, but its reflection upon these means that its future is not determined by them.

Through the prism of critical realism, we are invited to view self-identity as a phenomenon that, while arising from social interactions, remains distinct and cannot be wholly subsumed by them. This idea resonates with certain principles of social constructivism, as outlined by Burr (2002), which acknowledges that while society is a human construction, individuals must nonetheless navigate and respond to its structure. Moreover, critical realism positions us to appreciate the *emergence* of entities within the social fabric as a reflection of a world replete with uniquely interconnected properties – ones whose outcomes are not precut by any predetermination (Archer 2000, 2003, 2010, 2015; Archer et al. 2015; Bhaskar 1989; Caetano 2014, 2016; Fletcher 2016; Marks and O'Mahoney 2014; O'Mahoney 2011). This emergent ontology underscores the inherent unpredictability of interactions, fostering a deeper understanding of the dynamic and evolving character of the social world. As asserted by Marks and O'Mahoney (2014: 69):

> A stratified, emergent ontology allows realist researchers to conceptualise different levels or entities upon which identity construction may be dependent, but irreducible to (for example, memory or reflexivity), or levels or entities which may be dependent upon, but irreducible to, identity (for example, culture).

Acknowledging this nuanced understanding, the emergent ontology compels us to reconsider the interplay between personal experiences and societal structures. Archer (2000) and Marks and O'Mahoney (2014) steer us away from the predominant emphasis on societal discourse and static categories, advocating for the recognition of the potent role personal agency plays in crafting our identities. They challenge the conventional notion that awareness is a derivative of collective narratives, arguing instead for a renewed emphasis on the individual's decision-making prowess. This 'reclaimed consciousness' has substantial methodological repercussions, as it insists on interpreting situated experiences as heavily contingent upon individual responsibility. Consequently, the argument advanced in this book posits that acknowledging such agency is vital for perceiving identity as entirely intertwined with social constructs. Brown (2018) echoes this premise, asserting that comprehending identity as a subject of sociality necessitates a deliberate shift towards embracing personal agency and responsibility in the analytical discourse.

It is crucial to recognize that striving to grasp the objective or absolute essence of reality, as Bhaskar (1989) discusses, is an inherently futile endeavour. Our descriptions, limited by perspective, can never fully encapsulate the depth and vastness of reality; they merely reflect a singular viewpoint among countless others. Its significance, however, is embedded in the realization that the one-sided nature of descriptions of objects and interpretations of events is an indication of a non-binary relationship between the subject and other subjects and objects. As noted by Lanza (2009: 118), 'we "see" separation between objects only because we have been conditioned and trained, through language and convention, to draw boundaries'. More on this later. Currently, as we seek to comprehend the catalysts of speech and action, it becomes evident that personal discretion serves as the foundational 'internal judge'. This 'internal judge' acts as a critical intermediary, analysing and juxtaposing our inner desires and concerns with the external pressures of social expectations, as expounded by Archer (2000). This introspective process is the precursor that ultimately gives rise to observable actions (see Figure 3.2 representing the mind map).

The mind map, inspired by the insights of Marks and O'Mahoney (2014: 72), encapsulates the development of personal identity as an emergent property of the reflexive self, sculpted through the pursuits and initiatives of the individual. This visual schema brings to light the dynamic exchange between the individual's internal discourse and the encompassing context. It illustrates how the external world feeds into the reflexive dialogue, contrasting and intertwining with the individual's aspirations and concerns. Such a process gives rise to a continuous internal narrative, a reflective weighing of personal priorities, which is keenly observed but not spoken by the self. In this silent introspection, the self becomes both the subject and object of its own scrutiny, thereby shaping its identity and making decisions that resonate with its core values. It is important to acknowledge that this introspective machinery is not compartmentalized; the self and its internal dialogue are deeply interwoven, each infused with the other's presence – there is a self within the inner dialogue as much as there is an ongoing commentary within the self. While the term 'within' may be an imperfect linguistic tool to describe the intricacies of mental processes, it serves as a provisional term, alongside 'reflect', until language evolves to more precisely articulate these complex inner workings.

It is essential to recognize that the elements of the mind map are distinct, yet they constitute parts of a broader, intricate system. The adage 'as within, so without' reflects not just our internal narratives, but extends to how we

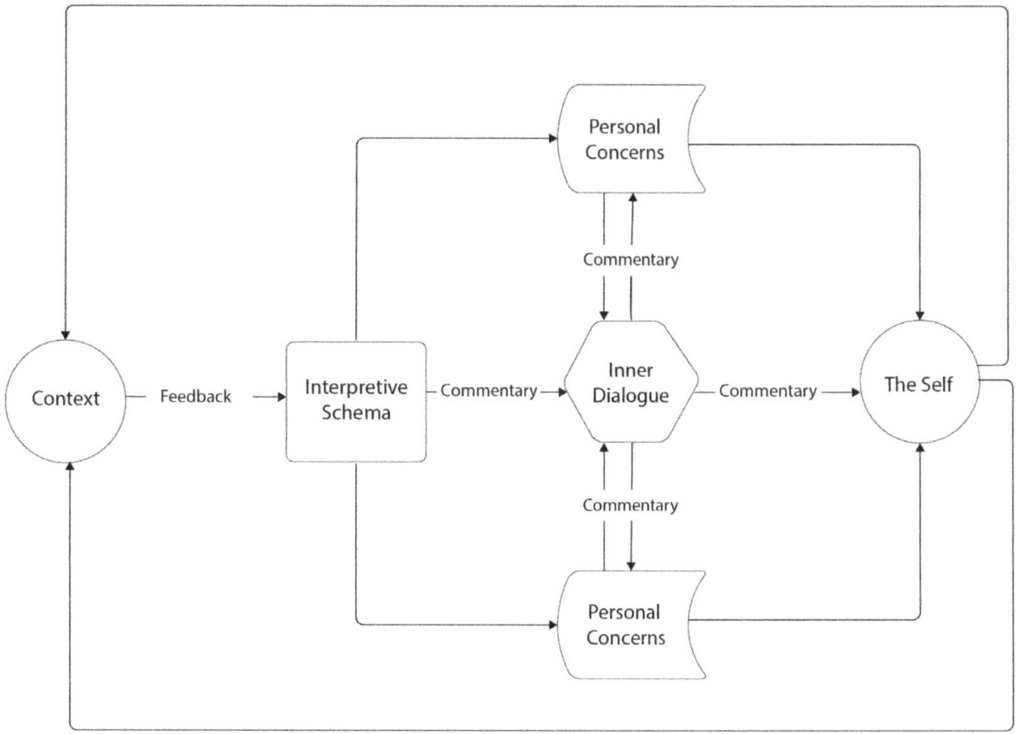

Figure 3.2. This figure is a processual representation of the stratified nature of self-identity. At its core is our self, which provides resources for seeing and acting in the world. The self precedes the creation and emergence of our valued concerns, which serve as a lens through which we assess and perceive the world. The relationship between the self and the world is not unilateral – our experiences of the world provide feedback that is used in reshaping of the self, but also our valued concerns and the schema with which we interpret the world. © Matija Radomir Djolic.

interact as individuals within any collective, such as an organization. No person is an island; my understanding of a colleague is inexorably linked to, and shaped by, my own identity – perception and self are entangled. Lanza (2009: 28) poignantly captures this with the statement, 'There can be no separation between the observer and the observed. Where there is division, reality ceases to exist.' This notion, considered a phenomenon, permeates our interactions – be it between thoughts, words, actions, or between individuals themselves. Consequently, the internal dialogue is not isolated but part of a layered ontology. It exemplifies how 'recognized' norms are but one dimension through which we perceive the social and individual selves. As noted by Peterson (1999: 34):

> Our hopes, desires and wishes – which are always *conditional* – define the context which the things and situations we encounter take on determinate significance; define even the context within which we understand 'thing' or 'situation'.

This allows me to say that the 'conditions' of our self-knowledge provide for a distinctively described 'external world' in the same way that the world distinctively described is reflective of our conditional (self-)knowledge. Therefore, that which is seen (or described) in the world (that is, the world described by the subject) is indicative of one's self-knowledge in so much as the 'inconceivable' or 'meaningless' is not actively perceived by the subject. In this instance, everyday speech becomes revealing of the layered ontology of self-identity whose amorphous structure *attains coherence* by an 'in-order-to' relationship between the spoken word and its subjective possibility. The second implication of the developed mind map is, therefore, that it avoids reducing ontology to epistemology because the description ventured is not an analogous rendition of the contents of one's thoughts. For instance, when someone speaks an 'untruth', it indicates a divergence between what is said and what is truly believed or experienced. This divergence – termed an 'in-order-to' relationship – implies that there is a deliberate intention behind the words spoken. This contrast between the empirical (what is expressed) and the sub-empirical (what is internally held true) can be seen as a 'mechanism' of self-preservation. Uttering an 'untruth' may serve as a protective strategy, allowing an individual to safeguard parts of their identity that they wish to remain concealed. As noted by Archer (2003: 156):

> We would produce a 'digest' *both* [emphasis in the original] for internal consumption and for external reporting (which are also unlikely to be identical). In short, we have to interpret ourselves synthetically before we can furnish any statement for external interpretation. All this is undeniable because we are indeed 'self-interpreting animals'.

This highlights the crucial epistemological distinction between thought and speech, framing self-expression as a 'because-of' capability intrinsic to the individual in pursuit of identity. Therefore, the act of speaking is not a standalone occurrence, but rather a component in a multifaceted system of meaning. It serves as a conduit for articulating one's intentional efforts to maintain and project one's unique perspective of the self, as well as to navigate the world of interpersonal relationships. As observed by Marks and O'Mahoney (2014: 70):

> Critical realism's depth ontology distinguishes real generative mechanisms from actual empirical occurrences, and both of these from what researchers believe they observe ... This depth allows identities to be researched as embedded within wider class or economic structures.

The third key insight from the elaborated mind map is that intentional deliberation forms an integral part of our daily awareness, as Archer (2000) identifies. Within our psyche, this translates to agency emerging from a continuous internal conversation, which functions as a balancing tool between personal and social identities, mediating our own desires against external expectations. The critical role of the 'internal judge' is ongoing; it imparts significance to even the most mundane activities by viewing them as extensions of our identity because these actions contribute to the maintenance of our ideal self. Consequently, a consistent pattern of discernment emerges, indicating that our actions, no matter how trivial or routine, carry imprints of our personal identity. In this way, every utterance we make is theoretically laden with self-expression. Thus, disruptions in our daily life are processed through the same individual-centric framework as our regular, habitual behaviours. Contrary to what Alvesson and colleagues (2008) might argue, identity formation is not confined to navigating the uncharted or unknown; even in stillness and reflection, we are actively shaping our identity.

The Interpretive Lens: An Integration of the Ontology and Paradigm

Prior to cementing our understanding of this philosophy's impact on the existential quest for self-identity, it becomes crucial to thoughtfully consider the counterarguments – those that challenge the significance of subjective worlds in comprehending the nuanced terrain of situated experiences. Challenging the subjective nature of 'ontology', Lacan's explication of a 'Lack' at the core of human subjectivity presents a significant counterpoint, as delineated in the works of Driver (2013), Knights and Willmott (1989), and through

Lacan's own elucidations (2006; Lacan and Miller 2018). This theory casts a profound shadow over the arguments advanced in this book by positing individual-specific ontologies – those frameworks of significance from which our actions stem – as mere illusory constructs. It argues that these personalized frameworks cannot serve as a foundational basis for interpreting situated experiences. To put it succinctly, the 'structural condition' of lack in subjectivity propounds that our desires, which we strive to fulfil, are inherently flawed and perpetually incomplete; this cycle of realization and inadequacy repeats endlessly. Driver (2013: 408–11) further notes the following:

> A sense that something is fundamentally missing in us and from our lives drives everything we do and say. Moreover, this sense of lack is not a personal shortcoming we can correct. Rather, even with psychoanalysis, the best we can do is to recognise lack as a *structural condition* [emphasis mine] and find a momentary release or freedom from a narcissistic image … . Every time we feel sure that we have fulfilled a desire, we find out that there is something missing still. We want more. We want something else. We want what eludes symbolisation, or what Lacan referred to as the *object a*, the surplus pleasure that is missing from our signifiers, *the peace of the real in the symbolic* [emphasis mine], the thing we really desire that they are placeholders for. We cannot say what but we know something is not right. In fact, at some level, we have an overwhelming desire that is impossible to know. But it is there nonetheless.

In essence, our experiences seldom align with our initial expectations; the anticipation of savouring a pizza, magnified by hunger, often surpasses the actual satisfaction derived from eating it. The theory suggests a layered view of being, distinguishing between action and its underlying precondition – the notion of 'lack'. This perspective offers a more nuanced understanding than the less complex ontologies found in certain post-structuralist and entity-centric theories. However, it simultaneously challenges the notion of a coherent self within the social sphere by acknowledging the inherent difficulty, as Heidegger posited in 1953, of defining a clear-cut 'subjectum' or subject of existence. As further asserted by Driver (2013: 410):

> We only learn from others and through the words of others what we desire and this does not seem to fulfil what we unconsciously desire. So, when we articulate our desire, it always turns out in the end to elude us, to be a desire for nothing. We try to overcome this lack by turning the self into a definable object that knows who it is and what it wants and can therefore obtain it. However, the process of constructing ourselves in this objectifying way consciously through language leads us to be subjugated and stuck, in what Lacan referred to as, the imaginary order. The problem is that the imaginary order is a misrepresentation and an illusion … all we obtain in the symbolic order is an encounter with an alienated self and others.

Since Lacan (Lacan and Miller 2018) underscores the critical importance of recognizing our inability to ever 'completely' and 'conclusively' articulate our own needs and desires, there is, however, a critical limitation in this stance: it tends to conflate knowledge (epistemology) with the very essence of existence (ontology). What is the grounds for this claim? The focus of my argument is not on whether each subject or object can be exhaustively identified but, more pressingly, whether self-expression is inextricably linked to a 'because-of' relationship with an individual's personally crafted world view and their relationship to the surrounding community. This inquiry is not about the probability of accurate self-characterizations. Rather, I aim to shed light on the 'mechanisms' that restrict the potential for self-expression. In more precise terms, my argument proposes that these mechanisms reveal a unique individual, not in the sense of an objective entity defined by exhaustive description. The argument is therefore fundamentally not epistemological – it does not attempt to validate whether perceptions of the self can be definitively realized, thus implying that our expressions are all-encompassing. As asserted by Bateson (2002: 124):

> It is nonsense to talk about 'dependency' or 'aggressiveness' or 'pride' and so on. *Only if you hold on tight to the primacy and priority of relationships can you avoid dormitive explanations* [emphasis mine].

The crux of advocating for individualized ontologies lies in exploring how a subject can initially grasp or interpret themselves and their world. This interpretive ability hinges on a relational ontology, the interplay between different layers of reality. For instance, recognizing a 'fundamental' deficit (i.e. lack) in human subjectivity assumes a prior understanding of 'reality' that informs our recognition of this structural deficiency. Put simply, the identity issue at hand is ontological, as previously mentioned. Symbolic constructs rely on the subject who imbues symbolism with meaning; thus, discussions on the ontological nature of human deficiency must consider our capacity to perceive our own subjectivity or an experience as 'lacking'. Following Peterson's (1999: 287) reasoning, if two entities are indistinguishable, they are not truly separate, and an entity without discernible characteristics is questionable in its very existence. Therefore, debating the underpinning concept of lack necessitates its comparison to a contrasting notion that renders it credible through their 'imminent distinction'. As Bateson[2] (2002: 64) writes:

> To produce news of difference, i.e., *information* [emphasis in the original], there must be two entities (real or imagined) such that the difference between them can be immanent in their mutual relationship … There is a profound and unanswerable question about the nature of those 'at least two' things that between them generate the difference which becomes information by making

a difference. Clearly, each one alone is – for the mind and perception – a non-entity, a non-being ... A sound of one hand clapping.

Our understanding of 'lack' as an intrinsic aspect of subjectivity demonstrates that its comprehension is rooted in the interplay of ideas, not their separation. Esteemed thinkers like Heidegger, Jung, Sartre and Schutz unite in the view that thoughts cannot emerge in a vacuum, but only from a foundation of pre-existing knowledge (McHugh 1971). According to Peterson (1999), it is within this interconnected framework of being that we discern 'lack', entwined with our inherent sense of possession and the concept of 'having'. Such insights can be drawn from both tangible experiences and theoretical frameworks (Bateson 2002; Peterson 1999). Consider the simple yearning for the perfect pizza: our longing is driven by the mental image of its flavour, without which our desire would lack form and substance. As noted by Peterson (1999: 71):

> Before we truly master something novel, we *imagine* what it might be. Our imaginative representations actually constitute our initial adaptations. Our fantasies comprise part of the structure that we use to inhibit our responses to the *a priori* significance of the unknown. (Emphasis in the original)

Sartre (2018: 573) also affirms this point when he states:

> Indeed, that is the character of the unity of the three temporal ecstasies: the end, or the temporalization of my future, implies a reason (or motive), i.e. it points toward my past, and the present is the arising of my act.

Drawing from Sartre (2018) and Peterson (1999), there is an inherent preconception underlying our goals, as we envision an objective and advance in a linear trajectory from the present towards the future (Peterson 1999: 29). In line with Lacan's thinking, self-expression could stem from a not-yet-realized possibility, such as the hunger that remains unfed, as implied by Heidegger (1953). Yet recognizing an unmet desire does not necessarily compel us to verify its accuracy or feasibility. More vital is the insight that our desires prompt a reflective evaluation of our environment, spur us to act, and mould our lived experiences. Thus, the key issue is not an enduring sense of 'self-lack' or incompleteness, notwithstanding its motivational force. Instead, it is the recognition that a yearning mirrors a measure of the self, a standard by which we can appraise our own 'realization' or 'deficiency'. Moreover, this measure allows us to perceive the realities we encounter as 'enabling' or 'limiting', following Archer (2000, 2003). In essence, our desires provide a benchmark that helps us gauge whether our actions are effective, shaping our understanding of success. As Sartre (2018: 567–68) states:

> Having, doing and being are the fundamental categories of human reality. Every type of human behaviour can be subsumed within them … These categories are not unconnected, and several writers have emphasized these relationships … *And, again, we point to a similar connection when we show a moral agent doing something in order to make himself, and making himself in order to be.* (Emphasis in the original)

Therefore, while situated expression may appear as a mere fragment within the grand tapestry of our ideas about the self and others, it is anything but transitory or illusory – a contrast to the post-structuralist view. This is because the essence of our spoken words and actions is rooted in a deeply subjective 'context' that is uniquely ours, a context that remains steadfast even amid the flux of interpretation and understanding. Indeed, proponents of critical discourse analysis have long acknowledged this as axiomatic, understanding that texts resonate differently among unique readers – a notion explored by scholars such as Fairclough in his 1993 and 2013 works. While our articulations may offer only a glimpse into our personal reservoir of meaning, this reflection is far from insignificant; rather, it forms the essential scaffolding upon which our capacity to 'abstract' is built – a process rendered meaningless without it.

It is neither my intent nor my philosophical stance to puzzle over the 'truthfulness' or 'completeness' of one's expressions as if engaging with a strictly positivist interpretation of experience. Instead, my goal is to illuminate the intricate links in the chain of meaning, exploring how the interplay of self-expression and subjectivity shapes our individual worlds out of the raw continuum of a more profound reality. This exploration acknowledges that self-expression acts as a sieve, filtering the overwhelming potential of our experiences down to a manageable milieu within our constructed interactions. Within this framework, our experiences defy simplification; they are multifaceted, often simultaneously lacking and rewarding. Therefore, it is critical to recognize that our experiences are not mutually exclusive, as if they could be as one-dimensional as what Bateson (2002) poetically termed 'the sound of one hand clapping'. As acknowledged by Sartre (2018: 574):

> In this way, the motive comes to learn what it is through the set of beings that 'are not', through ideal existences and through the future. In the same way as the future returns to the present and the past to illuminate it, so my projects as a whole turn back to confer on the motive its structure as a motive. It is only because I escape the in-itself by nihilating myself in the direction of my possibilities that this in itself is able to acquire the value of a reason or a motive. Reasons and motives have meaning only within a projected set that is precisely a set of non-existants. And, in the end, this set is myself as a transcendence; it is me in so far as I have myself to be, outside myself.

The foregoing discussion establishes a framework for identifying personal criteria that individuals use to comprehend their professional environments. Firstly, our philosophical examination reveals that our perception of the external world is deeply intertwined with the temporal tapestry of our subjective concerns – the diachronic narrative that individually resonates with each of us. Put simply, interpreting what we say necessitates an understanding of our personal histories and future aspirations. Secondly, the diversity observed in the observable and nuanced dimensions of communication suggests that our daily expressions are sculpted by an underlying quest for identity and self-fulfilment. This implies that the meaningfulness of our words is also inextricably linked to a recognition of our career-related interests, which encompasses our understanding of conditions that we perceive as either enabling or hindering our existence. As noted by Fairclough (2013: 309):

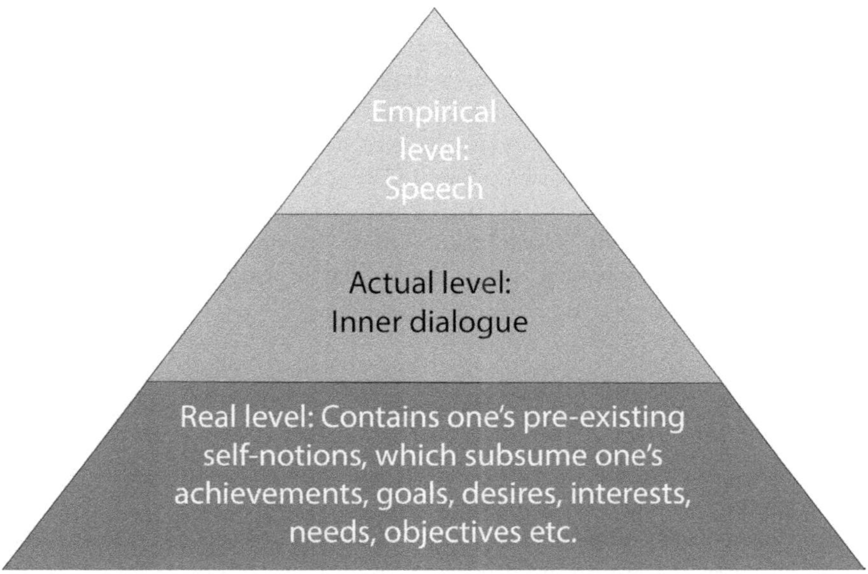

Figure 3.3. The stratified nature of the self comprising three strata: The empirical level represents that which is manifested as 'identity work' or situated identity positions (for instance, everyday communication and decision-making). The actual level represents identity work in the domain of internal dialogue. Internal dialogue is a question-and-answer process that emerges when the subject perceives something in the external world as being an enablement or a constraint to self-realization. The real level contains one's pre-existing self-notions, which subsume one's achievements, goals, desires, interests, needs, objectives and so on (Heidegger 1953; Peterson 1999). © Matija Radomir Djolic.

> From a relational perspective, any property we care to identify as significant 'distinction' in social life, including social class, is nothing other than *difference* [emphasis in the original], a gap, a distinctive feature, in short, a *relational* property existing only in and through its relation with other properties.

Lastly, and of critical importance, is the 'in-order-to' connection between two key factors: (1) the unfolding significance of personal values and experiences over time (the diachronic narrative), and (2) the individual's professional interests. Together, these factors weave the tapestry of bespoke ontologies that inherently restrict the range of interactions one can have within such a construct. Building from this, the nuanced ontology of self-identity I propose as an analytical framework is rooted in a tiered structure. This structure captures the interplay between empirical, actual and real dimensions of self-expression, delineating how each level contributes to the formation of identity as follows:

In practical terms, this implies that any expression of a person's aspirations towards self-realization is a mirror of their self-identity, and thus carries theoretical weight for the argument presented in this book. The pursuit of self-realization inherently encompasses a dialogue surrounding an individual's accomplishments, aspirations, desires, interests, necessities and objectives. These facets underpin our understanding of how people use language both in form and function – what Fairclough (1993, 2013) and Silverman (2013, 2017) describe as the modal and paradigmatic elements of daily communication. This understanding is instrumental in dissecting the dynamic interplay among self-identity, personal agency in everyday life and the context of lived experiences.

Synopsis

This chapter has laid out the case for understanding reality through a layered, or 'stratified', ontology. This nuanced conceptual framework challenges the binary viewpoints prevalent in existing scholarship – perspectives that previously obscured the notion of self-identity as a subject of our social fabric. By weaving in concepts from critical realism, it has highlighted how examining the interrelation of reality's different layers (such as the individual and society) circumvents the simplistic view of entities as mere constructs within power dynamics. Thus, the stratified ontology carves out a space for a bidirectional conversation among the distinct aspects of reality, which is indispensable for appreciating situated experiences independent of discursive rationalities as the sole source of meaning. Consequently, a genuine engagement with the interplay among self-identity, everyday agency and situated experiences necessitates a deep dive into the 'in-order-to' framework. This framework connects the expressions of daily life with their underpinning subjective intents, enriching our exploration of these concepts beyond surface-level interpretations.

Notes

1. 'Dasein' essentially represents everyone that lives within a society and interacts with other individuals in their everyday being-in-the-world. As explained by Cohn (2002: 8): '[Heidegger] does not speak of "human beings" but of "Dasein" … Heidegger, in using it to characterise *human* beings, pays attention, as he frequently does, to the literal meaning of the word: this is "*there*-being" or as we usually say "being-there".'
2. Although Bateson is a natural scientist, the argument he is making is phenomenological and one that emphasizes the non-dual relationship between subject and object as fundamental to 'reality'. As such, even though this study is a qualitative analysis of self-identity, its ontological arguments coincide with those put forward by Bateson (2002).

Chapter 4

The Map of Self-Experience

The subsequent short chapter offers a window into the design of the research programme that gave birth to this book. It will articulate the frameworks guiding the research design, delve into the context in which the research was situated and elucidate the methodologies employed in both data gathering and analysis. While it retains a theoretical underpinning, this chapter serves an essential purpose: it provides readers with a compass for navigating the intricacies of the research process and a foundation for comprehension of the empirical conclusions that will unfold in the pages that follow.

Design Frameworks

This book is based on research I conducted as a doctoral student. The study employed Smith's interpretive phenomenological analysis (IPA) (Smith et al. 2009) to answer the following questions:

1. How does one's self-identity shape one's situated professional experiences?
2. How do one's professional experiences (re)shape the process of (re)articulating (professional) self-identity?

As we prepare to examine the findings of this study, it is crucial to first delineate the methodological approach used – a process that will enhance the reader's grasp of the logical underpinnings of the contributions this book aims to make. Building on the ontological and epistemological discussions earlier in the text, it is important to recognize how the principles of interpretative phenomenological analysis align with the complex nature of accessing the substance of situated experiences. As Schutz (1945, 1967) argued, fully comprehending experiences during the act of participation, or 'acting-in-progress', is daunting, given the intricate challenges of navigating social engagement (Jung 1933).

At this point, we need to clarify a critical distinction within the IPA framework. It does not endorse the concept of 'unselfconsciousness' – the idea that individuals are unaware of the motivations underpinning their daily professional existence. Instead, what IPA delineates is the difficulty involved in conducting a 'double hermeneutic' – a reflective and interpretive analysis – of one's actions during their unfolding (Schutz 1945). This is not to be mistaken for a lack of self-awareness, but rather, it highlights the inherent challenges in examining and interpreting one's behaviour in the very moment of its occurrence. This distinction is also acknowledged by Husserl (1982: 95) when he states:

> So, when we are fully engaged in conscious activity, we focus exclusively on the specific thing, thoughts, values, goals, or means involved, but not on the psychical experience as such, in which these things are known as such.

The principles underpinning IPA underscore the importance of uncovering and understanding the less overt, or sub-empirical, elements of our multilayered self-identity – those that are crucial for a comprehensive grasp of situated experiences. IPA acknowledges that individuals do not have to be aware of the underlying reasons for their interests and actions in the midst of their occurrence, despite these reasons having a lasting influence. Take, for example, the act of diligently completing an assigned task: this might be driven by a subliminal quest for self-validation, a psychological strategy to mitigate feelings of self-doubt or incompetence. Such motivations often remain obscured without intentional and profound introspection. It is indeed a fascinating condition of humanity, to navigate our existence immersed in action, often without immediate insight into the underlying 'why' of our behaviours.

Therefore, given the inherent difficulty of critiquing our actions as we engage in them, we are prompted to adopt a reflexive standpoint, retrospectively examining our experiences to gain insight. In alignment with this methodological approach, the mind map introduced earlier serves as a tool to capture and interpret the introspective narratives of the individual – essentially providing a visual representation of the inner workings of the mind during attentive listening. This is aptly captured by Husserl (1982: 120) who says that:

> Focusing our experiencing gaze on our own psychic life necessarily takes place as reflection, as a turning about of a glance which had previously been directed elsewhere. Every experience can be subject to such reflection, as can indeed every manner in which we occupy ourselves with any real or ideal objects – for instance, thinking, or in the modes of feeling and will, valuing and striving. So, when we are fully engaged in conscious activity, we focus exclusively on the specific thing, thoughts, values, goals, or means involved, but not on the physical experience as such, in which these things are known as such. Only reflection reveals this to us. Through reflection, instead of grasping simply the matter straight-out – the values, goals, and instrumentalities – we grasp the corresponding subjective experience in which we become 'conscious' of them, in which (in the broadest sense) they 'appear'. For this reason, they are called 'phenomena', and their most general essential character is to exist as the 'consciousness-of' or 'appearance-of' the specific things, thoughts (judged states of affairs, grounds, conclusions), plans, decisions, hopes, and so forth.

The IPA methodology rigorously addresses 'unmet anticipation' as crucial subject matter (Smith et al. 2009). The search for understanding 'unmet anticipation' springs from its remarkable ability to reveal the deeper hierarchy of meanings ascribing significance to entities, events or individuals. Reflecting on our earlier discussions, recall how the tenets of self-identity persist within the fabric of ordinary events. This persistence extends even to the unexpected. Yet, in the quest to elevate these underlying tenets from the depths to a place of shared observation by the researcher and the researched, we find the most clarity at the outliers of our daily expectations – the domain of the unforeseen and the unexplored.

The reason is clear: relationality and activity dependence (Archer 2003) among the various layers of the stratified ontology of self-identity become starkly evident when confronted by the disruption of unfulfilled intentions and desires. In the wake of unmet expectations, the typically unseen constellations of our self-identity are stirred into consciousness. Indeed, negative emotions, carrying the element of surprise and the impossibility of their avoidance, serve as powerful conduits into the unique personal ontologies that also quietly shape our habitual and routine behaviours. The deeper exploration of these phenomena awaits in the next segment of this chapter. For now, let us recognize the essence of unmet anticipation through Heidegger (1953: 74):

> Something is unusable. This means that the constitutive reference of the in-order-to to a what-for has been disrupted. The references themselves are not observed, rather they are 'there' in our heedful adjustment to them. But in a disruption of reference – in being unusable for … – the reference becomes explicit … When something at hand is missing whose everyday presence was

> so much a matter of course that we never paid attention to it, this constitutes a breach in the context of reference discovered in circumspection. Circumspection comes up with emptiness and now sees for the first time what the missing thing was at hand for and at hand with. Once again, the surrounding world makes itself known.

Accordingly, the IPA methodology advocates that to unearth the intricate connections between self-identity, daily agency and situated experiences, one should concentrate on what subjects identify as 'disruptive experiences'. With this premise, the design of the research aimed to craft an environment conducive to eliciting 'confessions'. This set the stage for participants to offer detailed narratives on their interpretation of particular professional situations. Consequently, the analytic process was geared to benefit from a double hermeneutic[1] approach, enabling me to richly portray the nuanced individual-specific ontologies and simultaneously mitigate the influence of my biases on assessing the relevance of participants' expressions. Such considerations naturally influenced the sample size; in order not to dilute the depth and specificity integral to IPA's idiographic technique, the study was conducted with a select group of only three participants.

The Focus on the Experience

Focusing on emotionally charged experiences can serve as a gateway to understanding the layered complexities of our identities. Simply put, when we delve into moments that resonate deeply with us – those interactions and events imbued with significant emotion – we uncover the very personal frameworks that attribute such profound feelings to these experiences. These 'disruptive experiences' act as catalysts, bringing to light the often obscured, yet persistent, structures of meaning that silently shape our day-to-day existence. Clegg (1975), building on the existential philosophy of Heidegger (1953), suggests that it is specifically through disruptions, through the 'brokenness' of routine, that we are compelled to confront the essence of the things we typically take for granted. He posits that it is only when the familiar breaks down that we are jolted into awareness, into a reflection on the true nature of our concerns (Clegg 1975: 87). In this sense, it is the very act of breakdown – an object failing to function, an expectation not met or a sudden loss – that beckons us to contemplate and understand our reality in a new light. By examining these emotionally potent experiences, we prompt a philosophical introspection that reveals deeper truths about our identities. This method of inquiry not only enlightens us about the values and meanings we ascribe to our lives but also incites a transformation in our self-perception, inviting us to question and perhaps redefine the narratives we live by.

Let us consider the pervasive emotion of anxiety, often seen through the lens of psychoanalysis as a 'psychological burden' (Jung 1933; Peterson 1999). This 'burden' arises from the profound sense of potential 'loss' experienced when one is faced with the reality of unfulfilled expectations. The weight of this 'burden of loss', and the resulting waves of anxiety, draw back the curtains to reveal the internal world an individual strives to safeguard. It is within this preservation – where the continuity of one's beliefs about self and society is upheld – that a cloak of security is woven. Yet it is critical to note that my investigation into anxiety eschews the traditional analytic desire to quantify or dissect its psychiatric underpinnings – such as chemical imbalances – opting instead for an ontological lens. My fascination lies not in the biological litany of causes or symptoms, but in the existential arena where anxiety functions both as a condition and a descriptor of human existence (Cohn 2002). Anxiety is understood not just as a transient emotional state, but as an embedded facet of being that both characterizes and is characterized by our engagements with the world (Cohn 2002; Heidegger 1953; Husserl 1982). In advocating this view, I echo Panksepp's (2005: 341) call to explore emotional experiences – like anxiety – as foundational processes that undergird and shape human culture, from the arts to politics. By deciphering the subjective experiences of anxiety, we gain entry into the interpretive frameworks that define what is to be feared or otherwise, revealing the distinct 'ontologies' unique to each individual. In essence, to scrutinize the moments charged with emotional significance is to delve into the personalized tapestries that make up an individual's existential fabric.

Research Context

Mirbelia Projects (a pseudonym) is an Australian-owned and operated construction company that was founded in December 2001. Since 2001, Mirbelia Projects has grown exponentially and presents itself as a reputable construction firm working within the third-tier construction sector. Mirbelia Projects has dealt with top-tier project management and global architectural firms assisting in the delivery of major retail and hospitality construction projects. Mirbelia Projects' revenue for 2020 was $60 million. By 2020–21 its projected and forecast growth will be well in excess of $80 million. Mirbelia Projects employs 40–50 people, which includes both office and site staff.

Mirbelia Projects' structure is divided into five departments: projects, business development and marketing, estimating and estimating administration and support, quality systems and WHS,[2] and finance. Its structure is heavily hierarchical, with each department implementing a top-down system of management and control. Looking at the number of employees per department, the 'projects' and 'estimating' departments command the largest workforce. The two departments are central to the organization's operations and enjoy the highest level of resourcing and management attention. The company's directors are actively involved at all levels of the business.

Mirbelia Projects can be said to be representative of a typical mid-tier construction and project management company in Australia and is thus a representative case (Bryman and Bryman 2013) of an Australian construction and project management organization.

Data Collection

Data has been collected via the use of semi-structured interviews and participant observation. The observation was both formal and informal. Formal observation ensued from participating in meetings between the participants and other organizational members. I also shadowed (Czarniawska 2007) selected participants, conducting observations and making notes about how participants fulfil their day-to-day professional responsibilities and interact with other members of the organization. Most importantly, in the process of shadowing, the participants and I engaged in discussions in which the purpose was to reflect on everyday interaction episodes with other organizational members. Focusing on participants' reflections has generated rich descriptions of their professional worlds, which has allowed me to pursue the idiographic logic of IPA methodology (Smith at al. 2009: 51).

Involving participants in reflection on themes generated was a double hermeneutic methodology of eliciting individual-specific ontologies. By critically rationalizing their thinking, the participants were encouraged to attempt to understand why they see the world in particular terms (Smith et al. 2009: 51). In addition to eliciting rich descriptions of their professional experiences, this rather egalitarian strategy to 'making sense of data' has helped me eliminate my bias (ibid.). This is particularly pertinent in the context of a study that seeks to encourage 'full disclosure' of negative emotional experiences. Overall, involving participants in the research process and sense-making of generated themes not only aligned with the 'depth phenomenology' of IPA but has also, more importantly, helped me deal with the pre-established views I held about participants' 'identities' (Bryman and Bryman 2013).

Semi-Structured Interviews and Informal Interviews

Interviews were conducted to 'learn a great deal about a particular person and their response to a specific situation' (Smith et al. 2009: 51). On that note, the decision was made to interview participants on more than one occasion, both formally and informally (for instance, having general discussions over lunch, coffee or just in passing in an organizational context). The decision to interview participants more than once was made to permit rich descriptions of their professional experiences. Subsequently, informal interviews served in further refining the study's thematic insights generated in the formal interview episodes.

The interview schedule consisted of seventeen questions. The first four questions focused on the subject describing their immediate circumstance. Questions such as 'can you please tell me how you see your job fit into the work the organization performs?' and 'can you please describe the steps involved in fulfilling your professional responsibilities?' thus sought to highlight first-person rendition of the (*perceived*) professional context. The second part of the interview shifted away from descriptions of their immediate circumstances (which also included their professional responsibilities) towards discussing their professional experiences. Questions such as 'can you please describe the difference between a good and a bad day at work?' were aimed at eliciting reflections of emotional experiences in the context of the subject's goals, desires, objectives and concerns. This has helped me to develop an understanding of individual-specific 'hierarchies of meaning'. These 'hierarchies of meaning' formed the primary subject matter in the third section of the interview, in which the subjects were encouraged to engage in processes of meta-reflexivity[3] (Archer 2003). Questions such as 'can you describe how work-related anxiety affects your relationships at work?' encouraged the subjects to reflect on why they see things in particular terms. Lastly, the fourth section of the interview sought to attend to the problematic aspect of participants' perceptions and experiences respective to their self-knowledge. Questions such as 'how has work affected how you see yourself?' and 'how do you think your co-workers see you?' were aimed at highlighting the relationship between the subject's sense of self and how they perceived others' perceiving them. The last section of the interview thus allowed me to close the 'hermeneutic circle' (Smith et al. 2009) and construct a meaningful story of the individual. Overall, the tiered approach to the interview was aimed at highlighting the 'in-order-to' relationship between:

1. The subject's concerns about their social and professional conditions of existence.
2. The diachronic content of that which matters to the subject.

The primary aim of the interview schedule was to elicit the modal and paradigmatic aspects of speech (discussed in the previous chapter) and subsequently focus on reflexively unpacking emerging themes. This meant that in some sections of the interviews, the interview schedule was not followed stringently in such a way that answers were sought for all seventeen questions. The schedule was followed in a way that did not 'obstruct' the pursuit of participants' reflexive attitudes concerning claims and assertions. The aim was to understand how the subject's self-identity shaped their everyday professional experiences.

Observation

Formal observation was deployed in the meetings where estimating and project management practices intersected. I was present in one such meeting in which the three participants were also present. The aim of this strategy was to 'juxtapose' claims made by participants in interviews with the free following interaction between the study's participants and other organizational members. Theoretically speaking, this approach sought to utilize the significance of naturally occurring data (Silverman 2013, 2017). As suggested by Clegg (1975: 35), 'in a social science … everyday life as a display of actual performance of human activity must be the bedrock for any theorising, functioning as an analogous icon to that of nature in the natural sciences'. Ontologically speaking, the aim of this approach was to see how much of what is perceived by the subjects to be considered 'truth' is shaped by the subjects' goals, desires and concerns that were highlighted in the formal interview episode. For example, a conflictual situation between a study participant and another organizational member respective to their view on 'punctuality' was analysed not for the completeness and objectivity of the definition but rather to unearth the subjective 'context' that permitted particular views of 'punctuality'.

On the other hand, informal observation was conducted through general observation of the organizational setting and individual interaction within it. Informal observation helped me gain an understanding of the space and place in which participants operated (Heizmann 2011). I spent four months in the organization, observing, conversing and generally socializing with organizational members to gain insight into the 'everyday' aspects of the participants' organizational life. The process took account of the office set-up and the everyday 'banter' of organizational members. As such, informal observation assisted in uncovering 'issues' and 'demands' that subjects encountered while fulfilling day-to-day professional duties. The aim of this process was to gain an understanding of symbols and language used by organizational members in self-expression. The process also helped with understanding the sheer subjectivity of participants' accounts of organizational life.

Informal observation also extended to *shadowing* (Czarniawska 2007). I accompanied participants to numerous events outside of the organizational settings such as site inspections, site meetings and social events. This time was used for having general discussions with the participants about their lives, which included discussions about their past, their relationships with friends and family as well as their visions of a more desirable future. I took the time to reflect not only on events that ensued within the organizational setting but also events that the subjects experienced in domains outside of the professional context. The aim was to enrich and contextualize the sheer subjectivity of the participants' 'truth claims', providing a more complete understanding of the substantiveness of their reasoning. It is important to note that this approach was not deployed to ascertain truth and to render their observations within professional settings as plausible or otherwise but rather to unearth a more comprehensive meaning structure that shaped the subjects' everyday being-in-the-world of work. This is what is usually referred to as 'data saturation'.

Prior to moving on to data analysis, it is important to note that because of the intrusive nature of continuous recording and its potential to induce *reactivity* (Bryman and Bryman 2013), I decided to use field notes (in the form of journals) to capture data from informal observation and shadowing. I kept an analytic and self-reflexive journal that, in addition to expanding the transcribed data corpus, has assisted with documenting the significance of my initial observations and reasonings. The journal consisted of moment-to-moment reflections and personal reactions to participants' narratives and actions. As such, in addition to being a tool for reflecting on participants' comments, the journal also helped in analysing my own reflections and observations. This double-hermeneutic process proved to be essential for generating in-depth understanding of both the participants' and my own reasoning.

Coding and Data Analysis

At the heart of my ontological perspective is the axiom that a thorough exploration of self-identity and its entwinement with situational experiences demands attention to the tiered composition of identity. It is a precept I have reiterated time and again, underscoring its pivotal role: to decode the ongoing evolution of our sense of self through our encounters, we must probe its layered complexity. Every narrative shared by participants in a study serves a dual purpose. First, (1) it mirrors the unique contours of their individual psyches, their internal architecture of beliefs and perceptions. Secondly, and quite unintentionally, (2) it casts light on their personal construal of the world – reflecting a landscape they perceive as absolute but that is, in reality, both bounded and partial. Take, for instance, one's description of a colleague's skills and capabilities. On the surface, it may seem like an assessment of another's inherent abilities or a measurement against an objective performance standard. However, within our theoretical framework, such observations are prized for what they reveal about the observer's immediate psychosocial environment – their personal 'reality' – rather than as definitive commentaries on the colleague in question. This method of interpretation is what we term 'inverse-dialectics' (Fairclough 1993, 2013; Silverman 2013, 2017). We invert the analytic lens, steering from the realm of overt discourse and assertions to the underlying realm of personal subjectivity (Foucault 1980; Foucault and Sheridan 2002). Despite its roots in critical discourse analysis, or CDA, our focus shifts to the revelation of the 'self-fulfilling prophecies' born from individual-specific ontologies (Jung 1933; Peterson 1999; Silverman 2013; Wetherell et al. 2001). In this way, we invite a rigorous critique of the boundaries that such ontologies impose, opening avenues for a more expansive understanding of self and other. As noted by Fairclough (2013: 309):

> Relations in Aristotle are organised around a concept of *Relata*. *Relata* are *of other things*, or are said to be in some manner *towards something else*. They are so designated in virtue of their relation to another *Correlata*; the master is master *of a servant* – the servant is a servant of a master. Relata and Correlata are mutually defining; they are *simul natura*. If you suppress one of the pair, the other vanishes. (Emphasis in the original)

Accordingly, the methodological approach of the study positions our analysis to unpack participants' dialogue through the lens of their 'in-order-to' motives. This method connects the dots between (1) the personal significance participants ascribe to certain experiences over time and (2) their professional preoccupations. Thus, when sifting through interview transcripts and field observations, my initial task was to map out the personal metrics – what I term the 'self-criteria' – that participants use to navigate and make sense of their environment. These individual narratives were sketched out by identifying and classifying salient mentions of participants' concerns, aspirations, milestones and aims. This exercise was not merely about cataloguing goals; rather, it aimed to weave 'the life story' of each participant, illuminating their unique presence within the professional realm. The focus here was on capturing the essence of their existence in the workplace – to lay bare the subjective groundwork from which each participant launches 'truth claims', as Wittgenstein (1968) would say, about their ambient 'external world'. Building upon this foundation, the second phase of coding was directed towards assembling the world as constructed by the participants. In this round, I grouped together segments of interviews and notes that highlighted how participants saw their role in work, how they perceived others' work ethics, and their interactions with both peers and clients. The amalgamation of these perspectives aimed at sketching what participants deemed the objective schema of their reality. The overarching intention behind this two-tier assortment of codes was to discern the relationship between a participant's personal values – their 'subjective' essence – and their interpretation of the 'external' social landscape they inhabit.

Having illuminated (1) the individual 'context' of each subject and (2) their subjective construction of the world around them, the study then moved to unearth the underlying patterns of language that uphold the credibility of their perceptions. Wetherell and colleagues (2001) describe this as the 'paradigmatic' aspect of speech, which essentially enumerates the spectrum of conceivable alternatives and examines the select paths chosen by individuals within their communications. Armed with this understanding, the third stage of coding homed in on the discursive strategies participants employed to safeguard their self-concepts and their interpretations of others (Potter 2002). This step involved an analysis of modalities, a term used by Wetherell et al. (2001: 242) to refer to the varying 'degrees of commitment to truth or necessity'. Here, the thematic clusters were organized based on how effectively they conferred significance to actions and decisions under the subjects' perceived realities (Burr 2003; Clegg 1975; Weber 1968). Furthermore, beyond merely tracing the 'in-order-to' links between personal context and external reality, we teased out the subjects' self-ascriptive methods in rationalizing their experiences within these realms. This thematic grouping not only reinforced the participants' roles as agents in organizational life but also enabled a deeper, more nuanced critique of their existence within the professional world.

Limitations of the Research Design

The primary challenge faced by the research design is inherent to its idiographic focus. There exists a delicate balance between the depth of individual narratives and the breadth of participant diversity in such a study. To capture rich, textured accounts of the subjects' professional lives, an intentional decision was made to limit the number of participants. This, however, inherently constrains the study's scope for broad comparisons across a wider array of experiences. This intentional scope limitation inherently curtails the study's ability to produce what would traditionally be classified as 'generalizable knowledge' (Miles and Huberman 2014). Indeed, Harvey and Myers

(1995: 23) wisely note that 'without a substantive compendium of insights across varied scenarios, it becomes a challenge to establish expansive, generalised models that capture the essence of lived experiences'. Nonetheless, the aim of this study was never to pave the way for sweeping generalizations. Rather, it concentrated on generating a nuanced understanding of the intricate bond between self-identity and the experiences that shape it, and vice versa. Thus, the value of our conclusions should not be gauged by the yardstick of theoretical generalizability. Instead, they should be valued for their 'phenomenal significance' – for the revelatory insights they offer into the lived realities we set out to explore (Smith et al. 2009).

Notes

1. As noted (Smith et al. 2009: 35–36), a double hermeneutic process of analysis is one where 'the researcher is making sense of the participant, who is making sense of x. And this usefully illustrates the dual role of the researcher as both like and unlike the participant. In one sense, the researcher is like the participant, is a human being drawing on everyday human resources in order to make sense of the world. On the other hand, the researcher is not the participant, she/he only has access to the participant's experience through what the participant reports about it, and is also seeing this through the researcher's own, experientially informed lens.'
2. WHS stands for 'workplace health and safety'.
3. Meta-reflexivity is a term that highlights a process of being reflexive of one's own reflexivity (Archer 2003). It involved subjects in attempting to understand why they perceive things, events and people in particular terms.

Chapter 5

The Superimposed Truth

The Veil of Perpetuating Self-Ideas

Depth Phenomenology of Being-in-the-World of Work

The subsequent pages delve into the intricate realm of depth phenomenology[1] as it pertains to the perceptual and cognitive experiences of individuals within a mid-sized construction firm in Australia. This exploration is drawn from the rich fieldwork I conducted during my doctoral research, showcasing a myriad of phenomena that consistently emerge across various narratives of personal expression. Specifically, I shall engage in a detailed examination of the effects of perception and comprehension in three distinctive forms, which collectively influence and mould the ways in which organizational members construct and interpret their self-identity and that of their colleagues. These forms are categorized as follows:

1. Self-referential/reinforcing perceptions, which are inward-looking and contribute to the bolstering of one's self-concept, ensuring continuity and coherence in the individuals' world view.
2. Corrosive perceptions, which potentially undermine and erode one's sense of self and the mutual understanding within the organization, leading to discord and disconnection.
3. Self-preserving perceptions, serving as a psychological bulwark that individuals employ to maintain their self-concept against external challenges and internal doubts, thereby safeguarding their identity.

In the final leg of this discourse, I will illuminate the profound (4) ontological aspects of our self-ideas, drawing a significant correlation between their intrinsic nature and our capacity for perception and comprehension. Through this analysis, I will demonstrate how the content of our self-ideas is not merely reflective of our current cognitive processes but is also instrumental in shaping our ongoing ability to perceive and understand the world around us. This inextricable link underscores the importance of examining and comprehending the foundational beliefs we hold about ourselves, which, in turn, informs our experience of reality and our interactions within the organizational sphere.

The Primary Phenomenon of Self-Referential and Self-Reinforcing Being-in-the-World of Work

Summary of the argument: The data gleaned from the participants indicates that their conceptions of the 'surrounding world' are inherently shaped – and to some extent, constrained – by their established self-definitions. It becomes apparent that the participants engage with self and others through a self-referential lens, a modality characterized by a reliance on their own circumscribed base of knowledge. This approach to perception does not merely act as a passive filter but actively strengthens their entrenched senses of self and their understanding of others' worlds. The analysis suggests that when individuals interpret their environment through this self-referencing paradigm, they inadvertently bolster the credibility of their own knowledge claims. Our human inclination to seek consistency and continuity necessitates that our observations reinforce our existence as distinct beings. In other words, our need for personal perseverance hinges on the validation of our experiences as we navigate through life. This phenomenon reveals a symbiotic link between the veracity of our knowledge claims and the integrity of our self-identity. The more our perceptions of the world affirm our self-concept, the more secure and stable our identity becomes, creating a self-reinforcing cycle that underpins our sense of reality. This underscores the intricate relationship between our interpretive frameworks and the constancy of our personal identity – a dynamic that has profound implications on how we comprehend and experience ourselves and the world at large.

Each encounter with participants, whether it was in a formal interview setting or an informal discussion, entailed reflecting on the particularity of the organization's operations and the position participants held within the partner organization. Considering the classification of their circumstance, participants also reflected on experiences that made them feel anxious. What became apparent to me fairly quickly was that the 'position' held within the organization appeared not to be classified in terms of the 'objective' characteristics of the position in question, as defined by the organizational hierarchy, job descriptions or key performance indicators (KPIs). In discussions that ensued, the role of the individual within the organization was primarily classified on the grounds of personal criteria. For example, Mark, who holds a senior role in the organization's estimating[2] department, described his role by saying:

> The whole process feels like flogging a horse to see who will be able to sustain more of a beating ... I am expected to perform miracles while other people are given a free pass. Most people are very reluctant to take on responsibility while I always put up my hand to take on new projects even at my detriment. It is always the other guy who is at fault. Take George for example, the other day he was late to a site inspection and has expressed no concerns nor has he apologized for wasting everyone's time.

Margaret, on the other hand, who works in the project management department[3] as a contract administrator, asserted:

> I am expected to define scopes and negotiate contractors. But no one has ever shown me how to do that ... John just yells at me and sends me abusive emails about how I have done something wrong. Come and tell me to my face, don't send me emails. Act how a manager should act. Teach me how to do my job.

While Nick, who is a senior executive at the organization, began with the following:

> I am expected to wear many hats ... I need to be both a builder but also a psychologist. These days employees do not take responsibility for their work because they know there is always someone above them who will come in to pick up the pieces ... People in my position are expected to know everything and be on top of everything.

In every instance, it became evident that the delineation of participants' roles, as well as the roles ascribed to their peers, originated from the foundation of their self-awareness – their conceived sense of self. This personal self-awareness serves as the pivotal basis from which individuals discern and assign roles within the social and professional landscape, reflecting how deeply one's self-concept influences role perception and interaction with others. In the case of Mark; he has classified his job as 'gravely taxing' because of *his* ability to 'perform above standard', that is, sustain and manage what others would perceive as 'unmanageable' and 'excessively onerous' professional demands. Margaret explained her inability to perform her duties by drawing on the 'poor management' of her superiors. More importantly, Margaret presented the 'poor management' of her supervisors as an unquestionable description of their capability on the basis of her knowledge of what a 'good manager' does. Similarly, Nick's description of his professional world did not avoid the classification of employees today in reference to (diligent and hardworking) employees of the past, which he, in turn, represented.[4]

Considering the relational ontology of perception, it thus becomes evident that *because* Nick is a 'hard worker', he can recognize (particular forms of) 'laziness'; *because* Mark 'performs miracles', he can recognize 'reasonable' normative 'limits' of his role and in the roles of others; *because* Margaret is a 'good communicator, personable and sociable', she can recognize bad communication and insufficiency in the soft skills of her co-workers. The relational ontology of perception brings to light that participants categorize their environment through a lens that is reflective of their own self-knowledge and perceived identity. It underscores that the act of classification is not a detached process; rather, it is intricately tied to the ways in which individuals understand and identify themselves, suggesting that their world view is a mirror of their self-conception. Crucially, participants encounter in their professional domain certain 'objective' characteristics that, perhaps unconsciously, lend credence to their subjective self-perception. This discovery suggests that the attributes they ascribe to their work environment serve not only to define that space but also to reinforce and validate their personal identity. I therefore come to the following conclusion: *because* of 'who I am' → my classifications of the world become 'direct and objective' portrayals of reality → which are essential for maintaining the plausibility of my identity.

The interplay between the subject and objects, and between the observer and the observed, emphasizes self-referencing as a fundamental characteristic inherent in the participants' interpretation of themselves and others. It is through this relational ontology that we understand that the act of description itself is imbued with the essence of the describer's identity. As such, although participants' musings are indicative of attempts to construct identity 'in situ', the specificity and particularity of their descriptions[5] suggest that the classification of their roles as taxing (Mark), unreasonable (Margaret) and multifaceted (Nick) would be as arbitrary as saying their roles are 'dark', 'blue' and 'orange' (respectively) if it was not for their pre-existing self-knowledge, which endows their observations with sensibility. This is also recognized by Heidegger (1953: 83), who suggests that:

> The primary 'what-for' is a for-the-sake-of-which. But for-the-sake-of-which always concerns the being of *Dasein* [emphasis mine] which is essentially concerned about this being itself and its being.

This implies that particularized depictions of the surrounding world are born out of a bedrock of preconceived notions and perspectives regarding the subject matter, all of which are inextricably linked to a sense of self that cannot be disregarded. Revisiting the remarks from the central figures of the study, their self-characterizations, such as Mark's 'professional competence', Margaret's 'communicative and personable nature' and Nick's 'diligence and industriousness', cast a light on their immediate world, thereby delineating, by contrast, what 'others' lack in relation to their own attributes. This is also recognized by Ybema et al. (2009: 307) when they suggest that 'the images invoked tell a selective, frequently stereotypical and often dramatised story which scripts the "self" in relation to the "other" on a stage which magnifies differences'. I can therefore say that the referencing ontology serves to connect seemingly arbitrary concepts into a meaningful observation: for example, something is 'bad' or 'good' because **I** know what is 'bad' and what is 'good' and **I** know this because ***I am*** 'good' (or 'bad'). This can be recognized in the following statement made by Mark:

> It gives me great pleasure when a client compliments my work ethic to John [the company's director] … I love to take a new client on a journey; to be given a single sheet of paper and be able to produce an estimate that encapsulates his desires. To be able to help the client express what he likes and materialize it into a project that is feasible is very rewarding. This way you learn a lot but you also add value to the entire organization … It takes a lot of work to do something like that … The upsetting thing is when a project manager takes over from what I have set up and completely destroys all the good work by delivering the project late and not delivering on the quality; essentially, not doing what was promised (by me).

The phenomenon of self-referencing in perception extends beyond the mere incorporation of an individual's existing body of self-knowledge, however. It is worth highlighting that, instead of delineating their daily duties through what their roles 'objectively' encompass, such as referring to explicit job descriptions or measurable KPIs, the participants have also chosen to portray their 'professional worlds' through the prism of their aspirational selves – the embodiment of who they aspire to be. In Mark's case, his goal of 'gaining recognition for his achievements from the senior members of the organization' and 'maintaining high performing standards' is the nexus of his recognition of others' 'irresponsibility' and lack of effort. By the same token, Margaret's desire to become a 'decision-maker in her department' and to be given an opportunity to 'express her creative side and leverage her soft skills' allows for a credible portrayal of her immediate supervisors' managerial shortcomings as a hindrance to her professional fulfilment:

> I would like to become a project manager. I am very personable and outgoing and I think this role would be very suited for me unlike the one I am in now

> which requires me to do 'admin stuff' only. I would like to express my creative side and manage people and clients as opposed to being stapled to a desk all the time. Project management is all about good communications skills … You cannot be shy and be a project manager who is required to interact and speak to stakeholders all day every day … But how will I get there since no one will help me?

Ultimately, Nick's aspiration to develop the business to a point where he can 'pull back and spend more time with his family' imparts 'objective properties' onto the surrounding environment, contrasting the work attitudes of others with the behaviour necessary to achieve his personal objectives:

> I would like to one day be able to pull back and spend more time with my family. I know I have to work hard and I don't mind doing that. My father has done the same but he has gone too far and has worked all his life. I never used to see my father growing up. I don't want to do the same but I know that in order to be in a position to pull back from work, I have to give it my all now. This is the nature of the beast … But things have changed … Employees do not understand that this is life and they complain about things that are normal. This makes my job harder because I have to help them psychologically while also doing things for them that they should actually do themselves.

Therefore, although their stories describe different circumstances, they all highlight an inherent relationality between their existing self-definitions, future goals and desires, and the 'objective'[6] properties of the world(s) they inhibit. Consequently, we can reasonably deduce that a self-referential mode of perception inevitably engenders a unique cycle of being within the world. This cycle is initiated by an aspiration to authenticate personal knowledge by accentuating divergences or commonalities in comparison with others, as theorized by Ybema et al. (2009). Through this process of magnification, the existing self-conceptions are endowed with credibility, and thus, the potential fulfilment of future aspirations becomes conceivable – or even undeniable – on the subjective plane. The following framework develops:

Step 1: The subject, by accessing their pre-existing knowledge and comparing their sense of identity with 'the other', begins proactively seeking affirmation.

Step 2: The subject initiates the process of 'magnifying difference or sameness', utilizing this mechanism to discern and intensify distinctions or affinities between themselves and 'the other' as a means to situate their individual viewpoint as credible.

Step 3: This informed perspective serves to strengthen the subject's self-definitions, rendering them more tenable. The subject accordingly integrates these reinforced definitions into their identity, whether through deliberate intention or subconscious assimilation.

Step 4: The subject now experiences a strengthened conviction towards the realization of their future desires. Despite any inherent uncertainties linked with their aspirations, the subject regards these desires as achievable, bolstered by the confidence in their affirmed self-concepts.

The self-referential phenomenon of perception inadvertently instantiates a *self-reinforcing* relationship between (a) descriptions of the surrounding world, (b) who 'we are' and (c) who 'we want to become'. Here, it becomes difficult to delineate the boundary between the observer and the observed. This intertwining occurs as participants draw upon their self-knowledge to ascribe credence to their descriptions of objects in their environment. Bearing this in mind, consider a thought experiment: how credible would our goals and desires seem if they were not grounded in a genuine and accurate understanding of the current situation? To quote Nick, 'you need to work hard to achieve your goals and working hard means not being lazy like John'. I propose that our aspirations would dissipate if we were to acknowledge that we do not perceive a purposeful connection between them and our present actions or inactions. We could therefore contend that there is no dream devoid of our perception of possibilities and limitations, and likewise, there are no possibilities and limitations without our presence and discernment.

It is to some degree common sense to therefore state that subjects cannot go outside themselves to an independent world of knowledge with which to describe a circumstance. The 'arrows', however, also assume two directions: my classification of the present moment is also plausible because I perceive the present moment from the vision of who I want to become. We therefore also 'borrow' knowledge from the future self to classify and highlight meaning in the present moment. For example, my dream of becoming an ultramarathon runner assigns significance to behaviour in the present in the same way that my behaviour in the present allows for the realization of that dream. Nick's aspiration to retreat and dedicate more time to his family is, by his own account, achievable only through diligent effort, a conviction that gains certainty as he perceives what he interprets as 'laziness' in others around him. In this context, Nick's 'idea' crystallizes into a 'certainty', solidified by the credibility he attributes to his existing observations. To elaborate, without his current industriousness, validated in contrast to others' perceived idleness, his objective, which hinges on the requisite of hard work, would seem unattainable. This is also recognized by Peterson (1999: 26, 27), who states that:

> It appears, therefore, that the image of a goal (a fantasy about the nature of the desired future, conceived of in relationship to the model of significance of the

> present) provides much of the framework determining the motivational significance of ongoing current events … *The point is that some desirable future state of affairs is conceptualised in fantasy and used as a target point for operations in the present. Such operations may be conceived of as links in the chain* [emphasis mine].

The self-reinforcing relationship, as such, is multidirectional, resembling a web: Nick's continual existence within the world 'gains' plausibility, or is purged of 'doubt', by aligning with his goals and desires, which in turn 'achieve' certainty through his specific designation of both himself and others in his work-centred lived experience. As such, (1) his present choices to 'work all the time', which are driven by (2) his goals and desires, permit (3) particular designations of himself and others: his goal influences his perception of 'hard work' and 'laziness', while his 'capacity' to *distinguish* hard work *from* laziness sustains his goal, thereby allowing his 'dream to remain viable'. In support of this realization, Nick notes:

> (3) I am really tired of babysitting people. I wish employees took more ownership of their work. See Nigel for example, he comes in, works and leaves at 5 pm … Mark, on the other hand, makes it a big deal that he had to come in on a Saturday and he makes sure that we all know about it … (1) I never stop working, however, and I don't highlight it to anyone … Even when I get home, I get phone calls about projects and things other people are supposed to be taking care of. I cannot sleep sometimes because I am thinking about what needs to be done. I don't remember the last time I took leave and went somewhere with my family. (2) I would like to one day be able to pull back and spend more time with my family. I know I have to work hard and I don't mind doing that.

The phenomenon of self-referencing and self-reinforcing perception also ensues in the speech of other participants. Mark's choice to (1) persevere under 'abnormal circumstances' is influenced by his goal of (2) 'gaining recognition for his achievements', which permits for (3), a classification of himself as a 'miracle worker' and some of his co-workers' comportment as rather 'irresponsible'. Self-reinforcing and referencing perception is also embedded within Margaret's speech, whose choice (1) to 'not care' and 'give up' emerges in consideration of her (2) goal to be a project manager, which is hindered or made impossible by (3) her superior's 'incompetence', which 'obstructs' her self-realization.

The Epiphenomena of Corrosive Being-in-the-World of Work

Summary of the argument: As highlighted in the previous section, subjects monitor the external world and classify the comportment of others in terms of sameness and difference to their sense of self. However, through this comparative process, subjects (1) impose constraints on their self-knowledge, generating novel insights in the process. These newly identified boundaries of (self-)awareness are not just critical components of 'novelty' but also, and more significantly, (2) forerunners to the ascribed credibility of this new information. Thus, the 'objectivity' of novelty is rooted in the act of self-questioning. Ultimately, (3) the significance of this novel knowledge is aligned with the significance and perceived value that the subject attaches to their self-views, goals and aspirations within their lived reality.

The intriguing aspect of examining everyday discourse is the acknowledgement that self-referential and reinforcing perception invariably leads to self-monitoring, utilizing the very same standards applied when evaluating others. In simple terms, the way we monitor our environment also becomes the way we monitor ourselves. Inherent in judgement of others is therefore the challenge of self-reflection, a notion that becomes especially pronounced in competitive professional settings where benchmarking oneself against others is integral to professional growth. In continuation of the descriptions of his role noted in the previous pages, Nick asserts the following:

> This whole process of moving from a 'builder' to becoming a manager has been a steep learning curve for me. (1) Now I need to consider how people feel in addition to ensuring we deliver quality projects and make money. Going through the strategic restructuring of the company has been a big wake up call for me. It seems I lack understanding of how people around me feel. (2) I cannot read their emotions, and this has become very important to the role I have in the company. On top of everything, (3) I am now expected to work on my soft skills, improve my communication, dress better and consider other people's feelings.

During my dialogue with Mark regarding the 'challenges of being an estimator', he also underscored 'unacknowledged' aspects that bear relevance to his professional reputation as a 'high performer':

> Estimators get three weeks to measure a project. We get a whole pile of documents which we have to decipher in three weeks, account for everything and also produce a competitive bid. See this job I am working on now. Michael just came asking me whether I can fit it into my schedule. What he really expected was for me to commit to doing the job. Here I am now. (1) There is a week left and there is so much that needs to be done: I need to finalize the design of the job with the architect, match the client's brief, get subcontractors involved in the process, make sure I cover everything on the drawings while also be able to submit a competitive bid so we can win the tender. (2) I

> guess it is reasonable to expect these things considering how much I am paid. (3) However, when you come to review with the directors, they always find something they are not happy with, which overshadows all the hard work you have done.

Margaret's self-expression also brought forth new elements within her environment, which eclipsed her self-perception as an effective communicator, creative and approachable, attributes she considers essential for excelling in the role of a project manager:

> The project that I am working on now actually allows me to express my creative side. Michael has this client who owns many hospitality venues which he now wants to renovate and turn into [the] hippest places in the city. I love sitting down in those meetings and helping the client materialize his vision. I know a lot about development because my father has had, and still has, a very successful development business. (1) But for some reason I feel like the client ignores me. He always wants to speak more to Michael than to me about the design of the project. (2) I have a feeling he thinks I am still a junior and not a decision-maker which is why he does not want to waste his time with me. (3) I bet he would act differently if I had 'project manager' in my email signature as opposed to contract administrator. Being a contract administrator, the client probably thinks that I have no knowledge about designing and developing venues. Imagine if you were the client and you receive an email from a contract administrator about important project matters – would you consider them seriously?

In light of the foregoing discussions, the self-referential and reinforcing nature of perception – which, as demonstrated, is key to the participants' understanding – precedes the invocation of contingencies upon the subject's perspective of reality. Nick continues:

> It used to be much easier: I used to consider every member of this organization as a member of my family. I used to joke with everyone like I joke with my family and my approach to work used to inspire trust in people. (1) Now I have a mentor who I speak to once a week who is helping me better myself in areas of 'soft skills', but it has been a steep learning curve for me. (2) I just hope our employees can see that I care about them and if I sometimes offend them, it is not intentional. I cannot speak with many of them the way I used to … (3) Everything is becoming too professional and that is just not what I am used to … The other day I was told I was rude to Jessica … I would have never guessed that my behaviour was rude.

Mark also brings into question his professional capabilities, albeit in a more succinct way:

> (1) You always have a feeling like you could have done better. (2) It is definitely true when they say that you are as good as the last tender you have submitted … (3) You come to a point where anything that you do you know will be unappreciated … What they don't realize is that I can get a job anywhere … I can call a recruiter now and find another job … I guess if it continues this way, I can just move to another company to do the same things for more money and with less pressure.

Margaret also follows 'the trail' of self-negation by saying:

> I can just imagine what Michael [director] thinks of me. (1) Here I am being paid 100k to do virtually nothing. (2) Lisa, for example, is paid nearly half as much as me and she is a gun – she just puts her head down and smashes everything out of the park … (3) I want to develop my projects and do that which I am good at and it looks like this will never happen in this context because there is not much I am learning – nobody helps me with things. If nothing, I will just go back to working for my dad and doing my own developments.

It is important to acknowledge at this juncture that the fallibility of their knowledge is dispersed throughout their claims. In Nick's case, at no point has he highlighted 'objective' measures for defining the appropriateness of emotional management of employees, against which he can render his performance as 'not good enough'.[7] I am not sure if such a thing can even exist in a largely diverse workforce. More importantly, there is no way to know that his 'doubtful' performance in the domain of 'soft skills' will have a negative effect on his capacity to 'work hard' and preserve the arrangement of his existing goals and desires. Similarly, Mark and Margaret are unable to determine with absolute certainty if scenarios such as 'the client's preference to converse with Michael over me about the project' or 'the persistent sensation that I could have performed better' truly reflect their 'objective' professional shortcomings or serve as definitive benchmarks questioning their capabilities. This uncertainty, however, clouds their pursuit of personal ambitions – Margaret's aspiration to 'become a project manager and unleash her creativity', and Mark's desire for 'acknowledgement of his hard work'. Therefore, while the fallibility of their knowledge interlaces their narratives, the act of being both the subject and the object of scrutiny ushers in a novel dimension of plausibility initially beyond the subject's perceptual frontiers. Nick further notes:

> (1) Michael wants the company to grow but I sometimes wish I could go back to the days when I was just working on site and not having to worry about all of these things. (2) The transition from being a builder to having to also

> manage people has meant I am not focusing on that which I am good at – the building and quality control of our projects ... Michael [director], on the other hand, does not have a clue about what is happening on the ground and what I have to do on a daily basis. He goes off on his little sailing boat and comes in thinking things are just running smoothly on their own ... (3) When they are not, he makes a big deal about it thinking no one is doing their job properly. Essentially, I don't care, if he is not happy, I will just go back to doing what I used to do.

I came to the realization that by engaging in referential attribution of truth, the subjects expand the 'domain' of plausible knowledge with which to define the self and others. This stems from the fact that a claim acquires plausibility through its association with other claims, the interconnectedness and relational dynamics of which facilitate the drawing of inferences. In this context, self-referencing inevitably leads to the emergence of new insights that subject the existing self-knowledge to a contingent and evolving reality. For example, in the recognition of the validity of her world views, Margaret inadvertently introduces the burden of 'consensual recognition' (Archer 2003) and in doing so 'corrodes' her self-identity of being a 'good communicator' and 'creative'. By the same token, by referencing and reinforcing his self-knowledge, Nick (also done by Mark) places contingency upon the adequacy of his beliefs and his capability to realize his objectives. This is well articulated by Peterson (1999: 305), who recognizes that:

> The human being, by contrast, with a head full of alternative options (the abstract residue of individual ancestral choice), can use the internalised or freely offered opinion of the group to criticise spontaneous manifestations of subjective perception and motivation – to judge, alter, or inhibit pure subjectivity itself. This ability allows the human being tremendous interpretive and behavioural possibility, freedom, but lays subjective experience, untarnished instincts, bare to insult.

There are three implications emerging from these arguments. First, since every position entails its negative (Sharp 1991), the arguments accentuate that self-negation (or self-judgement) results from the self-referential and self-affirming qualities of perception (Archer 2000). The participants' utterances highlight the process as follows: the self-referencing subjects tell a story that magnifies difference (or sameness). However, in the magnification of difference and sameness (my hard work gives me capacity to see and judge laziness) the (1) self-referencing subject also produces new information, as suggested by Nick: 'although I am hard-working, some of my behaviour can be perceived as inadequate, depending on who we ask.' This means that being a subject and an object of analysis inadvertently brings forth novelty:

The self-referential and reinforcing nature of perception sets the stage for a fluctuation between stability and instability in the realms of self-assurance and self-understanding, which in turn is a fundamental precursor to sociality or the interplay of interactions among individuals (Archer 2000, 2003). What is true depends on where you sit, as Stewart Clegg regularly asserted.

Second, the significance of such 'corrosive' perception, or self-negation stated simply, is that it (2) precedes the validity of newly generated information. Given that understanding is rooted in the self-referential and self-validating nature of perception (as discussed previously), an expanded perception of reality arises amid self-doubt – the 'new' emerges from questioning what is perceived as established by the subject. The authenticity of the 'new' is not determined solely by additional references but by the magnitude of the doubt cast upon accepted truths. To illustrate, the encounter with a tiger invokes fear not merely due to its inherent danger but because it highlights the potential loss of one's familiar existence. The import of the tension between what a subject perceives as credible (like their self-concept and their world of others) and the doubt cast upon it lies in the potential to negate all previously held beliefs. Thus, the 'new' gains objectivity from the established objectivity of the 'old'. The point is not just that by challenging one's preconceptions, one encounters the compelling (and 'objective') nature of novelty, but that it is the substantiality of the disputed relevance of Nick's self-views, objectives and aspirations that lends a semblance of veracity and realism to the concept of 'soft skills'. Put simply, the value and significance we attribute to our current and aspirational selves suggest that any information capable of undermining these perceptions is worthy of consideration as credible.

Finally, (3) the scope of newly acquired information (or the number of 'valid' reference points) is contingent upon the significance we ascribe to our aspirations. As previously stated, self-monitoring based on the criteria we use to evaluate others generates novelty, akin to the concept that reflective scrutiny of our professional engagement yields fresh insights. Such novelty is then perceived as an objective characteristic of the world, as it challenges pre-existing perceptions held by the subject. This 'erosion' of the self-concept is crucial because it triggers an expansion of reference points through which subjects can define both themselves and others, doing so by introducing uncertainty as an ever-present facet of all subsequent experiences. As a result, the subject's confidence in their abilities wavers. Consequently, Nick might view each interaction with employees as a reflection of his 'inadequacy'; every client interaction could be seen by Margaret as a marker of her 'invisibility'; and each new project may represent a chance for Mark to falter and lose his reputation as an 'exceptional performer'. The participants' discourse thereby reveals that the complexity of the newly perceived world is intrinsically linked to the depth and breadth of the weight of our self-image, ambitions and desires – reminding us that the greater we perceive our potential loss to be, the more formidable the challenges we perceive to emerge.

The Secondary Phenomenon of Self-Preservation in Being-in-the-World

Summary of the argument: Subsequent to recognizing new constraints within their self-awareness, individuals exhibit self-protective behaviours. They attempt to maintain their identity by reshaping their narrative to accommodate the nuances of these newly discovered boundaries. However, this realignment is not achieved through the accumulation of a broader, more intricate web of reference points (such as gathering more data to attain 'perfection' or 'wholeness'). On the contrary, individuals often choose to reduce the intricacy and reach of their relevant reference points (for example, by lessening the number of benchmarks deemed significant). This is accomplished by reconfiguring their network of self-conceptions, ambitions and aspirations to establish (1) a hierarchy, wherein the most critical elements to the 'identity-seeking individual' rise to the top. More pointedly, the focused dimension of (restructured) subjectivity (2) constrains the potential variability of self-knowledge that is 'discovered in the external world', thereby diminishing (3) the unpredictability of the situation as it is now perceived. By prioritizing what bears the greatest importance in their 'subjective context', individuals streamline the complexity of the world as they reconstruct it, thereby unburdening their actions from the constraints they face.

The act of self-negation, or the onset of doubt cast upon one's previously solid self-awareness, creates a 'network of significance' that essentially defines the frontiers of the world that the subjects navigate. Remembering our earlier discussions, it is the considerable influence of the seemingly unlikely importance (that is, the negation) of Nick's self-views, ambitions and aspirations that lends a semblance of legitimacy and objectivity to the idea of 'soft skills'. In the context of this interconnected schema, the dynamic is self-reinforcing, indicating that the perceived validity and objectivity of the concept of 'soft skills', coupled with Nick's perceived shortcomings in emotional intelligence, imbue his established self-concepts, objectives and aspirations with notable importance.[8] Consequently, the significance network that informs behaviour comprehensively encompasses everything the subject embodies and lacks. It integrates both the 'expansion of new insights' and the 'intensity of existing self-concepts, ambitions and yearnings'. Following this line of thought, while the erosion of one's self-concept – through the imposition of fresh limits on one's self-knowledge – expands our cognitive universe and complicates its navigation, it simultaneously exposes the often overlooked network of concerns, desires, aims and goals that sculpt the specificity of 'immediate' situations the individual faces. This understanding allows us to realize that it is solely due to his 'miracle worker' self-image that Mark can experience a context where his performance is seen as 'lacking' and 'inadequate', and where the expectations set by his leaders appear 'irrational' and 'capricious'.

The profound consequence of 'self-negation' is that it reveals the underlying ontology of the 'network' that lies dormant within self-affirming identity work – the kind of agency that achieves its desired outcomes unimpeded by 'obstacles'. The 'elaborate descriptions' of the world (as understood by the subjects) are spawned from a 'because-of' relationship with their sensed shortcomings. By 'entertaining failure', the subjects therefore gave birth to a self-sustaining network of reasons, rationalities, self-descriptions, goals, desires and concerns all of which worked to validate their self-concept and the behaviours of others. Only when things are broken are we faced with their significance, to paraphrase Heidegger. I guess this is why romantics say that we do not know what we have until we lose it. Accompanying Nick to one site inspection,[9] I listened while he made the following observations:[10]

> My father used to always work. I remember, he used to come home very late and I used to see him only on the weekends. I really appreciate that my father sacrificed himself and made sure that we have everything that we need. He is the one that instilled the hard work ethic in me. This is how I approach my work today. However, I don't want to be like my father. I thank him but I don't want to see my kids only on the weekend and be a bystander in their upbringing. (1) This is actually why I work hard now. I would like this business to get to a stage where I can delegate and spend more time with my family. (2) However, I need to work hard now for this to be a possibility … But it is not all about hard work these days. I miss the time where I was on tools building things with my hands. Now I have to manage other people, be attentive to their emotions, entertain clients and network with them, all of the things I have never done before and do not like doing now. Michael [managing director] always complains about my behaviour in these areas of work … (3) Sometimes I just want to go back to what I used to do and if Michael doesn't like it, this is what I just might do.

The significance of self-negation, however, is not only that it exposes the 'network of meaning' that guides participants' behaviour. The significance of evoking contingency upon one's self-knowledge is that it also adds to what Heidegger (1953) refers to as the 'numbering of the self'. Let me explain. Given that the broadened domain of relevant and significant knowledge is scaffolded upon an individual's network of self-definitions, aspirations and desires (see previous section), Heidegger's concept of the 'numbering of the self' accentuates the dilemma in which subjects, as Sennett (2011: 45) observes, psychologically burdened by the increasing contingency of their self-knowledge, 'look to detail for some portent of meaning' in the pursuit of 'self-realisation' (also discussed by Archer 2000, 2003, 2010, 2015; Archer et al. 2015).[11] In this situation, the subject constructs a reality where all elements hold potential relevance. More critically, the subject shapes a world where this relevance is perceived as *uniformly distributed*. Such an outlook inadvertently engulfs the subject in perpetual uncertainty during interactions.[12] From the participants' narratives, this indicates a risk that individuals like Nick might overlook 'objective' emotional signals in communication with all colleagues.

This was acknowledged by Nick when he stated that 'the other day I was told I was rude to Jessica [and] I would have never guessed that my behaviour was rude'. Mark also perpetuates uncertainty within his daily activities by highlighting innumerable 'things' that need to be fulfilled (by him) to perform to *his* standard of being a 'miracle worker'. When speaking about the expectations of his superiors, Mark suggests that 'they always find something they are not happy with, which overshadows all the hard work you have done'. Finally, Margaret faces 'millions of things she has done wrong and others have done right' when she 'objectifies' the unfavourable stance of her capabilities (as perceived by others, supposedly). As my father would say, all subjects subsequently 'begin living someone else's life'. The significance of this argument is also recognized by Heidegger (1953: 125), who states:

> As the they-self, Dasein is *dispersed* [emphasis in the original] in the they and must first find itself. This dispersion characterises the 'subject' of the kind of being which we know as heedful absorption in the world encountered as closest. If Dasein is familiar with itself as the they-self, this also means that *the they prescribes the nearest interpretation of the world and of being-in-the-world* [emphasis mine]. The they itself, for the sake of which Dasein is every day, *articulates the referential context of significance* [emphasis mine]. The world of Dasein frees the beings encountered for a totality of relevance which is familiar to the they in the limits which are established with the averageness of they. *Initially* [emphasis in the original] factical Dasein is in the with-world, discovered in an average way. *Initially 'I' 'am' not in the sense of my own self, but I am the others in the mode of the they* [emphasis mine]. *In terms of the they, and as the they, I am initially 'given' to 'myself'. Initially, Dasein is the they and for the most part it remains so.*

To counteract the relentless relativism of their environment, as described by Sennett (2011), wherein everything holds sway, the subjects embark on a process of stratifying their subjective realities. In defiance of 'numbering of the self', they first conjure up alternative modes of existence within their current professional realms. As noted by Nick, 'essentially, I don't care, if he is not happy [with all the things I do], I will just go back to doing what

I used to do'. Mark also 'escapes' the complexity of the world within which everything is relevant by suggesting that 'if it continues this way, I can just move to another company to do the same things for more money and with less pressure'. By the same token, Margaret also deals with the 'swelling' of the totality of relevance by suggesting that she will 'just go back to working for my dad and doing [her] own developments'.

However, the subjects transcend the expanded domain of relevant and significant knowledge not merely by invoking alternative modes of being within their work world. More crucially, they achieve this by cultivating a single pointed subjectivity that transforms their network of significance into a structured hierarchy of importance. This implies that the subject's relational framework, made up of the entirety of their being and non-being that guides behaviour (the network of significance), is restructured so that elements previously diminished by self-denial now gain increased importance compared to those deemed 'relevant' through the act of self-negation. These aspects maintain their interconnection, yet the dynamic shifts from one of parity, as seen in the original network arrangement, to a hierarchy where the former holds greater weight for the subject than the latter.[13] The most significant aspects of the self are, as such, protected by virtue of the insignificance of newly perceived limits. For example, by assigning more significance to the 'hard worker' identity, Nick inadvertently 'downgrades' (by way of 'reduced significance') all reference points associated with the 'soft skills' paradigm. The same ensues phenomenally within the speech of other participants. Consequently, Nick's pursuit of alternate modes within his professional existence represents a gradation of subjectivity that simplifies a 'complex network' into a 'single-pointed' dilemma. As asserted by Nick previously:

> I really appreciate that my father sacrificed himself and made sure that we have everything that we need. He is the one that instilled the hard work ethic in me. This is actually why I work hard now. [So] if he [Michael] is not happy, I will just go back to doing what I used to do.

Margaret also simplifies the encountered surrounding world by underscoring her 'management and people skills':

> I want to develop my projects and do that which I am good at and it looks like this will never happen in this context because there is not much I am learning – nobody helps me with things. If nothing, I will just go back to working for my dad and doing my own developments.

Mark also escapes the 'numbering of the self' by preserving the significance of his 'miracle worker' self-identity:

> You come to a point where anything that you do you know will be unappreciated … What they don't realize is that I can get a job anywhere … I can call a recruiter now and find another job … I guess if it continues this way, I can just move to another company to do the same things for more money and with less pressure.

Accordingly, the gradation of subjective context not only streamlines the inherently uncertain nature of self-awareness but also, perhaps unintentionally, simplifies the complexity experienced in the wider world. By condensing knowledge reference points into a singular paradigm – 'hard worker' for Nick, 'competent communicator and project manager' for Margaret and 'miracle worker' for Mark – the subjects create a reality that is more straightforward to navigate. Consequently, by assigning varying levels of importance to reference points in the expanded domain of knowledge according to what is most significant to them, subjects decrease the unpredictability of their immediate circumstances, thereby liberating their actions from the constraints previously imposed. As such, as individuals narrow their self-definitions, goals and desires, the perceived breadth and intricacy of the world around them diminish. Thus, when subjects interpret their reality from a standpoint that safeguards the self,[14] they unburden their identity and perceptions of others from the referential attribution of 'truth'. In this way, unbeknown to themselves, the subjects act as their own sources of insight and guidance. These observations should not go unnoticed!

The Meta-Phenomenon of a Distinctive Self-Idea: The Organizing Idea(s) of Situated Experiences

Summary of the argument: The hierarchy of self-definitions, goals and desires is constructed around the 'in-order-to' and 'because-of' dynamics that interweave with the subject's self-idea. The distinctive self-idea represents a synthesis of the subject's perceived past deficiencies and the envisioned ideal self, a construct that crystallizes from these realizations. The self-idea establishes the ontological groundwork for perception, serving as the pivotal element in how individuals perceive themselves and others. As the foundational precondition for personal context, it is the essential criterion through which subjects sculpt and continuously refine their interpretation of the world around them. The organizing self-idea ontologically 'precedes' and informs the self-referential, reinforcing and preserving behaviours central to daily existence within the world of work – as outlined in the previous chapter. It delineates the perceived boundaries of the subject's world. Thus, the concept of situated experience is inseparable from the 'in-order-to' and 'because-of' relationship with an abstract, idealized self.

As emphasized in the previous chapter, an individual's network of significance is crucial to understanding and perceiving their environment. Take Margaret as an instance: the legitimacy of her self-identification as a 'good communicator' and the connected aspiration 'to run her own projects one day' is affirmed through her discernment of 'effective' and 'ineffective' instances of 'communication' and 'project management' in the external world. Engaging in referential attribution of truth, however, the subjects expanded the domain of relevant knowledge and self-knowledge. This dynamic has given rise to an inverse relationship between the subjects' self-perception and the significance they ascribe to the external world: as the relevance of all newly perceived elements in the world around them proportionately intensifies, their own self-definitions, goals and desires diminish in importance. On account of the subsequent 'corrosion' in their sense of self, the subjects have streamlined their 'network of significance' to prioritize elements paramount to the identity-seeking individual, consequently simplifying the breadth and complexity of the surrounding world. Take Nick's case as an illustration: it is through acknowledging his 'inadequate' interpersonal abilities[15] that he has managed to acknowledge and reaffirm the value of the 'hard worker' persona, thus liberating his actions from the constraints imposed by his perceived shortcomings in social adeptness. In Nick's own words, 'if Michael [the director] doesn't like it, I'll revert to what I was doing before.' On account of this shift, subjects began to comprehend and perceive the surrounding world through the lens of the 'hierarchy of significance'. On that note, among other (less significant) things that pertained to their sense of self, Margaret 'found' in the world *mostly* that which reflected her communications skills (or lack thereof); Nick 'found' in the world *mostly* that which reflected his 'hard work' (or lack thereof); while Mark 'found' in the world *mostly* that which reflected his capacity to (professionally) achieve what others cannot (or otherwise). Most importantly, therefore, the fact that such a shift in perception[16] unburdens the subject from referential attribution of truth matters not so much as does the realization that the *possibility* of single-pointed subjectivity is indicative of a pervasive 'subjectum' (Heidegger 1953).

The concept of 'subjectum' possesses depth that transcends the mere variance in self-expression. Although it reflects a distinctive subject, what is of significance, more importantly, is the phenomenon of *possibility* of a particular subjective context (or distinctive subject). Every subject develops a specific network of meaning, which evolves into a particular hierarchy of significance. Therefore, the profound essence of 'subjectum' is realized in the *deliberate embrace* of certain self-definitions, aspirations and desires – selected from a vast array of possibilities – based on the prevailing circumstances perceived by the individual. Subsequently, 'the choice' of referencing, reinforcing or preserving one's sense of self (see previous chapter) has to emerge from an understanding of the world in particular terms. This suggests that what is referenced, reinforced or preserved within speech (for example, a particular self-definition, goal or desire) has not only been intentionally appropriated, but more importantly has, in the first instance, been intentionally assigned with degrees of value – things emerge from the 'sea of inconspicuousness' by virtue of being comprehended and perceived by the subject as *more or less valuable because of something else*, and it is these (emergent) things that form the subjects' *immediate* 'surrounding world' (Heidegger 1953).

Empirically, this is reflected in the subjects' attempts to advance *specific conclusions* at the expense of others. On that note, while the arrangement within the network is self-sustaining in that self-definitions relate to and sustain specific goals and desires, and vice versa, the network of significance is not self-sustainable. As such, in the same way that a set of self-definitions is only sensible in terms of the goal to which they relate, the network of things that matter to a subject does not and cannot become meaningful in and of itself. Such 'uprooting' of significance would not permit the *gradation* of one's subjective content (see Chapter 7) by virtue of that which matters the most to the subject. Simply stated, it is *because-of* the story of participants that their perceived inadequacies *matter*. Furthermore, it is *because-of* their network of significance that the subjects and I were having the *particular* discussions in the first instance.

On account of these observations, it is because of something else that the network or hierarchy of significance (or both) *subsume* a particular content of value and subsequently *assume* their respective arrangements. This suggests that even though our self-definitions stand in a relationship with our subjectively conceived pragmatic ends – meaning that when one is perceived to be risked, the other also emerges as a point of contention – emphasizing a relationship between some more than others pinpoints an *organizing phenomenon* that *provides resources* for different[17] 'forms' of perceiving. What becomes evident is that subjects advance particular forms of subjective content (at the expense of others) on account of *their insight* about what constitutes a (more) representative, complete and adequate view of reality. In our (in-depth) discussion about his personal and professional life, Mark made the following observations:

> I began learning about building as a child helping my dad with the maintenance of our property in Texas. My father also had a small carpentry business, so he took us along with him every opportunity we had. He used to always use my siblings and I to assist him with everything around the house. We had a big land, a house and a barn like [the] typical Texas family that we were. Considering that I am one of eight, it was possible to manage his business and the land in this way. This meant that I was on tools since I was 13 years

> old … Living in such a big family also made it difficult to do what you personally wanted. Everything was always done for the sake of the family and this way it was difficult to develop your own identity; your likes and dislikes. When I was younger, I was never particularly good at anything … On the other hand, my father was very good with his hands, but he never had good business sense. This has meant that all he was ever known for is fixing things, but he never took it to the next level by turning his business into more of an enterprise. He liked doing things the old way – he thought that if he knew how to fix things, this is all that is needed to sustain himself and the family. However, because of this attitude, he has lost a lot of good business opportunities and as a result has found himself struggling to pay off the house we lived in. I think he still has a small mortgage on it and he is 70 years old. I respect my father and am grateful for his struggles. He made sure we had all we needed. I will try and do the same for my kids. But – and this is the reason why I moved to Australia – I want to embrace and explore new opportunities. If I stayed in Texas, I would have lived the same life as him and all my siblings. I would never end up doing anything on my own. This is why I love what I do now because, for the first time in my life, I am finally good at something and I have achieved it all on my own. I guess this is why I associate who I am with what I do. I consider being an estimator at Mirbelia Projects as part of my identity now.

The self-definitions, goals and desires of an individual not only mirror what is deemed significant and valuable within the context of existing circumstances, but also encapsulate our conceptions of the world and our place within it. They are reflective of our interpretation of both the past and present, and crucially, they shape our projection of a desired future.[18] On that note and with respect to the comments made by Mark, it is recognizable that the everyday 'conclusions' advanced in situ are supported by a narrative-like[19] structure. For Margaret, the constraints encountered in her environment that have influenced her adoption of self-definitions, goals and desires are rooted in her views on her father's life. This includes his interactions with her during her childhood, his relationship with her mother and his professional trajectory. Thus, her understanding of her 'immediate circumstances' has played a crucial role in forming what she considers to be a fuller, more precise and fitting account of the events that unfolded: Margaret's introspection into her father's life, as a lens to understand her own, has led her to establish a conceptual framework of advantages and disadvantages that guides her discernment of 'right' and 'wrong' in her day-to-day professional existence. Margaret notes:

> My father is a very successful man. He worked for a law firm for a long time and managed to become a partner. He was making a lot of money and has given to my sister and I everything we wanted. But because he worked so much, we were neglected emotionally. Work was his number one priority and

> that has not only strained his marriage but has also meant that my sister and I never had a father figure type of influence in our lives. After leaving the law firm, he began developing property, making hundreds of millions of dollars in the process. He is very business astute but as a result of his financial success, he lost the view of all of the things that really matter. My mother has left us as a result and he did nothing to stop her from leaving. On top of that, my sister has been struggling with depression for years and I cannot remember the last time I had a meaningful conversation with my father. Now, he is lost – he has all this money but is getting older and because of it, he is trying to compensate by dating younger women and buying things he does not need. See, I love my father and I love his work ethic and his approach to business. Business-wise, I want to follow in his footsteps. I want to one day have my own development company and manage my own projects. But I also want to have a family and spend time with my children and not sacrifice the things that matter for business success. I think you can have both.

By utilizing various methods of crafting self-identity in context – such as self-referencing, reinforcing and preserving, as detailed in the previous chapter – the subjects critically examine their fathers' constrained existences to forge a self-image imbued with 'revised' meanings. This *new* image, in their view, represents a more appropriately constituted *subject*. For example, Nick and Margaret retain their fathers' perceived work ethics as foundations of their self-identity, but embellish or extend them with the (revised) role that the family plays in one's professional undertaking. Conversely, Mark amplifies his father's work ethic by adopting a more 'business-oriented' mindset – manifest in his self-image as a 'miracle worker' and his ambition to be recognized and lauded for his diligence, all in pursuit of transcending the prospect of an 'average' life.[20,21] As noted by Jung (1933: 21), 'when it comes to the assimilation of content, it is never a question of "this *or* that", but of "this *and* that"'. In all accounts, as such, a new (ideal) world, with the subjects' self-identity at its centre, thus emerges from the perceived limits of the old.[22] As aptly asserted by Jung (ibid.: 115):

> It is true that widely accepted ideas are never the personal property of their so-called author; on the contrary, he is the bond-servant of his ideas. Impressive ideas which are hailed as truths have something peculiar to themselves. Although they come into being at a definite time, they are and have always been timeless; they arise from that realm of procreative, psychic life out of which the ephemeral mind of the single human being grows like a plant that blossoms, bears fruit and seed, and then withers and dies. Ideas spring from a source that is not contained within one man's personal life. *We do not create them; they create us* [emphasis mine]. To be sure, when we deal in ideas, we inevitably make a confession, for they bring to the light of day not only the best that in us lies, but our worst insufficiencies and personal shortcomings as well.

The insight from the 'drive to know' (Lonergan 1992: 28) subsequently served as the foundation for the constitution of the subjects' subjectivity. Furthermore, it provides the criteria for advancing some forms of (subjective) content at the expense of others. Crucially, it defined the contours of their personal worlds, inside of which they could carve out distinct identities, guided by the veracity of their insight. As such, the 'organizing phenomenon' reflected in participants' narratives (1) emerges as an *extension* to the perceived limitations in the world of actors, actions and contexts. The emerging phenomenon is an insight produced with respect to the question of identity (the 'who am I', and by virtue of implication, the 'how should I act' question). This insight then (2) foregrounds the formulation of one's ideas about oneself and the surrounding world of others. More importantly, to 'objectify' the insight and the self-idea, (3) the subjects then *(re)contextualize* the emerging conclusions by virtue of pragmatic correlates (goals, desires, objectives). This suggests that subjects seek to *prove* that which they abstractly formulate in the way they live their life. I can therefore say that the *novelty* of insight and the liberating experience of realization it engenders spearhead the ontological nature of the subjects' forthcoming ideas. On the one hand, this provides the 'insight' with context-specific applicability, sensibility and relevance, while inadvertently serving to affirm *truth* within its content.

Once a pertinent insight crystallizes into an idea[23] concerning the self and others, its substance solidifies into the core matters of concern for the individual, providing a basis for attributing significance to the self-definitions, goals and desires adopted in response to perceived circumstances. Crucially, the insights born from the 'psychic tension' inherent in questions of identity, along with the resulting self-concept, become entwined with one's continuous interactions with the world,[24] as they 'recede into habitual textures of the mind' (Lonergan 1992: 15). We resist compromising our ideas, for to do so would signify a betrayal of the insight that has granted us a distinct sense of self, differentiating us from the broader world. To betray this insight feels akin to betraying a force greater than ourselves – it is an affront to the foundational understanding that defines our individuality.

Synopsis

The arguments laid out thus far illustrate the dynamic cycle of existence that initiates with self-referential and self-reinforcing perceptions and culminates in the effort to maintain the uniqueness of one's self-concept. In particular, they underscore how our vigilant awareness originates from established self-knowledge reserves. Against this backdrop of self-understanding, we interpret the world around us and the actions of others as either resonating with or diverging from our self-perception and aspirations. Yet in viewing the external world through the prism of our own identity, we inadvertently apply the same evaluative criteria to our behaviour. This introspection breeds innovation that may erode our current self-concept by intensifying the certainty of 'who we are and wish to be'. Consequently, individuals remodel their network of self-definitions, goals and desires, often forgoing elements deemed less crucial in favour of those with a higher assigned value in their quest for identity. Ultimately, this discourse illuminates the deep-seated drive to safeguard and sustain the most valued components of our self-concept, anchoring and affirming our ideal sense of self.

Notes

1. This book aligns with Heidegger's definition of phenomenology. For Heidegger (1953: 58) 'phenomenology means … to let that which shows itself be seen from itself in the very way in which it shows itself from itself'. He continues by saying: 'to have a science "of" phenomena means to grasp its object in such a way that everything about them which is up for discussion must be treated by exhibiting it directly and demonstrating it directly' (ibid.: 59). This means that the study did not focus on highlighting truthfulness or plausibility of spoken words, but has however looked to unearth that which stands on its own, shines through and cannot be 'divided' further – that which lives on its own irrespective of the particularity of the spoken word.
2. A person working in an estimating department is called an estimator. Their responsibility is to scope and quantify projects prior to the construction process. It is the estimator who estimates the construction cost of the project, based on which the organization acquires new work.
3. Every construction organization is predominantly divided into two key areas: estimating, which tenders projects, and project management, which builds projects that have been tendered successfully by the estimating department.
4. It is important to reiterate that the study did not aim to establish the truthfulness of claims and whether what has been said by participants is factual or not. What the study aimed to highlight, however, is that our classifications of the surrounding world cannot be conceived as separate to who we are (or perceive ourselves to be).
5. Each participant articulated the essence of their roles ontologically in a uniform manner, yet their unique experiences and perspectives manifested in diverse ontic expressions.
6. What they perceive as objective properties *gain* their 'objectiveness' via their existing knowledge and self-knowledge, which also includes knowledge of who they *will be*.
7. It is important to note that given the book's positioning of the subject as central to the analysis of personal identity, and given the ontological nature of self-referential and reinforcing perception – which was explicated in previous sections – even if Nick's superior or an employee expressed how 'good' or 'bad' he is at managing employees' emotional well-being, their classification would be made from the vantage point of their own pragmatic ends (Archer 2010). As such, for example, the company's director could pass judgement against Nick's comportment in terms of his desire to manage the perceptions his clients have of the organization 'as a brand' (of which Nick is a representative). Classification of Nick's comportment from this vantage point would

be founded on a different set of substantive rationalities than would a classification rendered by Nick's colleague who pointed out Nick's insensitivity to matters of gender or cultural differences. Specifically, both represent classifications of Nick's 'soft skills' that are, however, founded on two different sets of concerns relative to the individuals making the classification. As a result of the inherent subjectivity of these classifications, they do not provide 'objective' guidelines for Nick that will assist him in managing his future comportment simply because their 'objectivity' is not referential to Nick's existing self-knowledge, which 'allowed him to previously joke with employees without worrying about what he says'. What these 'unknown' (to Nick) classifications, however, do provide for Nick is an expanded domain of relevance in that they highlight what he did not know, or did not consider, that *actually* matters. As such, the significance of newly introduced reference points is instantiated by Nick's desire to preserve *his* 'particular world' within which he can be a 'particular individual', and not because the colleagues' claims are objectively indisputable. As noted by Archer (2000, 2003), for something to matter, we must care about it enough, by virtue of which it becomes a matter of non-indifference to us.

8. For example, should Nick's ultimate goal be to become a songwriter, the importance placed on his performance in the newly introduced domain of 'soft skills' would be insignificant (or at least reduced) and the classification of his 'inappropriate' comportment a non-contention simply because his self-definitions would be tied to a concern that 'lives' outside of the organization's walls.
9. In construction organizations, site inspections are carried out at different intervals of the project to ascertain progress, meet clients or assist with overall delivery. The specific site inspection in question was for a tender interview, as the partner organization was shortlisted by the potential clients as one of the preferred builders, and as such the clients wanted to conduct a tender interview on the project site.
10. Quotations from Mark and Margaret on the same topic are presented in the following section.
11. The peculiarity of novelty, as such, pertains to the predictive nature of being-in-the-world, which 'pushes' one to evoke every possible contingency upon a potential event (both positive and negative) to protect oneself from a 'loss of face': subjects evoke the '(un)known' or '(im)plausible' to adapt to it in abstraction. On that note, the self is 'numbered' by the amplified internal soliloquy that suddenly becomes populated with an expanded domain of relevant and significant knowledge 'necessary' for self-realization. As such, in our attempt to improve our predictive capacities by learning more about the contingency of the surrounding world we inadvertently produce more points of reference that have the potentiality to 'corrode' our self-knowledge.
12. Peterson (1999: 40) explains this phenomenon by stating that 'It is particularly difficult to specify the value of an occurrence when it has one meaning from one frame of reference (with regards to one particular goal), and a different or an even opposite meaning, from another equally or more important and relevant frame. Stimuli that exist in this manner constitute *unresolved problems of adaptation* [emphasis in the original]. They present us with mystery which is what to do in their presence ... Such circumstances provide evidence that our systems of valuation are not yet sophisticated enough to foster complete adaptation – demonstrate to us incontrovertibly that our processes of evaluation are still incomplete.'
13. The hierarchy-of-significance arrangement is contrary to the network-of-significance arrangement because in a network arrangement, everything carries an equal weight of significance for the subject.

14. In terms of Nick, working less and spending more time with family or 'going back to what he used to do' both preserve his identity of being a 'hard worker'; for Mark, performing above standard or 'getting a new job' both preserve his desire to be recognized as a miracle worker; while expressing her creativity and being a decision-maker remain possibilities for Margaret if she decides to 'work for her dad and do her own developments'.
15. This was previously referred to as the multidimensional nature of identity work and is encapsulated in the acts of self-negation and self-affirmation simultaneously. In rearranging their self-definitions in the form of a hierarchy, subjects reinforced some aspects of the self at the expense of others.
16. The shift from perceiving the world through the network of significance to the hierarchy of significance.
17. As was highlighted in the previous chapter, when subjects 'comprehend' through a network of significance, their interpretation of the surrounding world is founded on a self-referencing and reinforcing modality of perception. On the other hand, when subjects 'comprehend' through the hierarchy of significance, their interpretation of the surrounding world is founded on a self-preserving modality of perception.
18. It is important to note that the complete particularity of our self-idea(s) can only be known by the subject, thus leaving much inaccessible to the researcher's analytic gaze. Irrespective of this conclusion, the rearrangements of subjects' goals, desires and self-definitions by virtue of importance is indicative of an organizing phenomenon that 'sits behind the inner dialogue' and informs different modes of speech (for instance, self-referencing/reinforcing/preserving).
19. Narrative, in this instance, does not just refer to reflexive reconstruction of past events, but also subsumes participants' future desired ways of being-in-the-world. For this reason, I find it more appropriate to refer to this self-narrative as a self-idea, since ideas reflect not only one's interpretation of past events, things and people but also one's vision of ideal ways of being. For this reason, the terms 'narrative' and 'idea' will be used interchangeably.
20. The study's findings do not highlight a deterministic outcome in which childhood events and their interpretation *had* to lead to the current situation. The findings merely highlight a relationship between subjects' experienced past, perceived present and projected future and recognize that there must be a plethora of additional interpretations, views and perceptions of one's past that have not been expressed in the participants' narratives. The findings merely emphasize the primacy of subjective constructs in shaping one's situated experiences and the narrative structure of our 'operating systems'.
21. My conclusions in this paragraph have also been confirmed by the subjects. I first came to these conclusions, which were then affirmed by the subjects as plausible in subsequent discussions and follow-up interviews.
22. I am not suggesting that subjects perceive the surrounding world exclusively on the back of realizations made at a particular moment in time. Nor do I suggest that the acquisition and accumulation of subjective content occurs in a linear and deterministic fashion, from past to future. I however suggest that one's being-in-the-world is regulated on the basis of insight that emerges as an extension of perceived limitations in immediate circumstance.
23. The fact that the self-idea – that is, a phenomenal extension of the perceived immediate circumstance – was capable of emerging suggests that there exists tension in one's psyche respective to making sense of the world and carving out a place for oneself in it. Whether or not there are pre-existing subjective frameworks with which the subject makes sense of circumstance is difficult to discern given the limitations of this study in time and

scope (see Leary 1977 on the eight-circuit brain theory). These frameworks can only be assumed on the basis that one cannot explain away the mind by virtue of emptiness of content. What is, however, evident is that subjects possess an intrinsic aptitude for inquiry, or better yet, that being-in-the-world is analogous with persistent sense-making, which cannot obviate the identity question since all sense-making is by definition self-referential: a system cannot go outside of itself for independent criteria of knowledge to make sense of circumstance (Clegg 1975).

24. This does not aim to suggest that a single insight shapes one's experiences, but rather and more importantly that the identity-seeking individual has an ontological drive to know themselves and others and as a result incessantly generates insight, which shapes their narrative, agency and situated experience accordingly.

Chapter 6

The Journey of the Distinctive Self

In the following pages I will discuss the 'journey' of the self-idea, a process whose essence is interwoven with the ability to trace how one's self-identity is moulded and reshaped. Initially, I will posit that the individual is, at the outset, unable to effectively engage with the ideas that influence their behaviour. Nevertheless, given that the self-reinforcing and self-referential nature of perception unintentionally generates new aspects within the self's understanding and the perception of others, I will contend that only through self-negation does the subject gain awareness of what structures their perception and cognition. A somewhat unforeseen conclusion is that this interplay of self-affirmation and self-inquiry ultimately 'brings us back to ourselves', by offering the chance to make choices congruent with the most significant aspects of our being.

Subsequently, I will explore the interplay of intentional engagement and distinct self-identity through the lens of the participants' reflections. The argument advanced proposes that the maintenance of '(self-)constructed environments' is essential for the abstract elements of the self to affirm their ontological essence. Put plainly, the narratives we craft must assume a semblance of truthfulness in order for us to sustain the continuity of our believed identities. Thus, intentionality is grounded in the essential credibility of both our self-narratives and our depictions of the world around us. This offers an ideal transition into examining self-identity as a distinctive phenomenon. I will suggest that the nature of self-identity is not only reflected in the definitively described surrounding world, that is, distinctive content advanced in situ, but also and more importantly in the distinctive subjective possibility without which nothing would be perceptible to begin with. Finally, the insights from these discussions will form the foundation for addressing the unanswered questions presented in Chapter 3.

The (Non-)Emergence of Self-Identity: The Journey of the Self-Idea

The *journey* of the self-idea is reflected in the relationship between the primary and secondary modalities of self-expression (see previous chapter). To begin with, our existence within the world cannot circumvent the self-referential and self-reinforcing dynamic of perception, as it is through our accumulated knowledge and self-awareness that we are able to 'understand' and 'observe' the world around us. On account of this realization we can say that everyday agency springs from the bedrock of pre-existing self-notions that 'subjugate' comportment to the sanctioning of its *exclusive* criteria – I act (and others act) as a result of what I know and my actions and the actions of others are rendered sensible or otherwise on the basis of that knowledge.

The classification of the others is thus ontologically *entangled* with our self-ideas. Therefore, the self-definitions we express verbally are not simply ephemeral musings but are instead substantial echoes of the situations we are currently navigating (Archer 2003; Heidegger 1953). This suggests that (a) the 'who' of a person manifests through an integration of external world elements united by their pertinence (for instance, what is deemed professionally demanding or straightforward is linked to Mark's perception of what those professional challenges entail); (b) these elements are animated by an underlying motivational priority (like how Mark's aspiration to be esteemed as a 'miracle worker' shapes his criteria for identifying what qualifies as a 'miracle' and what falls short); and (c) they facilitate the construction of a particularized reality populated by entities and phenomena that are 'discovered with regards to the fact that they are referred, as those being which they are, to something' (Heidegger 1953: 82). In a cycle reminiscent of the ouroboros, I turn inward upon myself, creating a situation where the world as I perceive it is the same world that I call into being. As asserted by Heidegger (ibid.: 105):

> Dasein understands its here in terms of the over there of the surrounding world. The here does not mean the where of something objectively present, but the where of de-distancing being with … together with de-distancing. In accordance with its spatiality, Dasein is initially *never here*, but over there. From this over there it comes back to its here, and it does this only by interpreting its heedful being towards something in terms of what is at hand over there.

The self-reinforcing and self-referencing modality of perception therefore first delineates the boundaries of participants' worlds within which they are *being* 'particular' individuals. Within *their* world(s), the individual evokes, or in the words of Peterson, determines the import, (of) a *particular* circumstance which they 'need' in order to 'exist' as a *particular* person. For example, it is the participants' hard worker, miracle worker and good communicator identities that permit for manifestations of laziness, irresponsibility and social ineptness respectively in the context of work. The workings of this phenomenon are also affirmed by Peterson (1999: 30–46) when he says that 'the plans we formulate are mechanisms designed to bring the envisioned perfect future into being. Once formulated, plans govern behaviour.'

The self-imposed guidelines for behaviour – reflecting our adapted notions of self-identity – used to ascribe attributes such as 'irresponsibility', 'laziness', 'diligence' or 'effective communication and management abilities' (Archer 2003), or to discern likeness or disparity in others, are simultaneously the metrics by which we gauge and govern ourselves, conferring significance (or the lack thereof) to our everyday actions. The ontological entanglement between ourselves and the world, as such, inadvertently permits for the emergence of novelty, since that which we see in ourselves also depends on where we sit (Clegg 1975). In a manner akin to the ouroboros turning in on itself, this creates a proliferation of reference points for understanding – we inhabit our distinct realities, yet these realities ebb and flow with the introduction of new information. Thus, I assert that the process of self-discovery is suffused with referential assignment of validity, which inadvertently instils a sense of contingency upon our views of (self-)credibility and (self-)authenticity. As affirmed by Peterson (1999: 238):

> All representations of objects (or situations, or behavioural sequence) are of course conditional, because they may be altered unpredictably, or even transformed, entirely, as a consequence of further exploration (or because of some spontaneous anomaly-emergence). The (anxiety-inhibiting, goal-specifying) model of the object of experience is therefore inevitably *contingent* [emphasis in the original] – dependent, for its validity, on the maintenance of those (invisible) conditions which applied and those (unidentified) contexts which were relevant when information was originally generated.

Consequently, our existence within the world unavoidably confronts a situation in which each assertion of plausibility regarding one's sense of self necessarily entails its negative (Archer 2000, 2003; Sharp 1991). To illustrate, I cannot lay claim to being an academic until such personal attributes are corroborated through adherence to social conventions that invest my assertions with validity. Crucially, even when the socially recognized norms of academia are satisfied, the individual's self-portrayal continues to be measured against a spectrum of 'degrees of acclaim' within the scholarly domain. As acknowledged by Heidegger (1953: 120):

> But even when actual, factical Dasein does *not* [emphasis in the original] turn to others and thinks it does not need them, or does without them, it *is* in the mode of being-with. In being-with as the existential for-the-sake-of-others these others are already disclosed in their Dasein. This previously constituted disclosedness of others together with being-with thus helps to constitute significance, that is, worldliness.

Thus, the import of my contention lies not solely in the awareness that self-concepts (such as self-definitions) are vulnerable to 'erosion', but more critically, that such erosion (as seen in self-critical stances) thrusts the entire spectrum of reference points, composing the individual's contextual world, into the limelight of their conscious engagement. Bear in mind that when we engage in acts of self-affirmation, we become 'oblivious' to the significance network that gives meaning to our daily actions. Put plainly, this notion of 'blindness' – the state of being 'unaware' of the connections between one's self-definitions, ambitions and desires, and their correlation with what we encounter in the external world – mirrors the seamless navigation of our routine objectives. A lack of obstacles in our day-to-day existence cultivates a familiarity with our environment, as our established patterns of perception (and behaviour) retain unchallenged legitimacy; they are not subjected to scrutiny (D'Alessandro et al. 2020). As suggested by Schutz (1945: 536), 'as long as I live in my acts, directed towards the objects of these acts, the acts do not have any meaning'. Expressed alternatively, the banality of the 'familiar' elements within our environment 'shrouds' the ontological underpinnings of perception – our understanding and self-awareness – with a veil of imperceptibility (Archer 2003). Recognizing the unselfconsciousness of self-affirming, Jung (1959: 79) describes the predicament as follows:

> His consciousness therefore orients himself chiefly by observing and investigating the world around him, and it is to its peculiarities that he must adapt his psychic and technical resources. This task is so exacting, and its fulfilment so advantageous, that he *forgets* himself in the process, losing sight of his instinctual nature and putting his own conceptions of himself in place of his real being. In this way, he slips imperceptibly into a purely conceptual [i.e. imagined] world where the products of his conscious activity progressively replace reality. (Emphasis mine)

On that note, the unobstructed attainment of pragmatic ends therefore 'distances' the knowledge of 'why' things are familiar from one's understanding. As noted by Peterson (1999: 34) 'those things we *take for granted* – and which are, therefore, *invisible* – determine our affective responses to the "environmental stimuli"' (emphasis mine). The 'ontological groundwork' of perception thus often goes unnoticed, due principally to the lack of contention experienced within an unchallenged professional existence. In simpler terms, the importance of our practical ambitions (becoming a project manager, achieving recognition as an exemplary employee, working less to devote more time to family) only becomes strikingly clear when its validity is challenged (Clegg 1975; Heidegger 1953). As noted by Peterson (1999: 287):

> non-existence appears as an inevitable consequence of the absence of limitations, or of oppositions. The absence deprives whatever constitutes the origin of a point of reference, distinguishable from itself – and, therefore, deprives it of existence ... Two things that cannot be discerned from one another are not two things, however, and one thing with no discernible features whatsoever may not even be.

This is also recognized by Heidegger (1953: 74), who states:

> Something is unusable. This means that the constitutive reference of the in-order-to to a what-for has been disrupted. The references themselves are not observed, rather they are 'there' in our heedful adjustment to them. But in a disruption of reference – in being unusable for ... – the reference becomes explicit ... When something at hand is missing whose everyday presence was so much a matter of course that we never paid attention to it, this constitutes a breach in the context of reference discovered in circumspection. Circumspection comes up with *emptiness* [emphasis mine] and now sees for the first time what the missing thing was at hand for and at hand with. *Once again the surrounding world makes itself known.* (Emphasis in the original)

Such realizations, therefore, suggests that a self-referencing or reinforcing subject who 'affirm[s] immediately the reality of all that is conceived' (Schutz 1945: 533) is, in the first instance, inhibited from seeing the significances that constitute their self-identity. In this instance, the subject does not know why they are experiencing the world in a particular way. As noted by Schutz (1967: 53), 'that which is irrecoverable – and this is in principle always something ineffable – can only be lived but never "thought": it is in principle incapable of being verbalised.' Subsequently, I contend that the process of self-negation should not be construed as deleterious, as its core function is to unveil the subjective paradigms that enable us to discern the world in distinct ways. Therefore, although 'it is through our knowledge and self-awareness that we can understand and observe the world around us', it is the questioning of this knowledge and self-awareness that enhances our perception of ourselves and others, allowing us to discover more about the world that was previously hidden from us. In this instance, 'the self … is no longer the undivided total self, but rather a partial self, the performer of this particular act that refers to a system of correlated acts to which it belongs' (ibid.: 7). Inadvertently, therefore, it is the 'subtraction'[1] in the sense of self that makes us more perceptive of the surrounding world, but also 'more accountable to ourselves' (more on accountability later). For now, let us recognize Heidegger's (1953: 42, 125–26) apt observations:

> The inauthenticity of Dasein does not signify a 'lesser' being or a 'lower' degree of being. Rather, inauthenticity can determine Dasein even in its fullest concretion … *Authentic being a self* [emphasis in the original] is not based on an exceptional state of the subject, detached from the they, *but is an existential modification of the they as an essential existential* [emphasis in the original] … [On that note], the self of everyday Dasein is the *they-self* [emphasis in the original], which we distinguish from the *authentic self* [emphasis in the original], that is, the self which has explicitly grasped itself … If Dasein explicitly discovers the world and brings it near, if it discloses its authentic being to itself, *this discovering of 'world' and disclosing of Dasein always comes about by clearing away coverings and obscurities, by breaking up the disguises with which Dasein cuts itself off from itself* [emphasis mine].

As noted earlier, a heightened awareness of oneself and others broadens the horizons of the world we encounter, thereby bringing new reference points, deemed relevant for self-actualization, into our purview. To uphold the coherence of this newly perceived network (that is, the cohesion of the 'I'), individuals allow further modes of contextual norms to infiltrate their conceptual perimeters, aiming to surmount their 'erosive' (or formerly unrecognized) idiosyncrasies[2] through processes like learning. The heightened uncertainty of what is known, together with the widened expanse of the unknown, subsequently immerses the individual in a 'spread of the indeterminate means', weighing down daily actions with the sense of (perceived) self-insufficiency. As suggested by Deetz (1994: 30), 'when the unity of the I is risked, the fixed self/other world configuration gives over to the conflictual, tension filled antagonisms out of which objects are differentiated and re-differentiated and preconceptions are given over to new conceptions'. Thus, I propose that gaining a deeper perception of oneself and others (via self-negation) amplifies the scale and reach of elements that are significant in the external world, leading to a form of self-restriction. Such self-inhibition diminishes the subject's potential for self-actualization. This 'loss-of-self' is aptly described by Peterson (1999: 52–53) when he states:

> We are protected from unpredictability by our culturally determined beliefs, by the stories we share. These stories tell us how to presume and how to

> act to maintain the determinate, shared and restricted values that comprise our familiar worlds … The orienting reflex substitutes for particular learned responses when the incomprehensible suddenly makes its appearance. The occurrence of the unpredictable, the unknown, the source of fear and hope, creates a seizure of ongoing specifically goal directed behaviour. Emergence of the unexpected constitutes evidence for the incomplete nature of the story currently guiding such behaviour; comprises evidence for error at the level of working description of current state, representation of desired future state or conception of the means to transform the former into the latter … *It is only when our goals have been destroyed that the true significance of the decontextualized object or experience is revealed* [emphasis mine].

Yet when our conceptualizations of entities (encompassing both self and others) become countless due to the boundless nature of ascribed credibility, understanding and awareness reconstitute themselves based on what is of utmost significance. Thus, it could be posited that when the world becomes 'overly vast', the network of significance takes on a hierarchical structure, with the most pivotal elements to the 'identity-seeking individual' situated at its apex. Consequently, although it is the uncertainty of our knowledge and self-awareness that allows us to expand our understanding of the previously (un)noticed world, it is the continuously growing scope of relevance that confronts us with the most essential facets of our self-identity. The process of self-negation reveals the comprehensive set of reference points that shape the subject's meaningful perception of their world. Moreover, being 'enumerated' by this entirety illuminates the ontological characteristics of the self, which typically elude conscious recognition when we navigate familiar territory. As noted by Schutz (1945: 533–34):

> our primitive impulse is to affirm immediately the reality of all that is conceived, as long as it remains uncontradicted … In this sense, it may be correctly said that a pragmatic motive governs our natural attitude towards the world of daily life.

As a result, when individuals point out shortcomings in others' abilities, they unintentionally cast doubt upon their own skills. Yet challenging our accepted truths allows us to break free from 'blinding familiarity' to highlight the indispensable elements of our ambitions; it brings to light not only the objectives we pursue but also the values and aspirations we aim to maintain and fulfil in our pursuit. The 'circular' nature of daily identity formation (or positioning) reinforces the (re)shaping of our subjectivity in such a manner that the imperative to uphold our core guiding principles is perennially reaffirmed at its basis (Figure 6.1).

This implies that through the interplay of self-affirmation and self-questioning, we ultimately come full circle back to our core selves, presented

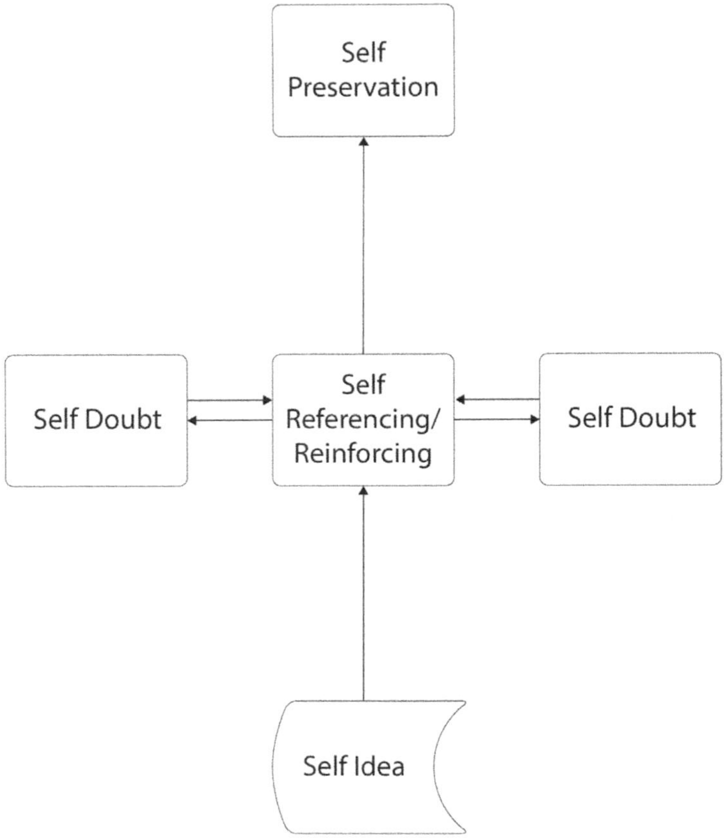

Figure 6.1. The 'circular' nature of daily identity formation (or positioning) reinforces the (re)shaping of our subjectivity in such a manner that the imperative to uphold our core guiding principles is perennially reaffirmed at its basis. © Matija Radomir Djolic.

with choices that resonate with the most crucial elements of our existence. Faced with challenges and constraints to our self-awareness, we are afforded the chance to select what matters most in our lives as individuals in pursuit of identity. This point takes on added weight when we recognize that the fundamental essence of what is truly significant often remains hidden when we adeptly navigate the details of our daily routines. Thus, the shift from a state of stability to one of volatility (in our understanding and self-awareness) grants us the occasion to uphold our ideals (such as visions of a more 'complete' reality and a 'better' constituted subject), thereby enabling us to 'reconnect' with the 'formative insight' that initially inspired our thoughtful consideration of everyday life.

The 'Intentionality' and 'Distinctiveness' of the Self-Idea

Our exploration thus far has unveiled a profound truth: our conception of personal agency, such as the embodiment of the 'hard worker' identity, gains its full significance only within an appropriate context. This means that the value we attribute to our diligent endeavours, those tireless exertions and steadfast commitments, truly manifest when aligned with specific objectives within the nuanced tapestry of our work circumstances. As we have previously established, there exists a deep ontological interweaving between an individual's self-conception and the milieu of their interpersonal engagements. This intricate connection suggests that our identity is not merely an internal construct but is inextricably linked to, and partially forged by, our interactions with others. Yet, in our quest to unearth the ontological bedrock of individual actions amid a myriad of others, we must acknowledge that the unique fabric of each person's situation weaves its own pattern of meaning. Take, for instance, the case of Nick, whose professional backdrop is painted with the dualistic hues of 'hard work' and its absence. Contrast this with Margaret, whose vocational landscape is accentuated with the elements of 'effective communication' and its counterpart. Meanwhile, Mark's professional realm is imbued with the motifs of 'exceptional performance' and its converse. It is these distinct and immediate circumstances that cultivate their personal 'contexts', each one a tapestry reflecting the subjective interplay of their distinct experiences and aspirations. As noted by Peterson (1999: 66):

> new procedures and modes of interpretation literally produce new phenomena. The *word* [emphasis in the original] enables differentiated thought and dramatically heightens the capacity for exploratory manoeuvring. The world of human experience is constantly transformed and renewed as a consequence of such exploration. In this manner, the *word* [emphasis mine] constantly engenders new creation.

This leads us to infer that the 'particular circumstance of work' is not merely a given, but rather sculpted from the broader canvas of existence by individuals. It is through this deliberate act of carving out their own niches that they weave the tapestry of their self-narratives, aims and yearnings into a meaningful symbiosis. According to Leary (1977), it is within this crafted space that these elements of the self come into harmonious correspondence with each other. The same is recognized by Heidegger (1953: 297) when he says that 'the self and world belong together in a single entity [Dasein]'.[3]

In this discourse, I propose that the essence of meaning exists antecedent to 'circumstantial particularity', establishing delineated frontiers that serve as the backdrop against which only certain actions can unfurl. This primacy of meaning acts as the canvas on which the details of context are drawn – it is the prelude that shapes the boundaries and contours of possibility for action. Bear in mind this pivotal truth: the conceptions we hold of ourselves act as filters, narrowing down the plethora of potential choices available in any given situation. Such an insight is at once profound and undeniably humbling, as it acknowledges the sheer impossibility of possessing omniscience – it is a recognition of our inherent limitations. In pondering this concept, we come face to face with the inescapable reality of self-imposed constraints on our perspective. Consequently, it becomes clear that the motivational forces prompting actions within the 'particular circumstance (of work)' do not spring forth from the situation itself, but rather from our individualized conceptualization of that situation. As rather poetically recognized by Nietzsche (2018: 72):

> let the youthful soul look back on life with the question: what have you truly loved up to now, what has elevated your soul, what has mastered it and at the same time delighted it? Place these venerated objects before you in a row, and perhaps they will yield for you, through their nature and their sequence, a law, the fundamental law of your true self.

Nietzsche (ibid.: 120) goes on to further note:

> To become what one is, one must not have the faintest notion of what one is … The whole surface of consciousness – for consciousness is a surface – must be kept clear of all great imperatives. Beware even of every great word, every great pose! So many dangers that the instinct comes too soon to 'understand itself' … The organising idea that is destined to rule keeps growing deep down – it begins to command, slowly it leads us back from side roads and wrong roads; it prepares single qualities and fitnesses that will one day prove to be indispensable as a means toward a whole – one by one, it trains all subservient capacities before giving any hint of the dominant task, goal, aim or meaning … At the bottom of us, really 'deep down', there is, of course, something unteachable, some granite of spiritual fatum [personal fate or destiny], of predetermined decision and answer to predetermined selected questions. Whenever a cardinal problem is at stake, there speaks an unchangeable 'this is I'.

Subsequently, it is not merely the fact that our reference to truth within a specific situation is prefigured by its subjective potentiality that holds significance. Far more crucial is the revelation that the 'self-constructed environment' – the realm fashioned by our own hands and minds – is indispensable for the abstract elements of the self to embody their undeniable nature. It is within these personalized constructs that our nascent identities assume their fullest expression. Take, for example, the case of Margaret. It is against the backdrop of what she deems 'inadequate performances' in work domains she holds as secondary that she firmly 'objectifies' the value of her 'good project management and communication skills'. This intentional foregrounding of her core competencies is underscored by her resolute back-up plan, articulated when she confidently declares that she 'will just go back and work with [her] father and build [her] own projects'. Such a statement does not merely reflect a potential course of action, it powerfully illuminates the essential role that her self-constructed professional identity plays in shaping her reality. As aptly recognized by Jung (1933: 126), 'if we don't know who we are, the world [within which we choose to dwell] will tell us'. On that note, both 'hostile' and 'familiar' circumstances are therefore equally approving of one's most significant realizations since their particularity is the 'playground' of the subject's identity. In Jung's (ibid.: 167–68) words:

> The self … is an archetype that invariably expresses a situation within which the ego is contained. Therefore, like every archetype the self … acts like a circumambient atmosphere to which no definite limits can be set, either in space or in time.

Therefore, even though the self and the world are intertwined into a single entity (Heidegger 1953), the integrity of our sense of self is *dependent on* the *plausibility* of the world we *choose* to carve out from its vastness, and vice versa. For example, since the validity of my 'academic' identity emerges from referential attribution of truth (completing my PhD → completing my PhD 'well' → becoming a lecturer → being a 'good' lecturer → publishing articles → publishing 'impactful'[4] articles … etc.), the *particular* immediate circumstance within which *the subject chooses to dwell* must be rendered as an *objective reality* for the 'academic' identity to sustain itself. Moreover, if my doctoral supervisors 'have given me the wrong advice', which has inadvertently led me to produce a substandard thesis, the quality of the thesis therefore does not affect my identity of being a 'good' academic as 'it was not my fault'. I am sure we all hear ourselves externalizing responsibility, on a regular basis, to maintain our visions of truth. The immediate circumstance, therefore, transcends the mere confines of a physical location, asserting its presence more critically as a conceptual framework. This framework's roots delve deeply into the underlying motivations of 'the reason behind my degree of choice' and reach out to the intellectual curiosities of 'the topic of interest I choose to explore' in the pursuit of academia. Moreover, it encompasses the scholarly endeavour of making an 'aptly delineated contribution to knowledge', which I endeavour to 'bring forth'. The acceptance and recognition of this knowledge underscore and legitimize the existence of the particular 'me'. Thus, the circumstance reveals itself as a mirror to the intricate network of our thoughts and intentions. This is affirmed by Schutz (1967: 102), who states:

> In [the] everyday world in which both the I and the Thou turn up, not as transcendental but as psychophysical subjects, there corresponds to each stream of lived experience of the I a stream of subjective experience of the Thou. This, to be sure, refers back to my own stream of lived experience, just as the body of the other person to my body. During this process, the peculiar reference of my own ego to the other's ego holds, in the same sense that my stream of lived experience is for you that of the other person, just as my body is another's body for you.

Accordingly, our very self-conception is imbued with an epistemological dimension – that is to say, it is through the practical application of our knowledge that our insights acquire ontological weight. This metamorphosis from notion to reality is captured in the concept of our 'tradition of knowing', coined by Jung (1933): where the revelations we have about the constraints of our immediate surroundings transmute into substantive ideas through the crucible of action. Without such 'contextualization' by way of praxis, any 'particular' insight remains an unanchored abstraction. Heidegger (1953) illuminates this interplay further, articulating how the ontological and epistemological facets of our lived experiences are intrinsically woven into the fabric of our consciousness. They are reliant on the integrity of a symbiotic relationship: that between the self and the world as the self understands and crafts it. It is, therefore, not merely 'where' we find ourselves, but reflecting more deeply, our interpretations of our location – the veracity of our thoughts about our presence – that are fundamental for our authentic existence. Consequently, what lies at the core of 'intentional action' is the self-idea in the act of releasing itself – an existential dance that materializes through the objectifying acts of thought, speech and deeds. As noted by Peterson (1999: 19):

> What is novel is of course dependent on what is known – is necessarily defined in opposition to what is known. Furthermore, what is known is always known conditionally, since human knowledge is necessarily limited. Our conditional knowledge, insofar as that knowledge is relevant for the regulation of emotion, consists of our models of the emotional significance of the present, defined in opposition to an idealised, hypothetical or fantasised future state. We evaluate the 'unbearable present' in relationship to the 'ideal future'. We act to transform 'who we are' into 'where we would like to be'.

The enduring fabric of our self-concept, then, is predicated on the current moment's convincingness. Yet this perception of what is plausible in the 'now' is not simply given; it is actively 'self-promoted'. It is precisely for this reason that individuals are impelled to reconfigure their self-definitions and the ends they have subjectively decreed as pragmatic, according to their perceived significance. Any disruption to this established order – the integrity of their significance hierarchy – signposts a potential disintegration of both their self-perception and the reality it informs (Higgins 1987). Thus, the 'concrete sensibility' of the present (Sartre 2018) crystallizes – as if through an existential alchemy – our previous experiences and projected identities into a tangible sense of being:

> In a system that is arranged hierarchically, we may choose to refer to the inferences at the lower level as perceptions and the inferences at the higher level … as beliefs, but we suggest that it is important to consider that similar processing obtains at all levels of the hierarchy … Although it is possible – and sensible – at one level of analysis to distinguish beliefs from perceptions … at another level of analysis – the one that we think is more useful – no distinction is called for. (Corlett and Fletcher 2016: 96–97)

The stratification we observe in our personal realms reflects that the narratives we articulate in our thoughts and utterances offer but a glimpse of the 'self-idea' amid the array of circumstances we perceive as immediate. Thus, the construction of a hierarchical scaffolding within our individual universe signals an ongoing process of value ascription, wherein each insight gains reinforcement through subsequent understandings gleaned from our engagement with what we deem to be objective slices of reality while navigating our existential trajectory ('being-in-the-world', particularly in a professional context). In light of this, it becomes untenable to posit an immutable link between bygone occurrences and current choices the individual faces; our meaning-making structures are not static archives but dynamic and fluid edifices, perennially reshaped by the confluence of experiences that have unfolded from our earliest moments to the present. The 'self-idea', therefore, is not an unchanging monolith but a living tapestry, perpetually woven and rewoven in response to the rich tapestry of life's encounters.

For instance, we observe how all three individuals purposefully nurture their most valued self-attributes by shedding those elements that prove incongruent with the 'new' contexts they are drawn to or aspire to engage with. Mark pivots towards the environment of a different organization, signifying his shift, whereas Margaret and Nick opt for the autonomy of self-employment. Crucially, in their attempts to safeguard their identity, these subjects not only preserve but also 'embellish' their defining traits within the framework of their present engagements. Consider Margaret, whose proficiency in communication and project management shines brightest when free from the encumbrance of needless bureaucratic trappings, 'not burdened' by the stifling constraints of rigid hierarchies and titles. Similarly, Nick's dedication and industrious nature are most palpable and valued when his 'soft skills' are not entangled in the assessment of his work ethic. Likewise, Mark's reputation as an effective problem-solver is contingent on recognition, which he finds to be lacking under the scrutiny of current superiors whom he deems 'unreasonable'. The unfolding journey into these new professional landscapes is bound to introduce fresh benchmarks of success – new 'referential' truths – that will further sculpt the subjects' personal narratives and shape the intricate lattice of what matters to them. Thus, the 'intentionality' inherent in the self-idea to actively 'sustain itself' propels the narrative forward, arguing for a dynamic and layered construction of insights upon which the edifice of the self is built. As recognized by Peterson (1999: 40):

> It is particularly difficult to specify the value of an occurrence when it has one meaning from one frame of reference (with regards to one particular goal), and a different or an even opposite meaning, from another equally or more important and relevant frame. Stimuli that exist in this manner constitute *unresolved problems of adaptation* [emphasis in the original]. They present us with mystery which is what to do in their presence ... Such circumstances provide evidence that our systems of valuation are not yet sophisticated enough to foster complete adaptation – demonstrate to us incontrovertibly that our processes of evaluation are still incomplete.

On that note, thrown into the world of others, the subjects inadvertently draw distinctions by way of comparison between things in their surroundings. More importantly, by drawing distinctions between the two things compared (for example, between Margaret and her father), the subjects generate *novel* ideas about the self and the surrounding world (Bateson 2002; Heidegger 1953; Peterson 1999; Sartre 2018).[5] Within this intellectual venture, newfound notions gently settle in as established mental frameworks, as per Lonergan (1992), becoming part of the 'habitual textures of their mind'. Through habitual practices and daily comportment, these concepts are 'objectified' and come to life by resonating with the 'necessary plausibility' of the subject's reasoning – a sort of cognitive litmus test in which to exist authentically, one's thoughts must reflect truth, and truth must echo one's thoughts (Sartre 2018). The process of 'inquiry', therefore, does not merely produce abstract insights – it actively shapes the very being of the subject and object alike, allowing the self-idea to crystallize through the lens of the individual's particular deductions. Thus, the self's distinctiveness unfolds uniquely for each person: while the outward manifestation of identities may leverage similar methods of verbal expression (as explored in the dynamics of self-referencing, self-reinforcing and self-preserving in Chapter 6), the cognitive substance behind each person's self-articulation remains profoundly personal and situation-specific.[6] Subsequently, it can be said that the substantive variance in what the subjects find meaningful is embodied in the distinctive descriptions of a 'single' professional context. As aptly asserted by Sartre (2018: 256):

> Every existing individual discovers himself in the moment that he discovers the world, and discovers himself in relationship with this other – with this group of brothers or partners; the individual is related to the world as soon as he is related to himself. Thus, he is connected to two different worlds – his senses and the plurality of the others … What is important is not what the Other reveals to me, but what he cannot reveal: that is, himself. It is then that his presence has meaning for me, when I realise that he exists only by transcending himself, when I taste the solitude which he can not communicate.

Thus, while the subjects actively craft their interrelational milieu so that their self-definitions, aspirations and longings align harmoniously within it, it must be acknowledged that the genesis of the self-concept cannot be divorced from the contextual dance of interaction in which the subject is engaged. Take Margaret's experience as a case in point: she found herself enmeshed within the world carved out by her father's 'actions', a reality whose interpretations furnished the crucial building blocks for her own identity's architecture. This rallying cry against determinism[7] underscores the argument for the inherently unique configuration of each individual's subjective framework. The very essence of personal distinction cannot simply be attained by extracting the subject from the web of interpersonal dynamics. Instead, it is through the careful demarcation and recognition of the emergence of personal interpretation within that very web of interactions that one's unique identity finds its expression. This is also confirmed and described by Bateson (2002: 64), who states:

> There is a profound and an unanswerable question about the nature of those 'at least two' things that between them generate the difference which becomes information by making a difference. Clearly each alone is – for the mind and perception – a non-entity, a non-being. An unknowable … a sound of one hand clapping.

With this in mind, the diversity of ideas presented in specific contexts serves as a testament to the definitive subjective possibilities that shape our valuation of importance and significance when juxtaposing two entities. It implies that the insights we garner on our 'quest for self-realization' are invariably tethered to a preceding intellectual journey – one that 'pivots from the concrete to the abstract', as Lonergan (1992: 30) articulated. Our capacity to reach conclusions, then, is inherently dependent on the distinctiveness of our internal states, allowing us to perceive and appreciate differences between self and others. Bateson (2002: 64), reflecting on this, notes that it is the recognition of difference 'which becomes information by making a difference'. Thus, the emergence of new insights through such comparisons is predicated upon an already existing awareness of distinctions, for, as Bateson further suggests, without this perceptual demarcation, 'each alone is – for the mind and perception – a non-entity' (ibid.). Therefore, the authenticity of self-concepts is not solely captured in the uniquely characterized external world – the particularities articulated in situ – but even more so in the realm of subjective possibilities. It is within this realm that our perceptions are given individual contour, without which the very act of perception would lose its differential quality, rendering all things either imperceptible or perceptually homogeneous. Thus, the act of grasping and interpreting the world around us extends beyond general self-awareness; it is specifically through the prism of our unique self-knowledge that the processes of comprehension and perception are made possible. Without the colour and contour that our personal insights lend to our understanding, the endeavour to fully engage with and decipher our environment would remain elusive. As noted by Heidegger (1953: 46):

> Every idea of a 'subject' – unless refined by a previous ontological determination of its basic character – still posits the *subjectum ontologically* [emphasis in the original] along with it, no matter how energetic are one's ontic protestations against the 'substantial soul' or the 'reifications of consciousness'.

Thus, the signature of uniqueness in our conception of self is largely the fruit of context-bound epiphanies. Consider Margaret, whose discernment of her surroundings has led to the crafting of an enriched, more comprehensive world view, one that inherently draws upon her self-perceptions. This layered tapestry of self-identity is woven from multiple threads: it begins with a pivotal insight, serving as the impetus to delve into profound queries of identity and existence (such as 'who am I and how should I act?'). This psychological and existential exploration gives rise to a refreshed understanding, which then actively informs and animates one's actions within the sphere of social interplay. Reflecting on this, we recognize that Margaret's self-idea cannot be claimed as wholly her own; it emerges from a wellspring that transcends 'one man's personal life', as Jung (1933: 115) elucidated. Yet it is precisely her uniquely shaped inner landscape, with its capacity to foster distinctive perceptions and responses in given situations, that carves out the individual landscapes of identity for each of our subjects. Nick, Mark and Margaret are distinguished by their discrete personal narratives, their distinct convictions and the personal metrics they use to measure their own triumphs and tribulations. These varied foundations inform their actions, and thus the essence of their existence. As aptly acknowledged by Sartre (2018: 246):

> The only kind of knowledge is *intuitive*. Deduction and discourse, which are incorrectly labelled as 'knowledge', are only instruments leading to *intuition*. When we reach the intuition, the means that were used to reach it are set aside;

> in cases where we cannot reach it, reasoning and discourse are left in the position of signposts that point towards an intuition that is out of reach. *Finally, if an intuition has been reached but is not a present mode of my consciousness, the maxims that I employ persist, as the results of operations that I carried out earlier, like Descartes's 'memories of ideas'* [emphasis mine].

At the heart of our existential quest is the transcendental aspect of our self-conceptions. These notions stem from an intrinsic yearning to better understand ourselves and others, with the ultimate goal of forging a more holistic self and comprehensively grasping the reality we are 'thrown into' from the outset of life (Sartre 2018). Our self-ideas are cultivated as a continuation of our perceptions, shaped by the immediate world around us, thereby anchoring them in our tangible experiences. Yet they simultaneously maintain a degree of 'independence' from the physical context. This is because our situated experiences are initially framed through the lens of personal interpretation – they are conceptualized on an internal plane before ever being associated with a specific locale.

Therefore, the tapestry of our situated experiences is intricately woven with the threads of our prior judgements about who we are and the nature of the world we inhabit. In this light, our circumstances perpetually strive to synchronize with the narratives we craft to shade our realities with specific hues.[8] Consequently, the self-idea does not merely emerge within the confines of contextual specificity, but soars above it. Our claims of identity within any given context are echoes of those pivotal realizations or judgements that have previously sculpted our sense of self at the moments of their inception and reaffirmation – each a brushstroke in the continuous canvas of our being, as discussed by Lonergan (1992), Sartre (2018) and Wilson (2016). In this way, our self-conclusions and interpretations of the world of others are reflective of our personal ontologies.[9] These internal conceptualizations are the lenses through which all aspects of existence can be discerned – they contour the visible and shape the perceivable.[10]

Answered Questions

Our examination reveals a critical flaw in the postmodernist assertion that casts identity solely as a product of discourse: this undervalues the significant role our self-conceptions, as well as our perceptions of others, play in the way we navigate the world. In parallel, essentialism neglects to acknowledge the fundamental influence of subjective constructs on the shaping of our perceptual and interpretive realities. The veracity and impact of these personal narratives do not hinge on their universal acceptance or acknowledgement as 'legitimate' or 'objective' in order to affect our daily perceptions and actions. Moreover, it is not necessary for these self-ideas to take form as linguistic constructs – though we often articulate them in words, their influence extends beyond the confines of language. Coherence and explicit definition are not prerequisites for these organizing principles of self to exert their powerful sway over our sensory experiences and encounters in the world. They rest on an ontological bedrock, underpinning the very essence of 'legitimacy', 'plausibility' and 'goal-directedness'. These self-ideas innately precondition our engagement with – and comprehension of – the world around us. As rightly asserted by Jung (1933: 115–16):

> Can experience with the objective world save us from subjective prejudgements? Is not every experience, even in the best of circumstances, to a large extent subjective interpretation? On the other hand, the subject also is an objective fact, a piece of the world. What issues from it comes, after all, from the universal soil, just as the rarest and strongest organism is nonetheless supported and nourished by the earth which we all share in common. It is precisely the most subjective ideas which, being closest to nature and to the living being, deserve to be called the truest. *But what is truth?* (Emphasis in the original).

Let us consider the implications of an opposing viewpoint, one that dismisses the influence of subjective self-constructs in defining our personal reality. Should such a stance be adopted, it would leave us bereft of a framework by which to interpret specific circumstances, stripped of the means to appraise them as meaningful. It is this deficiency in acknowledging the gravity of subjective constructs as authentic anchors of individual-specific reality that exposes a critical shortcoming in both essentialist and postmodernist theories of identity. Their analytical architectures risk 'alienating' the very individuals they aim to understand, by failing to accord due significance to the internal narratives crucial for personal meaning-making. This is also confirmed by Bateson (2002: 28–29), who states that:

> Experience of the exterior is always mediated by particular sense organs and neural pathways. To that extent, objects are my creation, and my experience of them is subjective, not objective. It is, however, not a trivial assertion to note that very few persons, at least in the occidental culture, doubt the objectivity of such sense data as pain or their visual images of the external world. Our civilisation is deeply based on such illusion.

Yet it must be acknowledged that the postmodern perspective does offer a valuable insight where essentialism might falter: in questioning the extent to which our conceptions of the world and of ourselves may be regarded as true and objective – indeed, as direct – portrayals of reality. In this respect, postmodernism provides a critical counterpoint to essentialist assumptions of a one-to-one correspondence between perception and the world as it is in itself. Grappling with the concept of universality, we inadvertently come to a point of realizing that our representation of the world and our self-conceptions are in the first instance subjective abstractions that (also) draw on a common stock of knowledge intersubjectively shared in specific communities of practice. Though they are subjective, however, one cannot assume their illusory nature (as recognized by Driver 2013), as such a position would suggest that only things that can be 'measured' objectively are worth analysing. Why, then, would there be a need to invent the microscope? This, precisely, is what research into self-identity has been calling for: a microscopic examination of our daily navigation through the world of work, culminating in the crucial understanding that our perception of the world is profoundly influenced by the essence of our being – by the unique amalgam of experiences, beliefs and attributes that constitutes our 'self' (Jung 1933). The preceding arguments thus assist us with answering the following questions:

1. How does one's self-identity shape one's situated professional experiences?

Answer: One's self-identity intricately informs one's situated experience, serving as a repository of interpretive resources that shape the perception and understanding of circumstances.

What I aim to elucidate is the intrinsic connection between our perception of circumstances and our consequent lived experiences. Drawing from the discussions in earlier chapters, it becomes apparent that our embodiment of a situation's unique nuances is an expression born out of our individual self-concept. Take, for instance, the articulation of adverse experiences: the characteristics we attribute to our external reality often echo a sense of 'loss' tied to our self-image – a reflection of diminishing personal aspirations or identity, rather than a mere cataloguing of 'objective' traits present in the situations we confront. It is important to note, however, that while the perceived or anticipated loss may pertain to tangible elements in the world – such as career status, advancement opportunities or lifestyle choices like family time – it is the underlying personal self-image (or its perceived absence) that orchestrates and colours their interpretation. Thus, our pre-existing notions of self construct the framework within which certain experiences are perceived and certain forms of agency are exercised. In essence, one's self-concept lays the interpretative groundwork that contours the nature of our engagement with circumstances, colouring whether we navigate them as pathways to self-fulfilment or as barriers to be overcome. The relationship between self-idea/identity and situated experience, as such, is expressed as follows:

Self-Idea ↔ Interpretation ↔ Perceived Circumstances ↔ Situated Experience

However, it is crucial to recognize that the interconnection between the self-idea, its interpretation and the ensuing situated experience is far from linear. The circumstances we perceive and the experiences they engender likewise exert influence on the manner in which we articulate ourselves. In a cyclical reciprocity, just as our self-ideas furnish the tools for interpreting experiences, those very experiences, in turn, inform and sometimes reshape how we understand and express our self-identity to ourselves and to the world. These arguments relate to the second question we have sought to explore since Chapter 3:

2. How do one's professional experiences (re)shape the process of (re)articulating (professional) self-identity?

Answer: The (distinctive) self-idea, or identity, undergoes a rearticulation into a hierarchy of self-definitions when circumstances are interpreted by the individual as obstacles to personal fulfilment or self-realization.

The self-idea subsumes a network of self-definitions, goals and desires that are referential to one another. In Nick's case, for example, his identity of being 'adaptable' and 'flexible' (for instance, the ability to 'wear many hats') is related to his other self-definitions as 'being a hard worker' and being 'emotionally astute' (for instance, the identity that is related to Nick's 'soft skills'). The sense of self is thus constituted by way of an in-order-to relationship (Heidegger 1953; Sartre 2018) between self-definitions and subjectively conceived pragmatic ends to which they relate. Their relationality (for instance, the relationality between one's goals and desires and one's self-definitions) suggests that the non-realization of pragmatic ends inadvertently corrodes the plausibility of self-definitions that support them. For instance, Nick's 'ultimate goal' – to dedicate more time to his family, and the identity bound up with that ideal – could be jeopardized if the certainty of his 'hard worker' persona is called into question, and inversely, the latter could be threatened by the former. In light of this, to avert the potential 'loss-of-self', individuals actively prioritize their self-definitions, assigning greater weight to certain aspects of their identity over others, in alignment with the immediate realities they perceive.

This revelation underscores the profound ways in which one's inner make-up is moulded by the fabric of particular social dynamics. Take, for example, Nick and Mark's unwavering commitment to their 'hard worker' identities or Margaret's steadfastness in preserving her 'good communicator, personable and sociable' persona. These are not mere superficial labels, but are core to their being, acting as cornerstones for each participant's projected future self. Against this backdrop, we see that by upholding his 'hard worker' image – while diminishing the role of his 'people person' identity – Nick strategically navigates his world to maintain the possibility of achieving his goal of 'spending more time with the family'. This interdependence lays bare a relational ontology: one's subjective constitution is interwoven with one's everyday actions. Through the lens of every experience, informed by each perceived circumstance, the rearticulation of self-identity is continually unfolding, with the individual calibrating the prominence of existing facets of their persona. In this way, the attributes deemed most vital are reaffirmed and anchored at the base of their daily agency, posited at the apex of their self-hierarchy as quintessential to their existence. Consequently, within the 'in-order-to' ontological framework that orchestrates the interrelations among various elements of their self-concepts, the subjects respond to feelings of uncertainty and limitations by recalibrating their 'subjective circumstances' – or subjective contexts. This recalibration seeks to safeguard the elements of self that they deem most precious and enables them to act decisively based on the fresh insights thus derived.

Conclusion

The philosophical ramifications of the foregoing discussion culminate in a refined understanding of the cyclical process that constitutes the evolution of self-identity. This process, as elucidated by the arguments presented, traces the arc from an initial insight through a phase of self-doubt – where one grapples with the sustainability of existing self-concepts that dictate one's behaviour (a phenomenon termed 'self-negation') – and culminates in the pivotal moments of choice that resonate with our most integral attributes. By acknowledging the ontological significance of our self-conceptions, I have illustrated how the purposefulness of our actions mirrors the imperative to uphold a coherent vision of the reality we perceive. This vision's veracity is indispensable for the continuity of our self-identity (and conversely, our self-identity is critical to affirming this vision). Crucially, the uniqueness of our self-identity extends beyond the immediate reflections drawn from experiences; rather, it is rooted in the uniquely constituted essence of our inner beings. Absent this distinctive inner framework, the individual would lack the capacity to derive insights that sculpt the experienced world with their own profound and personally resonant philosophy.

As we continue to piece together the existential puzzle of self-identity, we approach the threshold of a more coherent understanding, edging ever closer to completing the mosaic.

Notes

1. By way of evoking contingency upon our knowledge and self-knowledge and thus highlighting limits in self-understanding.
2. This means that a question like 'how are you doing with the project?' from our superior will be considered in a multitude of terms (positive and negative) that are in the first instance self-referential in nature. As we do not know exactly what the question aims to elucidate, unless we explicitly ask, the question will be interpreted and an answer ventured in our own terms, that is, in terms of all the things 'we have and have not done right' based on what we believe the 'right' thing is, that is, based on rules of comportment that resemble an individual of our perceived self-worth. The rules however pertain to all of the contingencies we 'find in the world', which we use to distinguish ourselves from others. The rules of evaluations are 'all the things we know' (and do not know), referential to our self-knowledge and knowledge of other-as-context. As such, the self-referencing subject continually places contingency upon their own pre-existing self-definitions to, rather paradoxically, ensure their perpetuation and subsequent realization of goals and desires, that is, to protect the pre-existing notions of self-worth. By evoking contingency upon their knowledge, all participants become acutely aware of that which is being 'jeopardized' and by coming into such knowledge, exercise their personal causal efficacy by 'devising' alternative ways of being-in-the-world with which to deal with the newly evoked limitations.
3. 'Dasein' is a German term that literally translates to 'being there', or 'presence'. It is a complex concept heavily used by the German philosopher Martin Heidegger in his work *Being and Time*, where it is used to describe the way that human beings exist in the world. According to Heidegger, Dasein encapsulates the unique ability of human beings to be aware of their mortality, to reflect on their existence and to give meaning to their own lives. It emphasizes human existence as being fundamentally tied to one's environment in terms of time, space and the collective existence of others.
4. Everything in inverted commas is open to indefinite referential attribution of truth, which opens the self to an indefinite cycle of questioning.
5. With respect to the question of identity, the two things that in their imminent relationship produce knowledge of their difference are the (perceived) self and the (perceived) other.
6. If one contended that the content advanced in situ is dependent on the position project managers assume in the organization, it would be akin to saying that all project managers have the same values, beliefs and motivators. This, however, is implausible.
7. This suggests that one cannot emphasize a deterministic relationship between a particular insight or a facet of the self-idea and a particular conclusion drawn in situ. On that note, one cannot say for certain that formulations of Mark's, Nick's and Margaret's are dependent on an isolated interaction they had with their fathers, for example. I want to emphasize, however, that the conclusions currently drawn are founded on a web of meaning that emerges respective to insight generated from perceived limitations in the subjects' immediate circumstances. The more complete and adequate view of reality and the vision of a relational subject serve as antecedents or inputs into the formation of preferences, significances, value and meaning. In the same way, the voiced (or otherwise) preferences, significance, value and meaning are reflective of the subjects' vision of a more complete and adequate reality and its relational subject.
8. By providing novel attributions of truth that we choose to deploy and participate within, the outcome of which is the revision of our network and hierarchy of importance.

9. A simple representation of this claim is the fact that every single participant in this study made sense, at length, of their professional identity in terms of their past, specifically in terms of their family upbringing and their lives as children (without being prompted by the researcher and the interview questions). This is not simply a retrospective reconstruction of past events into a meaningful whole, since their negative situated experiences were also a reflection of this 'abstract' narrative, or their existing body of knowledge and self-knowledge.
10. This is an ontological assertion and different to the argument about what we *want* to see and experience.

Chapter 7

The Self as the Centre of the Universe

In the ensuing chapter, my aim is to delve into the contributions to and expansions of the extant corpus of self-identity scholarship. Harnessing the foundational concepts outlined in Chapters 2 and 3 concerning the formation and manifestation of identity, my analysis will address key deficiencies in the literature – specifically, its occasional failure to portray a self-aware and distinct self without constraining it within the spheres of prescribed action and expectation. The discussion will begin by critically examining the prevalent portrayal of self-identity as fragmented or confined to certain predicates. Establishing self-identity as a construct within the social realm, I will proceed to elucidate the intricate, dialogical interplay between individual and collective identity. Furthermore, a particular emphasis will be placed on articulating how both self and society can be perceived as discrete yet intertwined entities, resistant to a deterministic framework. Ultimately, I will forge philosophical grounds for understanding everyday agency as a continuous, multilayered and multidimensional phenomenon. This exploration paves the way for a behaviour model, one that promises not only academic enrichment but also practical enlightenment for those navigating the existential quandaries inherent to the role of project management.

Contributions

The existing gaps in the extant literature highlight dominant thematic disagreements between essentialist and post-structuralist positions. At the core of their argument is the disputed existence of a distinctive self and intentional agency. More specifically, the literature reveals a lacuna in harmonizing (a) the concept of the evolving self that is perceived by the individual as cohesive and enduring; (b) the juxtaposition of autonomous selfhood against the influential forces of established role dynamics; and (c) the reconciliation of the unique or core self with the conventional, socially normalized identity. These pervasive tensions in the extant literature are thus reducible to a single argument – one which cannot seem to avoid an explanation of a self-conscious distinctive subject without imprisoning it in 'spheres of prescribed action and expectation' (Cerulo 1997: 388).

The problem with this theoretical stance is that, in its current form, it falls short of offering a tangible framework to navigate existential challenges within project management. Such a deficiency grows increasingly untenable in light of the alarming rates of mental health crises, including suicide, that afflict the construction and project management industry in Australia. Thus, the primary objective of this book is to confront these critical disparities in the literature, thereby setting the stage for a paradigm geared towards empowered self-regulation and management. To reacquaint and align the readers with the prior discourse, I will revisit and underscore the identified shortcomings within the prevailing scholarship, establishing a clearer backdrop for presenting my contributions. This effort will be buttressed by engaging with the salient identity-related conundrums that lie at the heart of the thematic contentions within self-identity research.

Is Identity a Predicate of Sociality or a Purely Situated and Fragmented Phenomenon?

Gap 1: In existing scholarship, identity and the processes of its formation are often considered through the lens of a Cartesian dualism, a perspective that cleaves the self from the object, and subjectivity from objectivity. This bifurcated model necessitates a move towards a more cohesive ontological stance, one that foregrounds the reciprocal and dialogical interplay among self and other, individual and collective, personal agency and societal norms. By centring on this interactivity, we allow self-identity to be examined both as the experiencer and as an aspect influenced by the intricacies of social relationships. Such a focus grants deeper insight into the ways personal identity is sculpted by the specific dynamics of interpersonal interactions.

We have seen from the preceding arguments and participant observations that we do not experience the world *directly*. To perceive the world directly would mean to see all the world there is to see, all at once. 'However, there is just too much of the world to see, just as there is too much past to remember' (Peterson 2018: 120). In general parlance, 'we restrict our limited vision and understanding to that which is of vital importance' (ibid.). This illuminates the inextricable link between our conception of the world and our self-conception: the values and priorities we hold implicitly enshrine our sense of self-worth, as noted by Gill (2015). The 'image' we hold of our surroundings is thus not an isolated construct but rather a reflection deeply intertwined with the 'image' we hold of ourselves.

The implications of these insights place the individual at the heart of their own (situated) professional 'experiences'. To say that an individual occupies the 'centre' entails a dual significance: (1) The subject plays an active role in the construction of their (professional) 'surrounding world', a setting in which only certain experiences are possible. The subject's complicity in this construction becomes apparent when we recognize that for any entity – be it a thing, event or person – to be characterized as either facilitating or impeding self-realization, it must be contextualized within a matrix defined by our own subjectively crafted goals. As Archer (2010) asserts, these entities take on the role of obstacles or facilitators based on their alignment or misalignment with our personal ends. The world we dwell within, therefore, engenders a particular creation and does so on the grounds of our *preconceived* ideas that we hold about ourselves (which do not preclude what we want, what we do not want, what we desire and strive towards). In this vein, it is critical to recognize that changes in the 'external world' – the pressures exerted by the environmental context – are not phenomena operating in isolation. As Archer (2000: 219) articulates, 'it is our own definitions of what constitutes our self-worth that determines which normative evaluations matter'. Therefore, when pressures from the 'surrounding world' influence our sense of self, they are initially filtered through the lens of our personal judgements before being perceived or dissected as signs of friction between the 'objective' and the 'subjective', or between the individual's identity and societal norms. Consequently, the envisioning of a personal goal must logically precede the complexities of the world, for it is through the conception of our desired self that the world becomes arrayed with challenges and opportunities. We cast a vision for our existence prior to the world manifesting as a landscape of potential obstructions or gateways, implying that our imagined selves create the narrative of our journey.

Secondly, (2) the experiential realm of the constructed surrounding world is inherently delimited by the contours of our self-conceptions. For instance, the perceived 'laziness' in others gains significance only through the lens of

Nick's personal standard of 'hard work', itself a reflection of the substance of his 'hard worker' identity. Consequently, any evaluation, assessment or categorization of one's circumstances – a process that necessarily encompasses others and societal norms – is intrinsically derived from the particulars of one's distinctive self-concept. Judgements thus make sense only relative to what is pertinent and meaningful to the individual's identity. From this, it follows that our daily observant engagement with the world is constrained by our self-concepts: we are attuned principally to that which resonates within the boundaries of our own self-understanding. Acknowledging this, the image we hold of ourselves operates as an ontological template for perceiving our milieu, determining the limits and possibilities of what is perceptible and experienceable within our personally sculpted reality.

The ontological precedence of our inner realities thus casts self-identity as the foundational subjectum against which all contextual distinctions take shape. Beyond the epistemic validity of this assertion, its ontological soundness stands firm, for the very consideration of any predicate logically entails the existence of a corresponding and relational subject. The implications of this are twofold: (1) *first*, it adds to the predicate-oriented conceptualization of identity that dominates the postmodern identity literature (see Ahuja et al. 2018, 2019; Alvesson and Robertson 2015; Alvesson and Willmott 2002; Alvesson et al. 2008; Beech et al. 2016; Brown 2015, 2017; Brown and Toyoki 2013; Driver 2013; Karreman and Alvesson 2001; Knights and Clarke 2017; Snow and Anderson 1987; Sveningsson and Alvesson 2003; Watson 2008). *Second*, (2) positioning the self-idea as a subjectum of society (or of an organization) recognizes 'identity as an issue central to understanding processes of social communication, negotiation, entrepreneurial behaviour, leading and following, decision-making, and strategizing' (Brown 2018: 11).

By doing so, my discussion responds to the challenge issued by Brown (2018), who advocates for 'exploring rich possibilities of identity' – a call to broaden the scope beyond the conception of identity as merely an emergent property of social interaction. In this light, my arguments make a vital contribution to the literature that often favours a predicate-centric view of identity. They underscore that our everyday modes of expression – our actions and self-descriptions – are rooted in our self-concept, which encompasses all that we perceive ourselves to be and aspire to become. The import of this perspective lies in its recentring of agency within the individual's domain. It contests the notion of the self as adrift in the currents of social relations and instead asserts the individual's capacity to navigate purposefully through the possibilities of identity. It is within this reclaimed autonomy that I determine my focus and carve out my path, actively shaping my observations and behaviours in the complex tapestry of interpersonal relations.

Following the thrust of these arguments, we see that attentive vigilance in our daily lives originates from our self-concept. My assertions underscore an inherent connectedness among diverse facets of identity, each differentiated by distinct moments in time and by their relative spaces. Positioning the self-concept as a foundational subject of social interaction implies that there exists a fundamental interrelationship within two realms: (1) among varied identity positions within the same sphere of interaction and (2) across identity positions within disparate spheres of interaction. Initially, as the relevance and significance of an 'action' within a particular sphere are inextricably linked to the individual's narrative identity, it follows that situated expressions of self are not merely sporadic gestures. They are embedded within a broader, coherent framework of personal meaning and awareness. More specifically, with our self-ideas delineating the boundaries of potential action and experience, the composite of situated identity positions is better understood as the unfolding of an individual-specific ontology, rather than an assemblage of unconnected deeds and declarations. Thus, the interconnectivity of different identity positions within a shared context finds its roots in the recognition that all perception, comprehension and articulation are mediated through the prism of self-knowledge. This self-knowledge, by demarcating a subjective slice of the world, enables us to attribute meaning and distinction to otherwise amorphous aspects of our shared reality.

Secondly, as every facet of identity is intertwined with the 'ontological foundation' of the self – a comprehensive construct that encapsulates who the individual currently 'is' and aspires to 'become' – a reciprocal relationship also persists among 'geographically dispersed' identity claims. Take, for example, our study participants: their present professional identities take root in self-concepts that originated outside the immediate professional setting. Nick's ideal of 'hard work' is an inheritance from his father's work ethic; Mark's drive to distinguish himself is born out of his experiences growing up in a large family; while Margaret's ambition to lead her own initiatives and harness her skills in project management stems from witnessing her father's accomplishments in property development. These personal narratives, though differing in origin and manifestation, are inextricably linked in contributing to the tapestry of each individual's professional self-definition. More importantly, acknowledging the self-referential and reinforcing nature of perception, which is grounded in ontological primacy, the self-definitions 'borrowed from elsewhere' are repurposed to evaluate the behaviour of colleagues in the present context. For instance, Nick's 'hard worker' ethos, once integrated into his self-idea, now functions as a lens through which he assesses both his own actions and those of his peers within his current organization. Similarly, the self-concepts of other participants act as benchmarks against which they measure the surrounding realities they navigate. Thus, it becomes clear that active participation in our environments, regardless of geographical location, is an extension of the subjective essence that encompasses our lived past and the future we aspire to create. Consequently, given that our every context is shaped by elements of our self-concept that surpass spatial and temporal constraints, self-attributions in any given situation cannot be viewed as discrete or standalone occurrences. Rather, they are continuous threads of a narrative that both reflects and informs the self throughout life's journey.

The *transcendental nature of the self-idea*, however, does not promote a reified view of the self (for instance, one's fixed personality) and the surrounding world, as suggested by proponents of essentialism (see Chapter 2 and 3 for related arguments). This is because the constructed narrative of the self is an accumulative phenomenon, emerging from the plethora of insights generated through comparison between different things, events and people one encounters throughout life. Therefore, we must acknowledge that situated identity positions are contingent upon a self-idea that cannot be said to reflect a single context exclusively, since its 'amorphous mass' remains subject to revision and change (by way of new insights) regarding the 'in situ' demands of the *perceived* normative order (Archer 2000, 2003). For example, before she immersed herself in the partner organization, the plausibility of Margaret's 'good' communication skills and her overall 'project management' identity was not contingent upon bureaucratic requirements (for instance, job titles). In light of this, we realize that self-identity cannot be perceived as either a subject or a predicate of sociality exclusively, given that the self-idea is an amalgam of both – one brings to (perceived) circumstantial particularity an idea about oneself that gets altered through interaction, albeit *not completely*. Such a realization, however, is *only* attained when theorizing of self-identity *begins* with the subjective possibility of a circumstance. Therefore, in the same way that one cannot speak of intersubjectivity without considering it as an 'offspring' of subjectivity, my arguments highlight that a discussion of the predicate-oriented, fragmented and precarious nature of situated identity positions is only sensible when recognized as a reflection of a distinctive and enduring *subject*.

The arguments therefore extend contributions of role identity theory (Snow and Anderson 1987) and do so by suggesting that one's self-identity is indeed shaped, although *not bound*, by 'structured role relationships' within which the individual participates. This distinction is very important. In undertaking this analysis, I endeavour to span the 'chasm' created by the literature's past shortcomings – the difficulty of conceptualizing a self-conscious, distinctive self without confining it to 'spheres of prescribed action and expectation' (Cerulo 1997: 388). More importantly, given that 'contextual particularity' of identity is nothing other than a synchronic reflection of a diachronic self-idea,[1] this book provides a more enduring rendition of pre-existing self-notions whose 'persistence' has been undermined by those who view identity as a 'precarious accomplishment' (Ahuja et al. 2018; also see Becker et al. 1961; Diver 2013; Knights and Clarke 2017; Pratt et al. 2006; Snow and Anderson 1987). What, then, is anxiety if not a pervasive sense of precariousness? We drift between concepts and beliefs, adrift in uncertainty about what is true and right for us, ultimately succumbing to the disquieting sensation of an anchorless existence. While it is beyond the purview of this book to thoroughly articulate the frustration and detriment wrought by postmodern thinking on individuals seeking agency over their fate, the acknowledgement alone of these phenomena is telling. Nevertheless, I must return to the main trajectory of our discussion.

By underscoring the role of pre-existing self-notions as foundational elements in shaping situated identity positions, I contest the perspective within certain scholarship that elevates discursive resources as the sole precursors of identity claims – a view held in works such as those by Ahuja et al. (2018), Beech et al. (2016), Brown (2017) and Knights and Clarke (2017). Therefore, by positing that 'context-specific identity' represents merely a transient aspect of an individual's overarching self-concept – a personal thread running through the fabric of space and time – I bring an alternative voice to debates often dominated by narratives of identity as an ephemeral, largely inconsistent, and fluid construct (Karreman and Alvesson 2001). Far from being concocted merely as a makeshift narrative for individuals striving to instil a semblance of coherence amid manifold vulnerabilities (Brown 2018: 10), identity, as I argue, is informed by a durable sense of self that informs and transcends immediate circumstances. The establishment of such a robust foundation – a solid springboard – enables the concept of self-regulation to be understood as sensible and practicable. Furthermore, by foregrounding the persistent and personally governed dimensions of self-identity, the discourse articulated in this book serves as an effective counterbalance to the narratives advanced by some scholars that portray self-identity through an impersonal, discourse-centric lens, or as a fragmented, rootless construct, vulnerable to the ebb and flow of circumstance (see Ahuja et al. 2018; Beech et al. 2016; Cerulo 1997; Driver 2013; Knights and Clarke 2017). The arguments herein advocate for an appreciation of the intrinsic cohesion and agency inherent in an individual's identity, accentuating the role of the self in intelligently navigating life's terrain.

Before I move on to the next arguments, I want you to consider the following analogy that will perfectly illustrate the absurdity of nihilistic claims of postmodernism (i.e. of an impersonal, fragmented, disjointed or precarious identity). The self-idea can be likened to the complex, thriving existence of a tree. Much like the intricate web of a tree's roots that extend deep into the ground, our identity is undergirded by an extensive network of experiences and insights that have shaped and nurtured us throughout our lives. These roots, representing the past, not only anchor us firmly in our history but also spread, reaching into the present and future, as a living testament to our continuous growth and evolutionary journey. The trunk, the core of our identity, stands strong amid the ever-changing landscape of life. It symbolizes our unyielding resilience and unwavering resolve to weather the storms and face the challenges that come our way. It is our enduring essence, the unique synthesis of individual characteristics and traits that distinguishes us from others. Branching out from the trunk, our self-identity diverges into various avenues, manifesting as an array of personal interests, relationships and aspirations. Each branch represents a different aspect of our lives, intertwining and interrelating with one another in a rich, flourishing canopy. The leaves, budding and blossoming, reflect the multitude of encounters, adventures and moments that adorn the tapestry of our existence, further enriching our identity and contributing to the vibrant and multidimensional nature of our being.

As a tree renews itself with each passing season, shedding its leaves and fostering new growth, our self-identity, too, is in a perpetual state of transformation. We, as individuals, constantly adapt to shifting circumstances, learn from experiences and cultivate new facets of ourselves. This dynamic metamorphosis not only echoes the vitality and life force that courses through our roots but also demonstrates the potential for continual self-discovery and personal growth. Ultimately, the analogy between self-identity and a tree captures the essence of our unique, evolving existence. The roots that stretch into the past and the future embody the foundational insights upon which our identity is built, while the trunk, branches and leaves exemplify the diverse and intricate manifestations of our lives. Like a tree amid the ever-changing seasons, we are perpetually transforming and expanding, navigating the journey of self-identity with resilience, grace and the vibrant life force that sustains our individual growth.

The axiom 'As within, so without; as above, so below' serves as a poignant reminder: our inner life animates our external engagements. Bear this in mind – without a rich internal landscape, the external world holds no substantive discourse. It is the essence that dwells within us that breathes significance into our encounters in the world beyond.

Is (Distinctive) Self-Identity a Discursive Illusion?

Gap 2: The identity politics and identity formation literature cannot seem to explain, ontologically, the possibility of a distinctive self and the distinctive other in the context of liquid modernity.

The sheer unpredictability of interpersonal interactions highlights that our subjectively conceived 'maps' of the world are not objective representations of reality. The subjectivity of it all, that is, the limitations of our 'interpretive map', are evident when we experience novelty. In this scenario, embracing an identity such as 'a hard worker' or being 'good at one's job' simultaneously uncovers latent inadequacies, such as deficiencies in 'people management', which, while previously regarded as peripheral, now surface as integral components of the self (as exemplified by Nick's self-concept) in light of the prevailing circumstances. This indicates that our cultivated self-concept inherently encompasses potential areas for growth or challenge, acknowledging its own boundaries and the prospect of continued evolution. Before moving on, let us recognize Heidegger's (1953: 75) observations: 'taking care of things always already occurs on the basis of familiarity with the world.' Therefore, the essence of what constitutes novelty is intrinsically personal, as each subject's recognition and embrace of the new is rooted in the fertile ground of their own unique concerns, desires, needs, aims and aspirations. As noted by Peterson (1999: 34):

> Our hopes, desires and wishes – which are always *conditional* [and conditioned – emphasis mine] – define the context within which the things and situations we encounter take on determinate significance; define even the context within which we understand 'thing' or 'situation'.

The apprehension of what is new, then, unfolds within the confines of what is already known to the individual. This implies that the recognition of novelty draws its significance in contrast to the familiar; without this juxtaposition, 'new things' would bear no meaning to the observer and would reside beyond the limits of our perceptual realm. On that note, in the same way that our self-ideas ontologically presuppose their own limits, every situated *known* identity claim also entails its *unknown* negative. The first (1) consequence of this insight is that it is through the interplay between opposites – the known and unknown – that we can trace the contours of our understanding and personal awareness. More precisely, the nexus of the familiar and the yet-to-be-discovered elements of reality demarcates the periphery of what is accessible to an individual's perception. More significantly, the second (2) implication of our understanding is that it is the very existence of 'the nature of two different things' – the known and the unknown, as delineated by Bateson (2002) – that permits discourse on perception and comprehension in the first place. As Bateson illuminates, 'relationship is always a product of double description' (ibid.: 123). Thus, the capacity to discern and contemplate relies intrinsically on the ability to differentiate one thing from another. Because two indistinct objects do not register as separate, and a solitary entity might not register at all (drawing on Bateson 2002 and Peterson 1999), it is through the limitations carved out by our self-concepts that we can recognize and reflect upon various 'things in the external world'. We come to understand, then, that entities (and individuals) become perceptible by virtue of their inherent distinctions; in the same manner, the self and the other are discernible through the delineations of their individual knowledge and self-awareness. As noted by Schutz (1967: 102):

> In the everyday world in which both the I and the Thou turn up, not as transcendental but as psychophysical subjects, there corresponds to each stream of lived experience of the I a stream of subjective experience of the Thou. This, to be sure, refers back to my own stream of lived experience, just as the body of the other person to my body. During this process, the peculiar reference of my own ego to the other's ego holds, in the same sense that my stream of lived experience is for you that of the other person, just as my body is another's body for you.

These arguments hold pivotal significance for two main reasons: (1) First, our capacity to articulate self-identity (and the identity of others) is grounded in our inherently fragmentary grasp of these concepts. In other words, it is precisely due to our partial awareness and self-knowledge that we ascribe varying levels of importance to different attributes. For instance, Nick elevated the value of 'hard work' within his personal schema, employing it as a benchmark against which he gauged not only his own attitudes and actions but also those of his colleagues. By prioritizing 'hard work' at the pinnacle of his value system, Nick effectively (re)shaped his own identity and the identities of those around him, relativizing and diminishing all other traits (such as people skills) by comparison. Thus, the structure of significance that underlies an individual's self-conception orchestrates the unique way in which they characterize themselves and others. The inherently provisional nature of our self-concepts allows for the expression of personal preferences, furnishing us with the means to discern and declare our individuality and that of our peers. As affirmed by Peterson (1999: 9):

> This means that *categorization*, with regards to value – determination (or even perception) of what constitutes a single thing, or a class of things – is the act of *grouping together according to implications for behaviour*. (Emphasis in the original)

Subsequently, **(2)** the act of distinguishing and comparing encountered entities not only aids in defining them but also sculpts a 'segmented' reality – one that is inhabited by elements of varied importance to the individual in pursuit of self-identity. From this perspective, we recognize that the nuanced attribution of significance to facets of one's self-concept extends to the way objects in the external world are perceived: individuals assign varying levels of import to different aspects of their environment, marking some as critical and others as incidental in their path to self-realization. The consequence of having such a selective and bounded framework of ideas (about oneself and others) is that it paints a vibrant world, one shaped to underscore or set the stage for daily engagements. In the vast expanse of potential stimuli, subjects distil and navigate towards those nuances that resonate with personal significance, thereby transforming erstwhile background static into features of compelling relevance. It follows, then, that the inherently provisional qualities of our self-concepts are what empower us to engage in meaningful actions; they enable us to differentiate and navigate through a hierarchy of relevance within the 'external world'. As Peterson (1999: 9) profoundly observes, 'thinking is also and more fundamentally a specification of value, specification of implications for behaviour'. Accordingly, just as a deficit of meaning can lead to inaction, the demarcated boundaries within our self-ideas sift out the immaterial, thereby liberating our actions from the quagmire of the inconsequential. This is also recognized by Archer (2010: 284) when she says:

> Increasingly, agents navigate by the compass of their own personal concerns. This growing reliance on their personal powers – whether deployed individually or collectively – has as its counterparts the demise of the generalised other and the diminution of socialisation as a quasi-unilateral process.

Indeed, the inherent restrictions of our 'interpretive maps' are a testament to the ontological reality of self-ideas. Were our sense of self only 'fragmented' and unrooted, without the anchoring threads of continuity and coherence, we would lack the ability to prioritize or assign 'weighting of importance' to the myriad aspects of our environment – a key prerequisite that enables us to act in distinctive and purposeful ways (such as, for example, choosing to abstain from particular contexts or interactions).[2] This intentionality was apparent in the narratives of the participants, as they expressed a readiness to take decisive actions, such as pursuing a career change, to safeguard their core values and aspirations. Mark contemplated seeking employment elsewhere to be in an environment where his contributions would be acknowledged; Margaret, recognizing her strength in people skills and creativity, contemplated starting her own venture; and Nick considered returning to independent work as a reaffirmation of his 'hard worker' identity. As Nagel (1989) posits, there is no 'view from nowhere'; our interpretations of the world are irrevocably rooted in subjectivity – '*there is only a perspective seeing*, only *a perspective "knowing"*' (emphasis in the original) (Gadamer 1975: 364). Thus, I posit that the distinct contours of our self-concept not only empower our agential endeavours but also provide the necessary framework for engagement, as our bespoke limitations inform and refine our capacities to think, speak and act. More specifically, a self that has been uprooted and rendered fragmented would find itself mired in constant inertia, unable to discriminate in assigning meaning and value across the expanse of its experiences. However, contrary to characterizations of the coherent self as an illusion, as posited by Driver (2013) and echoed by others (see Knights and Clarke 2017), the evidence provided by the participants illustrates that our self-concept serves as a navigational tool – one that overlays the world in such a manner as to enable precisely directed actions emblematic of a purposeful being. Thus, the discourse presented here challenges the notion advanced in some scholarly circles that the pursuit of identity is futile, and is an endeavour 'to turn the individual into a definable object that knows who it is and what it wants' (Brown 2018: 10), by affirming the importance of self-identity as an enabler of meaningful agency.

More importantly, by highlighting *the ontological nature of our self-ideas*, the arguments I put forward extend the literature that promotes an inherent 'lack in human subjectivity' (see Braidotti 2011; Lacan 2006) and argues for an illusory nature of self-identity (Knights and Clarke 2017). This brings us to the crux of the matter: the deliberate destabilization of the self all too often cultivates a breeding ground for anxiety. When we flit from one identity to the next in search of something grander – without truly discerning our core values – we fall prey to the perils of an existence lacking solid ground. Our research observed the phenomenon first-hand; participants became numbed by the continual introduction of new reference points for self-definition. It is essential, then, to propose an alternate perspective: our self-conceptualizations are not fixed mirrors of reality. Rather, they are malleable constructs that can – and should – be adapted to foster a more fulfilling life. Where postmodernist thought halts at the assertion that 'our self-definitions are not objective representations of reality', it inadvertently drops us into a void ripe for existential angst, potentially leaving us reliant on the figurative psychiatrist's couch. The journey we must undertake goes beyond this diagnosis; it involves reimagining our self-narratives with intentionality, sculpting them not as rigid truths but as dynamic frameworks within which meaning can be thoughtfully cultivated.

More precisely, my work builds on the foundation that acknowledging the inherent limitations in our understanding of the self and the world activates a form of preferential agency. This conceptual framework extends the discourse around identity, challenging views that deem our self-concepts a mere anthropocentric illusion – a belief that we hold dominion over the course of our lives, or as Becker described it, an 'anthropocentric deceit (and conceit) that we control our lives' (2011: 55). I contend that our very conceptions of self serve as cognitive schemas – lenses through which we filter and interpret our experiences. In this way, these self-conceptions emerge not as deceptive constructs, but as instrumental strategies in coping with the anxiety and insecurities that accompany human existence. The subsequent chapter delves deeper into the tactical role of self-identity in navigating the seas of existential uncertainty and its implications for our agency.

Against this backdrop, there exists a curious paradox: our very capacity to shape our identities and the external world is, in fact, a by-product of our inherently partial understanding of the self and others. Archer (2010: 300) captures this sentiment by asserting that 'these very different forms of social orientation are, indeed, interior to subjects' and inherently shape their divergent paths in society. The implication here is that while self-identity may assume an illusory veil – particularly when it is reduced to a mere facet of discourse – it gains tangibility and intentionality when cultivated from the fertile ground of our limited yet evolving self-awareness. By refining our conceptualization of identity formation – acknowledging it as a dynamic process enriched by the continuous emergence of insights drawn from our constrained knowledge and understanding of ourselves – we bridge previously irreconcilable paradigms. Positivism, interpretivism and constructivism have traditionally faltered in envisioning a coherent self that is at once enduring and in flux. It is through this nuanced prism that we can begin to perceive an identity both anchored in stability and susceptible to growth and transformation.

This crucial epiphany lays bare the fact that the conversation surrounding the 'fragile self, vulnerable to implosion' – a notion articulated by Watts (1951) and further explored by Becker (2010, 2011) – is predicated on the understanding that the self is not monolithic but deeply layered, comprising elements of varying importance. Akin to the layers of a tree, our self-identities are structured hierarchically, fostering the coexistence of both stable and fleeting facets of who we are. The enduring trunk remains resolute against the winds of change, while the leaves – the more transient aspects of our identity – seasonally come and go. Thus, by foregrounding the hierarchy that guides the salience of different self-concepts, my work enriches the discourse on 'liquid modernity' as proposed by Bauman (2000). It acknowledges the fluidity yet insists upon the continuity of a coherent subject within this framework, navigating the tensions put forth by theorists such as Braidotti (2011), Driver (2013) and Knights and Clarke (2017), as well as the psychoanalytic insights of Lacan (2006). The stratified self-dialogue shapes a view of identity as dually stable and mutable, thus reconciling the seemingly opposing qualities of selfhood's permanence, as suggested by Archer (2000), with its more fragmented, ever-evolving elements as discussed by Driver (2013) and Knights and Clarke (2017).

Is the Self in a Dichotomous Relationship with 'Society'?

> *Gap 3a* in the extant self-identity literature is embedded in the failure to delineate the dialogical relationship between the conscious agent and the *perceived* world of subjects and objects.

The ontological essence of one's self-conception diverges significantly from René Descartes' famous dictum – 'Cogito, ergo sum': 'I think, therefore I am.' This divergence is critical since a person's sense of self is subjected to a multitude of objective influences that extend beyond mere cognition (Archer 2000). As noted by Archer (ibid.: 215–16), 'the environment at any time was either dangerous or it was not, and this was a matter of objectivity for it was gauged by whether it damaged our bodies or was benign towards them – something which could be ascertained medically, that is without resort to human subjectivity'. It is imperative to clarify that the exploration of self-identity within the parameters of my study does not engage with first-order referential concerns, as per Archer (2000) and Peterson (1999); in simpler terms, it does not seek to map the 'objective' features of interaction between structure and agency. Instead, within the frame of this discourse, the imperative is to discern not the inevitability of pain following a sharp blow to the head, but rather to probe the deeper significance of such an event to us – as self-interpreting subjects. Before we move on, keep in mind Bateson's (2002: 123) claims:

> The mind contains no things, no pigs, no people, no midwife toads, or what have you, only ideas (i.e. new of difference), information about 'things' in quotes, always in quotes. Similarly, the mind contains no time and space, only ideas of 'time' and 'space'. It follows that the boundaries of the individual, if real at all, will be not spatial boundaries, but something more like the sacks that represent *sets* [emphasis in the original] in set theoretical diagrams or the bubbles that come out of the mouths of the characters in comic strips.

The exploration into the subjective meanings attributed to experiences, entities and relationships uncovers a multidimensional implication: First and foremost, I assert that a singular, all-encompassing normative framework does not govern interactions within any given context. This assertion is exemplified by the case studies in which 'self-definition' takes on distinct, personalized dimensions: Nick embodies 'a hard worker' not as a universal[3] standard but as someone who brings joy through humour; Margaret's claim to being a 'good communicator' is characterized by her non-confrontational style; and Mark's self-coined 'miracle-worker' status derives from his anticipatory prowess in meeting the needs of his colleagues and clients. These individual interpretations highlight the nuanced ways in which each participant internalizes and redefines the concept of 'people person' in alignment with their unique perspectives and priorities.

While a blow to the head with a sharp object will incontrovertibly result in pain, the subjective import of that pain is deeply personal and varies according to the significance each individual assigns to the event. For some, this might conjure feelings of shame connected to their 'sense of dignity, of worth, of how we are seen by others', as Archer (2000: 216) articulates, whereas others may remain emotionally unscathed. In a parallel fashion, an offhand inquiry from a superior – such as 'How are you doing with the project?' – may resonate differently with each person. It prompts a subjective analysis informed by one's inner narrative and priorities. To one person, it might evoke moments of perceived failure; to another, it represents an affirmation of exceptional effort. Still others may interpret the inquiry as overbearing, perhaps even taking it as a signifier that it is time to seek new career opportunities. These varied interpretations, born of 'error', 'misunderstanding' and 'disagreement', lend credence to Clegg's (1975) assertion that 'what we see depends on where we sit'. This phrase aptly captures the essence of a 'multiverse' of normative frameworks, each existing within the same space of interpersonal exchange, yet experienced through the diverse perceptual lenses of individual subjects. As noted by Burr (2003):

> each person perceives the world differently and *actively creates their own meanings from events. The 'real' world is therefore a different place for each of us.* (Emphasis in the original)

In light of this understanding, we might collectively acknowledge that society, a structure or an institution cannot 'interact' with the self unless such engagement is mediated by each party's interpretation of the normative orders at play. Thus, when contemplating the dynamics between self and society, it is perhaps more fitting to consider them a dance between the self, laden with personal interpretations of the normative order, and the other, equally endowed with their own subjective readings of that order. After all, sociality and the norms that ostensibly symbolize it lack the intrinsic capacity for interaction without the human tendency to ascribe agency where it inherently does not exist. Consider, for instance, the justice system and its courts, which enact laws that delineate the boundaries of acceptable conduct. These legal entities, in and of themselves, do not 'interact' with individuals. Instead, they shape the field of possible actions, influencing agency within the sphere that individuals deem significant to their lives. As asserted by Archer (2003: 218) elsewhere, 'there are evaluative standards, but their effect is dependent upon our feeling bad if we fall short of them and good if we live up to them'.

I propose that even though the normative standards of the partner organization – such as definitions of 'good people skills', 'good communication skills' and 'good performance' – exist prior to the involvement of the study's participants, it is the subjects who animate these norms through their engagement with them. They actualize norms by interpreting them in the context of their self-concepts and acting upon this personalized comprehension. Thus, the 'interaction' between self and society is initially an abstract process that takes place within the subject's reflexive interpretation of their environment. Schutz (1945: 533) underscores this subjective foundation of reality, stating, 'reality means simply relation to our emotional and active life. The origin of all reality is subjective ... whatever excites and stimulates our interest is real'. From this standpoint, it is essential to acknowledge, as Archer (2010: 275) notes, that while 'structure predates the actions that transform it', the interplay between them is catalysed by the subjective lens through which individuals perceive themselves and their social context. In essence, as Bhaskar (1989) articulated, the causal power of social form is mediated through social agency.

As this book shifts the locus of the relationship between self and society from objective discourse to one's subjective constitution, it becomes apparent that the assimilation of normative principles is far from straightforward – it is moderated by the unique hierarchy of significance within each individual. This personal lattice of values and priorities bestows upon choice and preference their roles as natural elements of our existence within the occupational sphere. Therefore, the normative order undergoes a subjective filtration process before it can integrate into, and possibly transform, our pre-existing conceptions. It is through this lens of personal 'orders of significance' that individuals classify and, subsequently, adopt the norms they encounter, intertwining them with the ongoing construction of their identities. These insights fundamentally recalibrate our understanding of the interplay between self and society. Firstly, they spotlight the individual as an agent distinct from societal constructs, a distinction grounded in the intentionality and discernment exercised when navigating various orders of significance attributed to experiences, objects and interpersonal relations. Echoing the sentiments of Müller et al. (2015: 87), we cannot presume that 'agents will completely behave in accordance with all conditioning influences'. This resonated in the study when participants actively managed their self-concept by eliminating certain attributes they previously deemed essential, carving out an identity in alignment with their deepest convictions of self-worth within the framework of the partner organization.

Furthermore, this perspective delineates the self and society as interrelated yet distinct phenomena, engaging in a nuanced dance of 'interaction'. It is illustrated by the selective assimilation of social norms and their personalized interpretation alongside individual self-conceptions. For instance, Margaret's recognition that her exceptional project management skills are independent of her challenge with 'mundane' administrative tasks underscores the individualized nature of 'appropriation'. The stratified construction of identity allows one to ascribe 'graded significance' to external influences based on a tiered structure of personal relevance and meaning. Thus, by positing that norms may be adopted, albeit not without reservation, and that the self reflects societal influence but remains autonomously defined, my argument sustains a meaningful distinction between the realms of self and society. This delineation is crucial, as it allows for the articulation of their relationship as inherently dialogical – a mutual exchange marked by agency and choice – rather than a rigid, deterministic interaction.

Considering these points, it is critical to understand that the preceding discourse is not intended to elevate the self-idea to a divine status, nor to diminish or sidestep the profound impact that specific contextual arrangements exert on the shaping and reshaping of participants' self-concepts. Nevertheless, a deeper comprehension of how context influences identity formation necessitates a more precise examination within the literature concerning the loci of these interactions. Through establishing that norms must be perceived as such before they can impact an individual, the crucial role of distinct personal perceptions emerges – a role that upholds the objectives of institutions through the eyes of the individuals that comprise them. The proposed analysis underscores a symbiotic relationship between the self and society, wherein 'oppressive' work conditions, for instance, are actualized through the individual's recognition and experience of them as oppressive. Thus, it is essential to acknowledge the existence of an external social order while understanding that internalization is key to one's emotional response; as Archer (2000: 217) elegantly puts it, 'there cannot be a sense of remorse without the personal acceptance that I have done something wrong'.

My work builds upon and expands the scholarship of managerial identities (Trethewey 1999; Thomas and Davies 2005), engaging particularly with the discourses posited by Foucauldian feminist theorists such as Weedon (1987) and Butler (2011). These theorists argue that individuals are inextricably bound by 'gendered discourses that constrain women's professional identities' (Trethewey 1999: 423). However, this contribution nuances these perspectives by suggesting that subjects are not merely passive recipients of discourse and power dynamics. Furthermore, this analysis offers a critical perspective on the prevalent subject–object dichotomy in understanding the interconnection between self and society. It challenges the prevailing notion, as articulated by Brown (2018: 14) and observed in Koveshnikov et al. (2016), that seeks to interpret identities as strictly 'effects of relations of power' that limit, shape or coerce identity trajectories and individual agency. Instead, it posits that identity is also actively constructed and navigated by subjects, even within the constraints of existing power dynamics.

By illustrating that norms are recognized as such through their resonance with an individual's unique self-concept, a distinct boundary emerges between a subject's personal intentions and the broader goals of institutions. Echoing Bhaskar's philosophical stance, as referred to by Archer (2010: 275), 'people and society … do not constitute two moments of the same process; rather they refer to radically different things'. This distinction underpins the relationship between the self and society, which cannot be conceived without the normative backdrop that must be engaged with – experienced, understood or challenged – before one can ascertain their respective properties. In this light, I argue that self and society would blur into indiscernibility if not for the personal meanings ascribed to social norms. The critical focus, then, is not solely on whether the external world wields the force to shape and constrain behaviour – through mechanisms ranging 'from accessibility of resources to the prevalence of beliefs' (Archer 2010: 277). Rather, it is the manner in which individuals perceive and engage with these 'control measures' that is paramount to understanding their role in shaping action and identity.

By positing that the convergence of subject and the enduring normative order is navigated through the terrain of self-preference, prioritizing those self-conceptions most deeply held, we preserve the individual's capacity for autonomy and choice without negating the influence of 'political processes and power constellations' (Koveshnikov et al. 2016: 1353). This perspective underscores the importance of the subject's elective engagement with normative frameworks, thereby charting a course out of 'central conflation' (Archer 2015; Archer et al. 2015). Such conflation either obscures the differentiation between self and society through monolithic action or errs by promoting a deterministic dynamic, rather than recognizing their true dialogical nature. This approach thus serves as a connective thread between the two poles of debate: on the one hand, those who assert that 'individuals are produced by discourses and organisational processes', and on the other, those who uphold 'considerable agency in matters of identity' (Brown 2018: 14). My discussion not only aligns with Brown's (ibid.: 15) call for integration across various theoretical and practical paradigms but also steers clear of the pitfalls of solipsism. The avoidance of solipsistic reasoning is vital; such an outlook would impede our engagement with existential issues by eroding the foundations of dialogue, thus undermining the possibility for truly grappling with social and ethical concerns like responsibility, empathy and justice.

Is Identity Work a Discontinuous and a Single-Dimensional Predicament?

> *Gap 3b* in the extant self-identity literature would, as such, be embedded in the failure to delineate agency as intentional and proactive, emerging from a 'head full of *pre-existing ideas*'.

The participants' narratives highlight that identity work is an ongoing, continuous, multilocal and multidimensional[4] predicament. However, before making claims that highlight the 'proactive' nature of identity work, it is important to explicitly elucidate how the arguments have permitted such conclusions.

That the genesis of the interaction between context and action is rooted in the meanings individuals attribute to the prevailing normative order necessarily addresses the debate on the locus of social influence – whether it should be conceptualized as residing wholly within the agent or entirely externally to them (Archer 2010: 273). This dichotomy is reconciled by the proposition that all interpersonal interactions originate from a standpoint of self-reference: Perception hinges on the interplay with one's accumulated self-knowledge. As Schutz (1945: 533) concisely puts it, 'to call a thing real means that this thing stands in certain relation to ourselves', emphasizing the subjective filter through which reality is construed and engaged. While the participants' narratives reveal a rich epistemic diversity, reflecting various self-descriptions, there exists an underlying ontological consistency – their perceptive engagement with their professional environment is unified by the distinctiveness of their self-concept as the main reference point for their daily existence within the workplace. A given object, event or person emerges from a state of obscurity into prominence by being infused with meaning by the subject, only to potentially fade into irrelevance once this personal significance wanes. Echoing this sentiment, Sartre (2018: 606) affirms that 'we choose the world – not in its inherent properties, but in its meaning – by choosing ourselves'. Thus, by navigating our world with our self-concept as the initial frame of reference, or more aptly, by interpreting our experiences through the prism of our self-idea, we come to realize that the contours of 'reality' and the constitution of the social order are intrinsically shaped by the unique perspectives we hold of ourselves and our interactions with others. As noted by Burr (2003: 19):

> Each of us develops a system of dimensions and meaning, which he calls 'constructs'. We perceive the world in terms of these constructs and our actions, although never predictable, can be understood in light of our construal of the world. Everyone construes the world differently, so in this sense we each inhabit different worlds, although it is possible for us to gain some appreciation of others' constructions.

Given that reality arises from subjective interpretation, as Schutz (1945: 533) posits, its essence is inherently transient rather than static. Burr (2003: 19) echoes this view by suggesting that 'we have the capacity to change our own constructions of the world and thereby to create new possibilities'. This understanding has profound effects on how we conceptualize the 'primordial purpose' of being-in-the-world. Our perception of the world is inextricably linked to the veracity and resonance of our self-definitions, ambitions and desires. This implies that the 'familiarity' we attribute to our surroundings is a reflection of our own internal coherence. As the insights from the participants illustrate, when our pursuits come into question – when the paradigm of interaction feels restrictive to self-actualization – the very definitions that undergird those pursuits become suspect. Archer's (2003: 195) analysis aligns with this notion, as she observes that commentaries on our experiences 'are thus relational to something, which is what gives them their emergent character, and that something is our own concerns which make a situation a matter of non-indifference to a person'.

The impetus to engage with the world around us is rooted in our need to validate and uphold the coherence of our 'interpretive schema' (Peterson 1999) – the lattice of self-definitions, ambitions and yearnings that form the bedrock of our reality. This scaffold of understanding is what allows us to ascribe meaning and truth to our experiences. Ever-present in this exchange is a pre-reflexive vigilance, a state that Schutz (1945: 533) describes as one that 'affirms immediately the reality of all that is conceived'. It is from this deeply ingrained inclination to preserve the harmony of our personal network of meaning that 'active exploration' takes flight. Such exploration is the spontaneous and intrinsic quest to secure the intricate web of significance that shapes our identity and our world. Absent this fundamental drive, self and environment would meld into an indistinct amalgam, devoid of individuality or structure. As aptly depicted by Wilson (2016: 2–3):

> The human mind behaves as if it were divided into two parts, the Thinker and the Prover. The Thinker can think about virtually anything ... As psychiatrists and psychologists have often observed (much to the chagrin of their medical colleagues), the Thinker can think itself sick, and can even think itself well again. The Prover is a much simpler mechanism. It operates on one law only: Whatever the Thinker thinks the prover Proves ... If the Thinker thinks the sun moves around the earth, the Prover will obligingly organise all perceptions to fit that thought; if the Thinker changes its mind and decides the earth moves around the sun, the Prover will reorganize the evidence ... Of course, it is fairly easy to see that other people's minds operate this way; it is comparatively much harder to become aware that one's own mind is working that way.

It is imperative to acknowledge that both the articulation of self-identity and the interpretation of our environment are predicated on a fundamental need to maintain our self-knowledge. This insight further reveals that the domain of discursive agreement and symbolic interaction, as proposed by Brown (2015), only partially encompasses the realm of identity work. The intricate relationship between the coherence of our self-concepts and the structure of the social world intimates that the primary landscape for identity work is, in fact, intrapersonal. The individual must recognize in the external realm reflections that resonate with and uphold their self-perception before they can thoughtfully engage and negotiate their identity within social discourse. Consequently, as our outward expressions and claims are inherently undergirded by the solidity of our self-concepts, identity work must be understood as a multi-local phenomenon, spanning both internal cognizance and external interaction.

This reveals that the genesis of identity work – encompassing the formation, sustenance, adjustment and enhancement of self-concepts – extends beyond active dialogues with others, originating from the more subtle act of upholding one's intrinsic tendencies. Recognizing this, my argument addresses the vibrant 'focal area of contention' identified by Brown (2015: 24), which challenges the presence and meaningfulness of identity work during seemingly mundane life encounters. Moreover, by tracing the roots of identity work back to the 'intrapsychic domain' (Brown 2018), it is posited that identity work is not merely episodic or confined to moments of particular challenge or change, as suggested by Brown (2015: 25), and supported by the explorations of Ibarra (1999), Beyer and Hannah (2002), Collinson (2003) and Kaufman and Johnson (2004). Instead, it is an unceasing process, quietly yet persistently interwoven into the fabric of daily existence, reflecting a dynamic interplay between the self and the myriad facets of lived experience. As affirmed by Sartre (2018: 603):

> The *first phenomenon* [emphasis mine] of being-in-the-world is the original relation between the totality of the in-itself or world and my detotalized totality: I choose myself in my entirety in the world in its entirety. And just as I come *from* the world *to* a particular *this* [emphasis in the original], I come from myself as a detotalized totality to the sketch of one of my particular possibilities, since I can only grasp a particular this against the ground of the world in the circumstance of a particular project of myself.

The continuous process of identity work does not imply fixed demarcations within our interpretive schema. Rather, this insight holds dual significance: Firstly, it frames identity work as a harbinger of the emergence of the 'unknown'. To rephrase, one must engage with the known before encountering the unknown within it. Peterson (1999: 19) accurately encapsulates this dynamic, noting that 'what is novel is of course dependent on what is known – is necessarily defined in opposition to what is known'. Thus, identity work acts as a precursor to innovation and discovery, just as it cultivates a sense of familiarity and order. The duality of every proposition, where each assertion entails its negative (Sharp 1991), implies that identity work not only precedes but also engenders the birth of new experiences. This concept challenges the notion of an absolute divide between identity work and 'external' forces. In reality, we are co-authors of the pressures and tensions we face, an understanding that has profound implications for existential inquiries – explicated further in subsequent discussion. These arguments inform debates that traditionally regard structural changes as ontologically preceding transformative actions, positing instead that it is the very actions informed by the peculiarities of the normative order that contribute to structural continuity and change.

Moreover, the presented arguments refine our understanding of identity work by examining the varied degrees of agency available to the subject. For instance, through its role in the acknowledgment of novelty, identity work is instrumental in broadening the 'domain of relevance' by which subjects ascribe meaning to themselves and their interrelations with others. This process was exemplified in earlier discussions, where the act of interpreting others' actions in a self-referential manner brought to light new, hitherto unnoticed, reference points essential for self-actualization. Yet the role of identity work is multifaceted; while it can expand the scope of what is recognized and understood by a subject, it can also focus and distil the expanse of the interpretive schema down to a singular focal point. Such a distillation serves not necessarily to reinforce existing self-knowledge, but to refine or recalibrate the self-concept around a more select array of influences, experiences or commitments. In response to novel experiences, all subjects instinctively recalibrate their personal significance network, elevating to the top those elements they deem non-negotiable. This act reveals that our sense of personal agency and autonomy is amplified when we recognize and prioritize different values in our perceptions of self and others. It implies that a coherent self-identity, coupled with the adeptness to tread into the realm of the unfamiliar, becomes more marked when we attribute varying degrees of importance to our experiences, rather than valuing them all equally. On that note, we can say that 'affirm[ing] immediately the reality of all that is conceived' (Schutz 1945: 533) is a different form of identity work to one that assigns shades of significance to things, events and people, since the latter reflects a more (self-)conscious subject. More on this later.

The arguments presented here underscore the multidimensional nature of situated identity positions by showing how a single speech act can both reinforce and diminish different facets of the self. Essentially, a situated position can mirror both self-affirmation and self-negation at one and the same time. Take Nick's case as an illustrative example: his admission of lacking 'soft skills' for staff management – a mode of self-negation – simultaneously acts as a reaffirmation of his identity as a 'hard worker', positioning it as the singular defining characteristic of value in light of his current context. As noted by Peterson (1999: 10), 'to act is literally to manifest *preference* [emphasis mine] about one set of possibilities, contrasted with an infinite set of alternatives'. This offers us a chance to understand that the act of prioritizing particular aspects of the external world inherently involves undervaluing others, a process often evident within a single expressive moment. As Peterson (1999) suggests, significance emerges in direct relation to what is deemed insignificant. In this light, it is critical not to mistake routine expressions for the sole manifestations of identity work, as such a narrow view would disregard the strategic 'choice to remain silent' as inconsequential, overlooking its potential impact on self-identity. Strategically navigating silence and speech reflects the exercise of agency and supports a conception of autonomy that broadens beyond discursive analysis to appreciate the active meaning-making efforts by subjects regarding things, events and people in their lives.

Synopsis

The insights garnered from these discussions offer a pathway for understanding self-identity as an intrinsic element of social and organizational life. By elucidating the unique aspects of self-identity, I trace the iterative path of the self-idea – a cyclical process of identity formulation that starts with self-identity as a core concern of social existence and concludes with self-identity as a crucial determinant of social engagement. Furthermore, by highlighting the deliberate aspect of agency, my analysis emphasizes the role of the individual in effecting choices, thereby acknowledging that the aspect of self-identity related to outcomes cannot overlook the individual as the primary architect in the evolution and reshaping of identity. These insights pave the way for a reciprocal interplay between self-identity and social norms, offering a middle ground between the constructs of structure and agency rooted in one's personal interpretive lens. The implications for current debates within self-identity scholarship are profound, fostering theories that transcend the confines of binary interpretations of identity phenomena. My arguments posit self-identity as a composite of both consistency and transformation, being both distinctive and fluid – a duality that is essential for identity work to fulfil its intentional role. This process aims not only to construct and adjust self-concepts but also to uphold a sense of continuity and individuality. Moving ahead, the subsequent chapter will delve deeper into the mechanisms of identity work, examining how it successfully regulates one's sense of coherence and distinctiveness, thereby charting a course for self-navigating existential challenges.

Notes

1. Otherwise, claiming that identity positions are exclusively disparate and situated phenomena (devoid of a foundation that connects them) would be akin to claiming that the situation has created the criteria for understanding and speech 'by itself' and separate to the minds of interlocutors.
2. It is important to note at this juncture that all three participants have resigned since I exited the partner organization. This affirms that one's self-identity (self-definitions, goals and desires) cannot be considered illusory, since it is by virtue of its content that subjects make decisions that shape materiality – all subjects have shaped the context of interaction in the partner organization by choosing to not participate within it any longer.
3. One cannot even contend that there is a 'universal' definition of particular discourses within a specific contextual arrangement, as that is suggestive of a closed system of organizing that cannot be said to signify a modern organization (Burr 2003).
4. This means that it can encapsulate a self-affirmation and a self-negation simultaneously.

Chapter 8

The Self-Fulfilling Prophecy of Existential Dilemmas

The following paragraphs will address the self-fulfilling aspect of our self-ideas and the problematic aspect of adopted self-notions. The previous chapters have highlighted that subjects perceive and experience *with* (or through) their existing body of knowledge and self-knowledge. With this foundation in mind, I will address the implications that existing self-notions have on situated negative experiences. The aim is to acknowledge that not all acts of identity work can be deemed successful, as certain forms of perception and comprehension may elicit a sense of incoherence. This recognition holds significant relevance in the context of project management, the challenging demands of which have predominantly been elucidated through the lens of institutional isomorphism. In undertaking this task, I will offer a more individualized account of existential dilemmas encountered by project managers in executing their daily responsibilities.

What is (Un)successful Identity Work?

Gap 4, identified in the intersecting literature of project management and identity, pertains to a shortfall in accounting for individual capabilities to navigate the pressures inherent in project management practices. In contrast to current depictions, identity work should not only serve as an agentive conduit between external expectations and personal aspirations but should also be examined for its effectiveness in mitigating the often stressful cycle of

> self-scrutiny and doubt intrinsic to the profession. By adopting a 'responsible' lens through which to view situated agency, we can better support initiatives aimed at overcoming the tendencies toward uniformity that institutional isomorphism promotes in project management. This approach emphasizes an individual-centric assessment that recognizes the nuances of personal relevance and tackles the systemic issue at a more meaningful level.

In regard to identity work, a successful endeavour would be one that assists with the process of 'forming, repairing, maintaining, strengthening or revising the constructions that are productive of a sense of coherence' (Sveningsson and Alvesson 2003: 1165). However, since situated experience is shaped by our self-ideas, arguments for (in)coherence in the sense of self must not preclude recognition of one's subjectively constituted view of reality. Thus, it is important to recognize that the processes of forming, repairing, maintaining and reinforcing our self-conceptions are not invariably successful instances of identity work, particularly when they overlook the 'self-fulfilling prophecy' inherent in our self-concepts. In the words of Waley (2013: 87):

> Watch your thoughts, they become your words; watch your words, they become your actions; watch your actions, they become your habits; watch your habits, they become your character; watch your character, it becomes your destiny.

Given that we perceive and experience the world from the springboard of our self-knowledge (see Archer 2000, 2003; Heidegger 1953; Jung 1933; Peterson 1999), the *problematic* aspect of this self-referencing nature of perception is that our 'successes' and 'failures' are not objective properties of our abilities. The stress and anxiety often rooted in a mistrust of our abilities do not necessarily arise from objective impediments to self-achievement situated in the 'external world'. Instead, these feelings are more accurately the by-products of a specific self-perception and world view. For the concept of identity work to hold,[1] it is essential to acknowledge the necessity of two underlying phenomena: Firstly, the pursuit of coherence in one's self-concept requires that the individual possesses self-consciousness, meaning an awareness of their personally adopted self-conceptions. Secondly, intentional agency must be directed towards safeguarding and maintaining elements of the self that the individual considers valuable.

Brown (2015) has tackled the prevalent 'lack of construct clarity' that beleaguers much of identity research. To distil the concept further, consider the following: an acute awareness of our life's priorities often surfaces when we confront its antithesis – our sense of self-inadequacy. In the realm of the familiar, we remain oblivious to the full spectrum of significances that compose our self-concept. The catalyst for this sense of inadequacy is an encounter with the unfamiliar, which stops us in our tracks. The very unfamiliarity acts as a barrier to self-actualization, for it thwarts our ability to utilize known channels of agency. In this light, constraining conditions are not merely obstacles; they serve as telltale markers that cast doubt upon the authenticity and feasibility of our professed self-awareness and our projected capability to realize our 'true' selves. Sveningsson and Alvesson (2003: 1165) guide us through the labyrinth of circumstances that influence our evolving self-conceptions, distinguishing these experiences based on their impact. Enabling circumstances act as affirmations, echoing back our pre-existing beliefs about ourselves, reinforcing our sense of plausibility. Conversely, constraining circumstances introduce a challenge. They present a mirror reflecting the previously unrecognized 'implausibility' in our self-conceptions and, in doing so, provoke deep introspection. For us, as beings in constant pursuit of identity, these moments of constraint do more than unsettle – they catalyse an awakening. This process prompts a re-evaluation of what is genuinely significant in our lives, leading to actions that stem from an emergent understanding of self.

Therefore, in the milieu of 'enabling' circumstances where the self and others are accepted without critical weight, I propose that 'unsuccessful identity work' manifests as a relentless self-affirmation. This continual self-endorsement inhibits the revelation of our personal hierarchy of significance, a subconscious framework that orients us within the world. To articulate this differently, a 'desensitized' existence – as Heidegger might describe it, an unthematic being-in-the-world – precludes us from actively discerning the interconnectedness of our self-conceptions, ambitions and desires relative to their actual value in our lived experience as purposeful beings. In moments where we navigate life through the familiar lens of our accumulated self-knowledge, we tend to default to a stance of disinterest towards the nuances around us. The absence of novelty breeds an expectation of monotony; we look beyond the surface because we forecast no surprises in the depths we have already charted. Schutz (1967: 47) touches upon this phenomenon when he posits that 'as long as my whole consciousness remains temporally unidirectional and irreversible, I am unaware either of my own growing older or of any difference between past and present'. This observation serves as a cautionary reminder: if perception merely echoes the known contours of our identity, it is not actively contributing to its evolution. Our agency, as suggested by thinkers like Archer (2003, 2010) and Peterson (1999), with an echo of the earlier insights of Jung (1933), falls short of effectuating transformative identity work when it fails to grapple with the uncharted and the unexpected.

In this discourse, I posit that successful identity work emerges from a dynamic and introspective process – one that does not shy away from the rigours of self-interrogation. As evidenced in the narratives shared by our participants, the journey towards self-understanding often begins by scrutinizing others. This examination acts as a mirror, reflecting both commonality and divergence, catalysing a deeper analysis of our own knowledge and limitations. Yet such scrutiny invites critical self-doubt, which paradoxically becomes the impetus for reconfiguring our inner architecture around the elements that hold the most profound meaning for us as beings in pursuit of identity. For instance, when we cast a sceptical eye on our aspirations and yearnings – perhaps challenged by an external truth claim, like Nick's newly acknowledged deficiency in interpersonal skills – our matrix of significance is reshuffled. A value hierarchy materializes, reshaping our self-understanding as certain elements surge in priority, drawing a road map for our identity's evolution.

Our 'worry' acts as a beacon, illuminating aspects of our lives that lingered unseen, regarded as givens while we proficiently navigated our routine duties – until now. Such worry uncloaks these taken-for-granted elements, inviting us to wield our agency in transformative ways, reshaping and refining dimensions of our self-identity based on their newfound significance. Rolfe et al. (2017: 740) encapsulate this when they observe, 'an inauthentic response is one in which the need for certainty and security overcomes an opportunity for the curiosity of questioning'. Indeed, the uncertainties and perceived restrictions that arise in our understanding of the self should not be viewed negatively in the context of self-evolution. Rather, they provide fertile ground for the reconfiguration of our self-conceptions, aspirations and desires, enabling us to act with a renewed authenticity that is aligned with an integrated sense of coherence and uniqueness.

It is through the meticulous process of reassessing our self-definitions that subsequent actions take shape, affording us the chance to consciously align our choices with our deepest values (such as through the decision to resign in pursuit of one's dreams[2]). Embarking on actions that resonate with our core concerns imbues our lives with a profound sense of purpose, coherence and distinctiveness. Thus, successful identity work transcends mere affirmation of self-devised agential pursuits. It signals a deeper, more introspective engagement with one's sense of self. Acts of self-affirmation, when not stemming from this reflective practice, may reveal the presence of a less self-aware individual, one who operates on autopilot rather than through deliberate, self-aligned intentionality.

Despite this, there remains a certain opacity to our self-awareness during moments of action. Schutz (1967) describes a 'retrospective gaze' that enables us to organize our myriad self-definitions into a hierarchy, yet the subtleties of this process often escape us as we engage with the world. This observation from participants' narratives suggests a profound difficulty in recognizing how our unique personal existence aligns with the broader tapestry of our world view in real time. To illustrate, each participant attributed intense stress and anxiety in their routine tasks to external pressures from colleagues, bosses or clients. This perspective overlooks the potential interplay between external challenges and internal objectives – how these external pressures are interpreted and internalized in relation to the participants' personal aspirations and desires, as expounded by Archer (2010). The external environment is perceived as inherently anxiety-inducing, without considering whether these impediments to self-fulfilment might actually reflect a deeper, more personal struggle with aligning external demands with internal goals.[3]

The scope of my inquiry delved beyond validating the veracity of participants' accounts; instead, it probed the problematic essence of the self-perceptions they have adopted. Such 'ontological blindness' is revealed distinctively in two spheres: (1) In the process of confirming our beliefs about ourselves and our world, we exhibit an apathy towards the intricate interplay of 'sameness' and 'difference' that textures our interactions and helps sculpt our identities. (2) Even when participants entered into acts of self-denial, acknowledging intricate and previously unexplored aspects of themselves, they nonetheless continued to assign the source of their anxiety to extant qualities of the external world. This betrays a problematic oversight. They failed to recognize how an altered set of ambitions and desires could fundamentally shift their experience of the external environment, illustrating just how deeply our internal drives mould our perception of reality.

(Successful) identity work, therefore, can be nuanced as a *multi-order phenomenon*. The (a) *first order* of the process requires us to perceive our self-notions in terms of the significance they attract in our life as identity-seeking individuals, and the necessity they acquire for the realization of the desired pragmatic ends to which they relate. For example, Nick must be a hard worker if he is going to realize his goal of spending more time with his family in the later stages of his life. Deploying a 'retrospective gaze' over the existing network of self-definitions permits us to rearrange them in the form of a hierarchy at whose peak sits that which matters to us the most given perceived circumstances at hand. Subsequently, what makes such reflexive processes 'successful' identity work is the ability to embody agency that attends to the preservation of our primary needs. However, although 'success' in identity work can be found through forms of agency that preserves the chain of 'something in order to for something else' (Heidegger 1953), such agency can nonetheless still *restrict the experience of circumstantial particularity* to a predetermined (and narrow) number of possibilities.

Despite participants' engagement in acts of self-negation yielding a heightened sense of coherence and uniqueness, their portrayal of the external environment as inherently anxiety-inducing overlooks the ways in which their self-conceptions actively shape their experiences of specific circumstances. Moreover, while these individuals exert agency reflective of personal choice – in an attempt to secure their established self-image – this perceived liberty is paradoxically constrained by a self-imposed binary divide between self and others. The truly problematic dimension of this situation is that it perpetuates certain recurring experiences, some of which are negative, because the choices available to the subject are bound by a self-crafted world that, unbeknown to them, limits their potential choices. To rephrase, unless Nick comes to understand that his definition of hard work is not an absolute but a personal interpretation, he is likely to encounter similar obstacles across various situations.

In light of the above, given that different orders of successful identity work suggest that the ability to 'choose' subsumes various degrees of freedom, the success of the identity work process, therefore, must also be considered in terms of our ability to have a conscious effect on our situated experiences. To achieve this nuanced understanding, perception must be accompanied by an aptitude that interprets (1) perceived self-inadequacy not as a fixed measure of one's abilities but as a situational challenge that interplays with the importance we assign to our practical objectives and (2) the context in which this perception arises. This necessitates a conscious recognition that the external world is interpreted through our subjective lens, acknowledging that 'obstacles' are intimately connected to our specific worries and aims, as they contribute to perceptions of unfamiliarity or anxiety.[4] This imparts the insight that the character of our experiences, whether uplifting or discouraging, is, to some extent, self-imposed as a result of the expectations we project onto our engagements with the world.

Consequently, even though our actions may be deliberately aimed at safeguarding our most cherished values (a fundamental aspect of successful identity work), a lack of awareness regarding the self-fulfilling nature of our interpretive frameworks can inadvertently confine us to the boundaries of our current understanding. This becomes particularly pertinent in the context of professional discomfort and regular negative emotional experiences.[5] In other words, my supervisor's opinion of my performance holds significance only if I perceive them as the sole arbiter of truth. This unease then relates to concerns regarding supporting my family and ultimately culminates in my most pressing consideration – am I a competent father if I lose my job? This final inquiry binds me to the capriciousness of my superiors, irrespective of the sheer improbability concerning the connections between concepts that our minds impose to construct a specific rendition of reality. A que sera, sera attitude towards life, however, liberates us from the bondage of these in-order-to chains. The (b) second order of successful identity work would thus not require a 'retrospective gaze' in so much as it would a *lateral* one that permits seeing that our knowledge and self-knowledge determines the import of the surrounding world. As aptly asserted by Ralph Waldo Emerson, 'wherever there is life, the world bursts into appearance around it'.

The uniqueness of self-expression is anchored deeply in what we prioritize in our quest for identity; thus, successful identity work at the primary level yields valuable perspectives for organizational theorists exploring the roots of decision-making, entrepreneurial endeavours and prevailing communication trends (Brown 2018). Alternatively, placing the individual at the core of scrutiny, the secondary level of successful identity work enables a dissection of daily life through the lens of how our intellectual frameworks shape specific realities. Consider the perceptible mutual distrust among followers of divergent religious beliefs – this stems from distinct 'maps of meaning' that hold profound significance within the realms of project management and existential therapy. These intricacies and their broader implications will be dissected further in the subsequent sections.

(Un)Successful Identity Work, the Crises of Project Management and Existential Therapy

The foregoing discussions highlight that within the frameworks of project management and existential therapy, the journey to understanding begins with recognizing the individuality of a person's self-perception and its interplay with their sociocultural context. This approach posits that our 'lived experiences' cannot be extricated from the web of our established self-concepts, ambitions and yearnings. For example, interpreting situations as hindrances to self-fulfilment can undermine the solidity of someone's sense of self. Thus, our interpretation of events, objects or people is intrinsically tied to the narrative we construct about ourselves – the 'project of the self'. Without the interpretive lens of identity, happenstances may lack meaning, affirming that significance is conferred by the individual engaged in the ceaseless pursuit of self-definition. Thus, considering that objects deemed insignificant linger beyond the edges of our perception, addressing the emotional weight of 'burdensome', 'restrictive' or 'inequitable' situations demands a departure from philosophies anchored in Cartesian dualism. Regrettably, this dualistic perspective – differentiating subjects and objects – has largely prevailed in the existing literature on project management (Rolfe et al. 2017). As noted by Van der Hoorn and Whitty (2019: 374–75):

> By shifting the focus from the so-called 'project management' equipment to what project managers are *directed towards*, we can reveal the common ground that links those who manage projects ... A focus on *comportment* can

> break us free from the terminology of the practice guides and their instrumentation focus as called for by the critical project management and 'lived experience' agendas ... Such a structure would assist in mobilising a context sensitive perspective of project work in the project management classroom with the focus on what the project managers are trying to achieve. (Emphasis in the original)

Thus, the twin tiers of successful identity work (referenced in the preceding section) may equip project managers with a proactive approach to manage what might otherwise be paralysing existential disturbances (Rolfe et al. 2017: 739). This approach is grounded in a deeper appreciation for the subject's lived experiences. For instance, engaging in the first tier of successful identity work begins with acts of self-negation that uncover the previously unnoticed hierarchy of personal values that permeates one's daily professional existence. The importance of such an uncovering lies in the awareness that the impediments one faces are intimately linked to the essentials of self-fulfilment. Consequently, perceived 'existential disruptions' are actually pivotal in spurring purposeful actions that uphold and affirm one's most deeply held self-concepts. Thus, the recognition and navigation of these disruptions are not mere hindrances but rather integral to the continuation of intentional, identity-affirming endeavours.

Thus, any exploration of existential therapy that commences with 'institutional theory' (Baker and French 2018) risks overlooking the profound importance of personal significance in confronting the adverse impacts of self-'dissonance'. In this light, the first order of successful identity work reveals a paradox: the emotional turmoil that accompanies the recognition of personal barriers is the very currency of increased self-awareness. It is through the prism of self-negation that an individual becomes more alert and attuned to their existence. Consequently, existential disruptions should not be viewed as detrimental within the pursuit of personal identity (as in the existential queries of 'who am I?' and 'how should I act?'). Instead, they act as catalysts, coaxing into the light the latent intentions and aims that underpin our daily engagement with the world, breaking the spell of rote habits and unexamined living. As aptly acknowledged by Wilson (2016: 1):

> The transition to a higher order of functioning – or hooking onto a higher neural circuit – is often accomplished by considerable anxiety or a turbulence in personal life which seems as if the organism were falling apart or breaking up. This phenomenon of instability is really the way that every living organism – societies, human primates, chemical solutions, etc. – shakes itself, as it were, by myoclonisms or similar convulsions into new combinations and permutations for higher and new levels of development.

Nonetheless, even within the first tier of successful identity work, there remains a potential for 'emotional entanglement' – an indicator of an as-yet unresolved consciousness – given the profound complexity and import that our most valued beliefs carry for our understanding of self and others. Engaging deeply in the validation of our self-conceptions, aspirations and desires, we uncover a richer landscape of significance where the self attributes weight to elements critical for its fulfilment. This is akin to acknowledging that the spaces we hold sacrosanct in our identity compel us to be hyper-vigilant against even minor impediments that may threaten their validity (Peterson 1999). Thus, the sense of alignment and clarity we achieve by selectively attributing significance to our self-concept and our relationships with others (as facilitated by the first order of successful identity work) represents a transitory state. Its 'solidity' relies not on the varying contexts we elect to engage with but on the foundational values we are determined to uphold. Consequently, even making life-altering decisions, like resigning for the sake of our most deeply held convictions, does not strip away the ingrained 'content' that shapes our unique emotional narratives. This entrenched personal perspective may hinder the ability to engage in 'a reflexive questioning of taken-for-granted assumptions about managing projects' (Rolfe et al. 2017: 740), leaving untouched the underlying assumptions that guide our experiences.

Building upon these considerations, any action intending to safeguard what is deemed significant, without recognizing that the constraints we face are not fixed features of the world but rather reflections of our subjective outlook, fails to grasp the interdependent nature of the self and the world. Heidegger (1953: 32) articulates this nuance: what no longer simply reveals itself, but, in pointing to something else, lets something be seen as something, gains with this synthetic structure the potential to obfuscate. The crux of this reflection is that such actions are incapable of thoroughly addressing the roots of 'existential disruptions', given their insensitivity to the inherently subjective origination of experience (Schutz 1967). To reiterate in simpler terms, the issue arises when individuals treat anxiety as an inherent aspect of external situations, thereby reinforcing and perpetuating problematic, limited interpretations of the world. Thus, the advanced practice of successful identity work posits that in order to confront existential anxiety within project management, we must first dispel 'ontological blindness'. This dissolution of obliviousness is facilitated by the recognition that our reality would fundamentally shift with a change in our aspirations and passions. To put it differently, the veil of ontological blindness lifts when individuals realize that their thoughts and beliefs require validation to truly exist. Therefore, while the initial stage of successful identity work indicates that acting in alignment with our most crucial personal values can cultivate a sense of coherence, the more profound, second stage reveals that by striving to uphold our most treasured self-definitions, we inadvertently craft a complex and challenging world for ourselves to traverse.

By assigning an *object* to existential anxiety (that is, one's self-idea), these arguments extend what the extant project management literature considers as an 'experience which is both objectless and nameless' (Rolfe et al. 2017: 740; see also Baker and French 2018; Buckle and Thomas 2003; Chasserio and Legault 2009, 2010; Clegg et al. 2020; Clegg and Courpasson 2004; French et al. 2013; Gale and Cartwright 1995; Lindgren and Packendorff 2006). Crucially, when we attribute existential anxiety to specific objects, we also create a prescribed way of addressing it. For instance, the lines of reasoning I present suggest that when a woman acknowledges the prevailing gender dynamics within project management as significant, she unintentionally gives rise to gender-specific barriers in her path to self-actualization. Paradoxically, by focusing on these gendered boundaries, she contributes to solidifying them in her external reality. Therefore, if a woman refrains from prioritizing social norms that fail to value her unique qualities or, conversely, if she refrains from critically examining her societal role beyond prescriptive gender narratives, she inadvertently internalizes these norms within her self-concept. This internalization can act as both a compelling force and a formidable hindrance, becoming the wellspring of both fulfilment and frustration (Peterson 1999).

Hippocrates is identified as the source of a common expression: 'before you heal someone, ask him if he's willing to give up the things that make him sick.' By the same token, Müller et al. (2022: 25) recognize that 'managers achieve self-development through the redescription of their lived experiences'. We can deduce, then, that alleviating existential anxiety involves a process of extending one's perspective beyond personal preoccupations. Yet this outward orientation is not conducted in isolation from oneself, as all thought is intrinsically influenced by our internal knowledge. More precisely, *to think beyond oneself* is to gain a penetrating insight that illuminates the ontological foundation of our self-concepts (Cohn 2002). In essence, it is to recognize that our self-interpretations act as both the architects and jailers of our mental edifice (Jung 1933).

Considering the previous discussions, it becomes apparent that postmodernists rightly perceive our identities as being constructed upon a bedrock that is distinct from the fluid and various situations we encounter over time. Nonetheless, this 'separation' does not render these foundational elements irrelevant, as they play a crucial role in shaping our individual experiences. Thus, postmodernists may fall short in appreciating the inherent significance of *Dasein* – 'a being that *can* [emphasis in the original] "choose" itself in its being, it can win itself, it can lose itself, and it can never and only "apparently" win itself' (Heidegger 1953: 42). Similarly, project management 'existentialists' (referred to in Rolfe et al. 2017; Van der Hoorn and Whitty 2019) exhibit a degree of myopia when they dismiss anxiety simply as 'not related to [one's] unselfconsciousness or conflicts between different parts of [one's] inner self' (Rolfe et al. 2017: 740). By adopting such a stance, they inadvertently relegate the resolution of existential challenges to structured methodologies like existential hermeneutic phenomenology (EHP), potentially negating the individual's agency. In contrast to both perspectives, I argue that our very notions of self are entwined with existential questions. Recognizing this, I posit that effectively navigating existential crises necessitates an appreciation for the multifaceted reality we inhabit – a reality that affords us the autonomy distinct from our own ruminations and empowers us to determine which thoughts evolve into spoken words and which crystallize into deeds. My work thus aims to forge a path towards a more personalized methodology in combating the stresses commonly encountered in project management – going beyond the institutional rigidity that is often pinpointed as a source of professional discontent (Baker and French 2018; Buckle and Thomas 2003; Chasserio and Legault 2009, 2010; Clegg et al. 2020; Clegg and Courpasson 2004; French et al. 2013; Gale and Cartwright 1995; Lindgren and Packendorff 2006).

Limitations of the Research and Findings

This book is grounded in a research project that, despite its depth, is not without limitations, which, in turn, pave the way for future inquiry. The theoretical framework that underpins this study implies that the production of novel contributions to existing scholarship is inherently shaped by the researcher's own foundational beliefs about the nature of being and knowledge – an ontological and epistemological stance. Through a meticulous investigation of subjective phenomenology, drawing on the insights of seminal thinkers such as Heidegger (1953), Peterson (1999) and Archer (2000, 2003), the crux of the book's argument is anchored in a fundamental aspect of the self that is beyond negotiation. Nonetheless, the primary limitation of this study emerges from what I describe as 'the leap of faith': an acceptance and application of the contributions of these theorists – Heidegger, Peterson and Archer – as the groundwork for my own arguments. This study, therefore, does not purport to establish the unique nature of the self as an incontrovertible fact but offers a conceptual framework through which the self might be perceived as distinctive, predicated on the ontological and epistemological postures we assume (May and Perry 2017).

The study's second limitation emerges from the inherent confines of its chosen methodology – interpretive phenomenological analysis (IPA). This approach predicates itself on an intricate phenomenological engagement with the participants' individual perceptions of self, a process inextricably linked to the researcher's subjective lens. Consequently, the interpretive act of discerning meaning in the participants' narratives is invariably shaded by the researcher's introspections and self-awareness. Therefore, the act of deciphering and understanding others' lived experiences is inevitably influenced by my own interpretive framework. In this light, IPA does not – and perhaps cannot – fully disentangle my perception from that of the participants when analysing how they navigate and comprehend their worlds.

This study is, at its core, an endeavour to underscore the profound insight that our conclusions are inextricably tied to our personal cognition and self-perception – a testament to the ubiquitousness of the self in our interpretation of the world. It posits that true phenomenological understanding arises only upon the recognition that our perceptions of the world are reflections of our own subjective constitution. This awareness transforms the interpretive process into what can genuinely be termed 'phenomenal'. Consequently, the emphasis of this analysis shifts away from evaluating the veracity and likelihood of everyday assertions, redirecting focus to the examination of subjective 'aptitudes'. These inherent qualities simultaneously facilitate and circumscribe our capacity for self-expression, thereby revealing the nuanced interplay between identity and perception.

The intimate depth characteristic of phenomenological research often raises questions about the generalizability of its findings, which may lead some to question the significance of its theoretical contributions if viewed through a lens seeking broad applicability. It is important to note, however, that invoking concerns of generalizability misconstrues the intent of this research project – it engages in a different paradigm of inquiry altogether. The study was meticulously designed to unveil the underpinnings of subjective experience, a goal necessitating a deliberate limitation on participant numbers to afford a rich, idiographic analysis. Consequently, while the study's focused scope may limit its ability to yield widely generalizable outcomes as conventionally understood (Miles and Huberman 2014), the influence of a potent exemplar should not be overlooked as an engine of scientific progress. In the words of Flyvbjerg and Sampson (2001: 76), it is imperative to acknowledge that 'knowledge cannot be formally generalised [which] does not mean that it cannot enter into the collective process of knowledge accumulation in a given field or in a society'.

Future Research Agendas

For Project Management Practice

This book frames self-identity as a cornerstone of organizational dynamics, laying down an ontological scaffold for the application of existential therapy within the corporate milieu. It invites future research to delve into the domain of identity work, exploring empirically how individuals can consciously and constructively mould their professional experiences. The aim is not to vindicate the veracity of my prior assertions but to enable individuals to grasp the liberating notion that consensus is not a prerequisite for personal truths. It is our beliefs, more than some objective 'truth', that shape our interactions with the world. As such, subsequent inquiries could explore 'self-distanciation' – the intentional cognitive departure from one's ingrained perspectives – and the transformative impact this could have on managing the often challenging terrains of professional life. Research focused on the subjective experience holds significant promise for fields like project management, particularly recognized for high stress levels, as identified by Love and Edwards (2005: 88):

> Aspects of occupational demands and their deleterious consequences on the psychological well-being of construction project managers have received limited attention in literature. Yet it has been widely reported that construction project managers have been experiencing increasing levels of occupational stress; the generic definition of work-related stress is the inability to cope with the pressure in a job.

As Love and Edwards (ibid.) go on to say, the situation is invariably unacknowledged in practice:

> Previous research has revealed that the most significant stress factors identified by construction project managers are work overload, long working hours, role ambiguity and conflict, the diverse range of personalities encountered in the project environment, poor communication, limited resources, insufficient time spent in the family/home environment and financial pressures (work-related and personal). However, it would appear that many construction contractors are unaware of the level of occupational stress being experienced by their construction project managers because of the limited theoretical and empirical research applied to occupational stress within the industry.

The perspectives I advance represent an innovative trajectory in project management research, as they directly engage with the roots of work-related stress by shedding light on how it is inherently embedded in the self and its identity constructs. In parallel with the insights of Müller et al. (2015) and Drouin et al. (2021), who assert that 'the essence of being perceived as an effective leader is rooted in adept self-management' (Müller et al. 2015: 3), my work lays the groundwork for future explorations that posit self-management as the linchpin of enriching professional life. This idea offers a lens through which stress in project management may not just be managed but transformed, proposing self-management not merely as a skill but as the foundational strategy for achieving positive and fulfilling work experiences.

For Archer's Meta-Reflexivity

Archer's (2000) concept of meta-reflexivity invites us to recognize that individuals possess the capability to thoughtfully examine their reflexive processes, discerning the underpinnings of their perspectives in given situations. This intellectual viewpoint allows for a nuanced understanding of one's interpretive frameworks. Earlier sections distinguished between the immediate recognition of salient aspects in one's life, which constitutes the first tier of successful identity work, and the more profound realization that our world views are intrinsically shaped by our individual selfhood – a reflection of the second tier of successful identity work. This latter understanding marks a critical phase in the reflexivity journey; it is not merely about identifying what matters to us but about grasping the deeper truth that our perceptions are echoes of our distinct personal identities.

Take, for instance, the recognition that our irritation with a colleague stems from a competition for a promotion – this is an insight into the situational drivers of our discomfort. However, this understanding is fundamentally different from realizing that our perception of this colleague might change if our sense of self-worth were not so closely tied to professional advancement. The second tier of successful identity work, which was not explicitly reflected in the participants' responses, emphasizes that mere awareness of our reflexive patterns differs markedly from understanding how these reflexive judgements influence the creation of our external reality. Recognizing the motivations behind our perspective on a specific event is one thing, but grasping how our perceptions actively shape our experiences of that event is quite another. This deeper level of identity work involves seeing the intertwined roles of perception and circumstance – not just interpreting situations but understanding the role perception plays in constituting those situations.

This discourse extends Archer's (2003) idea of meta-reflexivity by proposing that reflexive contemplation goes beyond merely recognizing the rationale behind a given assertion. It encompasses an understanding of the self-imposed constraints that shape our interpretation of the external world. Meta-reflexivity is therefore not solely concerned with the reasons behind a stated opinion (for example, 'he aggravates me because he lacks social skills'), but with comprehending the specific 'why' chosen out of countless possible explanations. Further research could enrich our understanding by exploring the extent to which individuals actively participate in the construction of their own experiences, and by advancing a more intricate interpretation of Archer's (2000) meta-reflexivity. This expanded concept would encompass individuals' capacity to extricate themselves from their internal narratives, thus exerting more deliberate agency in their daily professional lives. Such inquiries would notably complement studies addressing stress in demanding workspaces, particularly in sectors like consulting and project management, which have been well documented for their stressful nature (Clegg and Courpasson 2004; Gill 2013).

For Phenomenology of Unselfconsciousness

The distinction between two levels of successful identity work refines our understanding of Smith et al.'s (2009) concept of everyday 'unselfconsciousness'. I posit that our day-to-day existence within the framework of work is characterized by varying depths of consciousness. For instance, while we enact a form of reflexively mediated agency in affirming our sense of self, the awareness of such acts – particularly when linked to identity – is comparatively muted against moments of introspection that include self-examination or self-challenge. Additionally, it is important to acknowledge a gradient of awareness even within acts of agency aimed at upholding core elements of one's identity. Individuals may remain unaware of how their perceptions are silently shaping their experiences, thereby perpetuating certain narratives or experiences without recognizing their role in that creation. Such degrees of awareness, or lack thereof, spotlight the intricate dynamics between consciousness, agency and the ongoing construction of self within the world of work.

Unselfconsciousness encompasses more than simply lacking awareness of one's personal interpretative frameworks, which conventionally occurs during the affirmation of one's knowledge and self-understanding. This concept also captures the often overlooked dynamic wherein our ambitions and desires silently influence what we deem to be the 'objective' qualities of our external environment. It is crucial to note that an individual may remain oblivious to the cyclical process in which situated experiences are filtered through and reinforce one's unique conception of self. Looking ahead, it would be fruitful for future research to investigate how varying levels of self-awareness intersect with the distinctiveness of an individual's lived professional experiences, thereby unpacking the nuanced interplay between consciousness, intentionality and the authentic embodiment of one's role in the workplace.

Demanding work environments undoubtedly compel us to stretch our limits and capabilities. While I maintain that circumstances are initially perceived through our subjective lens, it is undeniable that certain organizational settings pose greater challenges than others, a stark reality underscored by the troubling high incidence of suicides within the construction project management sector in Australia (as documented by Baker and French 2018). Nevertheless, within these adversities lies a silver lining: such rigorous conditions can catalyse the development of a subject who is distinctively articulate and resilient. It is through navigating these trying circumstances that individuals often forge a more defined and durable sense of self.

Synopsis

The preceding sections elucidate a 'distributed model of distinctive self-identity', which serves as the foundation for our daily interactions and self-perception. This conceptual framework helps us evaluate the efficacy of identity work – a process that encompasses modifying, refining and repairing the narrative threads that contribute to our sense of coherence and individuality. Embedded within this framework is the paradox that while individuals have the innate ability to craft their identity through an awareness of their perceptual limitations, the endeavour of identity work involves a delicate balance. This balance pivots on the subjects' efforts to reassess and possibly transform their self-conceptions, aspirations and ambitions, particularly when these elements face critical examination. Unsuccessful identity work often results in an individual's self-concept merely echoing pre-established notions and self-doubts, a sort of acquiescence to the familiar. In contrast, successful identity work is characterized by proactive self-negotiation and redefinition, a form of constructive self-challenge that breaches the comfort zones of habituated perceptions and beliefs.

The phenomenon of self-fulfilling prophecies underscores the complexity of self-identity by demonstrating that our observations and interactions with the world are invariably coloured by our existing preconceptions. To refine our understanding of successful identity work, we can delineate it into a dual-phase process. The initial phase prompts the individual to re-examine and recalibrate their inner narrative in response to what holds particular significance in their life – this aspect often remains latent when circumstances align with expectations. The second phase facilitates a horizontal expansion of perspective, enabling us to assess our subjective constructs by juxtaposing them against external realities. This two-pronged approach to identity work is invaluable not merely for comprehending the context-bound nature of experiences, but also for actively sculpting, transforming and rectifying the components of our self-conception. It is in this dynamic interplay with life's inconsistencies that our self-ideas grow, adapt and establish a more harmonized narrative.

Notes

1. Identity work is the process of 'forming, repairing, maintaining, strengthening or revising the constructions that are productive of a sense of coherence' (Sveningsson and Alvesson 2003: 1165).
2. It is important to point out that since I have exited the organization, all three participants have resigned (there have been more than three resignations in the partner organization, so stating this still protects the identity of the subjects).
3. As indicated previously, the ontological nature of self-referential or reinforcing forms of perception suggests that one's classification of other's 'laziness' is only sensible in terms of one's perception of what constitutes hard work: for Nick, others were lazy because 'they complained about every little detail of their work' while he never did; for Mark, others were lazy because 'they did not go over and above to address clients' needs', which he did; for Margaret, on the other hand, laziness and incompetence was referential to her quality of being a people person, whereby any behaviour of her co-workers that did not highlight the characteristics of what she believed this competency entailed attracted a classification of inadequacy.
4. For example, choosing to resign from a position on the grounds of 'unreasonable working conditions' must be considered in terms of what is perceived to be 'reasonable' in the life of the identity-seeking subject (otherwise a change in context might not bear desired results). This becomes particularly important in the context of this book, since all three individuals interviewed have resigned since the beginning of the study.
5. This is not to say that one's knowledge and self-knowledge can be obviated; it is to say that particular experiences can be explained as subjective constructs, thus providing more opportunity for the identity-seeking individual to discern the 'gravity' of events and ideas that they serve.

Conclusion

My motivation for writing this book stemmed from a deep curiosity about the ways in which an individual's professional self-identity informs and moulds their day-to-day actions, particularly within the realm of project management. Although my initial interest was personal, I quickly realized that the role of self-identity in shaping routine communication, decision-making and entrepreneurial tendencies is a surprisingly neglected subject in scholarly research (Brown 2018). This spurred my investigation into current academic literature, with the objective to unearth whether there was an acknowledgement of the profound impact that pre-existing subjective frameworks exert on one's perception and, by extension, on their agency. Delving into the research on identity formation and identity work, I encountered pervasive tensions that have stymied scholarly efforts to fully integrate self-identity within the discourse on organizational life. A recurring struggle within these discussions is the difficulty in articulating a self-aware and distinctive self without subjecting it to a preordained set of behaviours and expectations – a dilemma described by Cerulo (1997: 388) as the entrapment within 'spheres of prescribed action and expectation'. This book, therefore, is an exploration of that middle ground, seeking to illuminate how self-identity operates within – and sometimes against – the grain of organizational scripts and norms.

Current literature on identity work and identity formation has struggled to reconcile the concept of a distinctive self with the prevailing philosophical climate of liquid modernity. This difficulty is largely due to an ontological stalemate where foundational views clash without resolution. For instance, the dominance of Cartesian ontological principles has led self-identity studies to characterize interactions between the self, others and society predominantly through the lens of causality – a perspective that inevitably entangles discussions in narratives of dominance and power. The ramifications of this are widespread, but in the purview of the arguments presented here, the consequence is a tacit reduction of social phenomena to what is assumed to exist ontologically prior to them. If, hypothetically, society is deemed to ontologically precede the individual, then the self is relegated to being a mere by-product of social conditions. One of the critical theoretical outcomes of this stance is that self-identity is treated as a derivative of social interplay, thereby negating the individual's capacity for intentional action and purposeful existence. Moreover, such a viewpoint overlooks the influence of subjective history on current actions, thus revealing an academic blind spot – the inability to acknowledge and describe the unique, individualized strategies people employ in navigating the challenging demands of project management practice. This book seeks to shift the focus towards a more nuanced understanding of the self, one that appreciates the complex interplay between individual subjectivity and societal structures.

The core arguments in this work emphasize the intricate interplay between the empirical manifestations of self-expression and the subtler, sub-empirical elements that underpin and shape our experiences. I put forth the notion that self-identity is inherently 'stratified', existing not only in outward expressions and internal dialogues but as integral to our conceptual 'operating systems', as proposed by Peterson (1999) – essentially, as a unique 'self-idea'. The philosophical groundwork laid by thinkers like Heidegger (1953), Peterson (1999) and Archer (2000, 2003) underscores the importance of acknowledging the layered nature of reality, affirming that 'our way of looking at things is conditioned by what we are' (Jung 1933: 117). Our stratified self-identity is deeply woven into the fabric of all perception, supplying us with interpretive frameworks that govern our daily interactions and existence. These frameworks, which delineate what we perceive as opportunities and limitations for self-fulfilment, are invariably interlinked with adverse or challenging experiences. This insight holds particular relevance for project managers contending with existential quandaries, especially since much of the discourse in their field is centred around the concept of institutional isomorphism, often neglecting the individual's capacity for personal agency. The most poignant consequence of such an oversight is the resultant incapacitation of individuals in addressing personal challenges – an issue that my work seeks to confront and redress.

At the heart of every social phenomenon lies an individual, a repository of beliefs and conceptions about themselves and the confluence of otherness that constitutes the world. It is these deeply held convictions that sculpt our perceptions and, in turn, subtly influence and shape the contours of our experiences. The question of identity, then, is not a peripheral aspect of rationale, as every act of reason intrinsically reflects a self-referential mode of perception and understanding. By centring the discourse on the individual's subjective constitution, this book offers a counter-narrative to the dehumanizing tenets that have often prevailed in the discourse on self-identity. Moving past the constraints of overly reductionist views, the content presented here delivers a layered interpretation of self-identity, intricately linked to the processes of decision-making, entrepreneurial behaviour and communicative patterns (Brown 2018). Recognizing that perception is the crucible within which experiences are forged may magnify the sense of responsibility we bear. Nevertheless, this acknowledgement comes hand-in-hand with the ennobling realization that it all begins with our own perspective. While daunting, this insight empowers us with the opportunity to shape our destiny in meaningful ways – providing the key to unlocking transformative potential in our personal and professional lives.

This book melds the concept of a distinctive self-idea with the deliberate nature of human agency, thus building upon and extending discussions that have previously dismissed self-identity as merely a discursive construct. By embracing the dynamic interplay of self-identity, everyday agency and situated experience, I have introduced a conception of the self that acknowledges its uniqueness without ignoring the complex fluidity of contemporary social structures – a task often oversimplified by essentialist arguments. Drawing from the robust frameworks of critical realism, phenomenological philosophy and the introspective depth of psychoanalysis, this work lays a solid philosophical groundwork. Such a foundation is essential for future identity-focused research that aims to incorporate a nuanced understanding of self-identity at the outset of social analysis. It is through this confluence of disciplinary insights that the book sets a precedent for comprehensively examining how our inner narratives shape – and are shaped by – the world we navigate.

This book achieves a crucial task by offering a tangible framework through which to understand existential quandaries. It does so by pinpointing the genesis of challenging emotional experiences in the efforts to uphold the ideologies that encapsulate our unique self-identity. By adopting this perspective, we move beyond generic coping mechanisms for managing negative emotions and delve into personalized strategies. In recognizing that we are inextricably intertwined with our beliefs, or more precisely, that our self-concepts play a pivotal role in the experiences we encounter, the book advocates for a tailored approach to address the rigorous demands faced in project management practices. It suggests that by understanding and negotiating the ideas we hold about ourselves, we can navigate professional pressures more effectively. This individual-centred orientation offers professionals not just a method to handle stress but a means to orchestrate their professional lives with greater awareness and self-congruity.

Keep in mind that the tapestry of our self-knowledge serves as the bedrock of our lived experiences, offering a repository of reflective tools that help us assign meaning to the world around us in relation to ourselves. In turn, the fabric of our professional lives informs and shapes the evolution of our (professional) self-identity, enabling us to recalibrate our internal narrative and our perspectives on the external environment. This recalibration is guided by the elements we deem most critical to our sense of self. It is within this recursive dynamic – between self-perception and experiential feedback – that the cycle of self-development is perpetuated, enabling growth, transformation and deeper self-understanding.

Glossary

Being-in-the-world: Being-in-the-world is a central theme in existential philosophy, particularly within the work of Martin Heidegger. It suggests a fundamental ontology that looks at the inextricable link between an individual's existence and the world in which they live, emphasizing an integrated, holistic understanding of one's being.

Central conflation: Central conflation is a term used in sociological theory to criticize approaches that fail to distinguish between the agency of individuals and the structures of society. It refers to the mistake of merging or blending these two distinct concepts into an indistinguishable whole, thereby losing the ability to understand their separate effects.

Constructivism: Constructivism is an epistemological viewpoint in the philosophy of science that asserts that all knowledge is constructed rather than discovered. It holds that individuals form or construct much of what they understand of the world and themselves through experiences and reflection on those experiences.

Dasein: Dasein is a German word that translates literally to 'being there' or 'presence'. In the context of Heidegger's existential philosophy, it refers to human existence or the experience of being that is conscious of and defined by its own existence.

Discourse: Discourse in philosophy refers to written and spoken communication. In social sciences, the term denotes ways of thinking and producing meaning, with emphasis on dominant narratives that construct social realities and individual identities within specific contexts.

Epistemology: Epistemology is the branch of philosophy that studies the nature, origin and limits of human knowledge. It addresses questions about what knowledge is, how it is acquired and the extent to which it is possible for a given subject or entity to be known.

Fragmented ontology: Fragmented ontology refers to a world view or belief system where there is no singular, cohesive reality; instead, it posits multiple realities or understandings of reality that may not be universally shared or consistent.

Institutional isomorphism: Institutional isomorphism refers to the process by which institutions within an industry or sector become increasingly similar to each other over time. This concept suggests that organizations are under pressure to conform to accepted norms or standards, leading to homogeneity.

Interpretivism: Interpretivism is a qualitative research approach that involves studying phenomena in their natural settings, interpreting them in terms of the meanings people bring to them. This approach often seeks to understand how individuals create, modify and maintain social structures through their actions and interactions.

Liquid modernity: Liquid modernity is a concept developed by sociologist Zygmunt Bauman to describe a contemporary, globalized society where social forms and institutions do not solidify for long and are constantly changing, leading to instability in individual identities and relationships.

Normative determinism: Normative determinism is the idea that normative forces – such as societal expectations, rules and conventions – determine individual behaviour and social arrangements, often allowing little room for deviation or individual agency.

Ontology: Ontology is the philosophical study of the nature of being, becoming, existence or reality, as well as the basic categories of being and their relations. It seeks to determine what entities exist or may be said to exist and how such entities may be grouped and related within a hierarchy.

Positivism: Positivism is a philosophical system that holds that information derived from logical and mathematical treatments and reports of sensory experience is the exclusive source of all authoritative knowledge. It asserts that there is valid knowledge (truth) only in scientific knowledge. Knowledge outside of science is subjective and should be discarded.

Project control group: A project control group, often part of project management, is a group responsible for monitoring and controlling various project aspects to ensure that objectives are met, typically within defined constraints such as time, quality and budget.

Scientific management: Scientific management, also known as Taylorism, is a theory of management that analyses and synthesizes workflows to improve economic efficiency, especially labour productivity. Developed by Frederick Winslow Taylor in the early twentieth century, it focuses on the management of work and workers by scientifically studying tasks to design optimal work processes and incentivize performance.

Social identity: Social identity is a person's sense of who they are, based on their group membership(s). This concept from social psychology examines how group affiliations (e.g. nationality, religion, occupation) can impact an individual's behaviour and self-perception.

References

Abbott, H. 2008, *The Cambridge Introduction to Narrative*, Cambridge: Cambridge University Press.

Ahuja, S., Heizmann, H. and Clegg, S. 2018, 'Emotions and Identity Work: Emotions as Discursive Resources in the Constitution of Junior Professionals' Identities', *Human Relations* 72(5): 988–1009.

Ahuja, S., Nikolova, N. and Clegg, S. 2019, 'Professional Identity and Anxiety in Architect-Client Interactions', *Construction Management and Economics* 38(7): 589–602.

Alvesson, M. 2010, 'Self-Doubters, Strugglers, Storytellers, Surfers and Others: Images of Self-Identities in Organization Studies', *Human Relations* 63(2): 193–217.

Alvesson, M., Lee Ashcraft, K. and Thomas, R. 2008, 'Identity Matters: Reflections on the Construction of Identity Scholarship in Organization Studies', *Organization* 15(1): 5–28.

Alvesson, M. and Robertson, M. 2015, 'Money Matters: Teflonic Identity Manoeuvring in the Investment Banking Sector', *Organization Studies* 37(1): 7–34.

Alvesson, M. and Willmott, H. 2002, 'Identity Regulation as Organisational Control: Producing the Appropriate Individual', *Journal of Management Studies* 39(5): 619–44.

Archer, M. 2000, *Being Human: The Problem of Agency*, Cambridge: Cambridge University Press.

——— 2003, *Structure, Agency and the Internal Conversation*, Cambridge: Cambridge University Press.

——— 2010, 'Routine, Reflexivity and Realism', *Sociological Theory* 28(3): 272–303.

——— 2015, 'The Relational Subject and the Person: Self, Agent, and Actor', in P. Donati and M. Archer (eds), *The Relational Subject*, Cambridge: Cambridge University Press.

Archer, M., Sharp, R., Stones, R. and Woodiwiss, T. 2015, 'Critical Realism and Research Methodology', *Alethia* 2(1): 12–16.

Ashforth, B. and Mael, F. 1989, 'Social Identity Theory and the Organisation', *Academy of Management Review* 14(1): 20–39.

Baker, M. and French, E. 2018, 'Female Underrepresentation in Project-Based Organizations Exposes Organizational Isomorphism', *Equality, Diversity and Inclusion* 37(8): 799–812.

Bardon, T., Clegg, S. and Josserand, E. 2012, 'Exploring Identity Construction from a Critical Management Perspective: A Research Agenda', *Management* 15(4): 350–66.

Bardon, T. and Josserand, E. 2010, 'A Nietzschean Reading of Foucauldian Thinking: Constructing a Project of the Self within an Ontology of Becoming', *Organization* 18(4): 497–515.

Bateson, G. 2002, *Mind and Nature: A Necessary Unity*, Cresskill, NJ: Hampton Press.

Bauman, Z. 2000, *Liquid Modernity*, Cambridge: Polity Press.

Becker, E. 2010, *Birth and Death of Meaning*, New York: Free Press.
——— 2011, *The Denial of Death*, London: Souvenir Press.
Becker, H., Geer, B., Hughes, E. and Strauss, A. 1961, *Boys in White: Student Culture in Medical School*, Chicago: Chicago University Press.
Beech, N., Gilmore, C., Hibbert, P. and Ybema, S. 2016, 'Identity-in-the-Work and Musicians' Struggles: The Production of Self-Questioning Identity Work', *Work, Employment and Society* 30(3): 506–22.
Benner, P. 1982, 'From Novice to Expert', *American Journal of Nursing* 82(3): 402–7.
Berger, P. L. and Luckmann, T. 1991, *The Social Construction of Reality: A Treatise in the Sociology of Knowledge*, London: Penguin.
Berman, A. M., et al. 2001, 'The Process of Exploration in Identity Formation: The Role of Style and Competence', *Journal of Adolescence* 24(4): 513–28.
Berzonsky, M. D. 1989, 'Identity Style: Conceptualization and Measurement', *Journal of Adolescent Research* 4(3): 268–82.
Beyer, J. M. and Hannah, D. R. 2002, 'Building on the Past: Enacting Established Personal Identities in a New Work Setting', *Organization Science* 13(6): 636–52.
Bhaskar, R. 1989, *The Possibility of Naturalism*, Hemel Hempstead: Harvest Press.
Bourdieu, P. 1990, *The Logic of Practice*, Oxford: Polity Press.
Boussebaa, M. and Brown, A. D. 2017, 'Englishization, Identity Regulation and Imperialism', *Organization Studies* 38(1): 7–29.
Braidotti, R. 2011, *Nomadic Subjects: Embodiment and Sexual Difference in Contemporary Feminist Theory*, New York: Columbia University Press.
Brown, A. D. 2015, 'Identities and Identity Work in Organizations', *International Journal of Management Reviews* 17(1): 20–40.
——— 2017, 'Identity Work and Organizational Identification', *International Journal of Management Reviews* 19(3): 296–317.
——— 2018, 'Identities in Organization Studies', *Organization Studies* 40(1): 7–21.
Brown, A. D. and Starkey, K. 2000, 'Organisational Identity and Learning: A Psychodynamic Perspective', *Academy of Management Review* 25(1): 102–20.
Brown, A. D. and Toyoki, S. 2013, 'Identity Work and Legitimacy', *Organization Studies* 34(7): 875–96.
Bryman, A. and Bryman, D. S. S. A. 2013, *Social Research Methods*, Oxford: Oxford University Press.
Buckle, P. and Thomas, J. 2003, 'Deconstructing Project Management: A Gender Analysis of Project Management Guidelines', *International Journal of Project Management* 21(6): 433–41.
Burner, J. S. 2009, *Actual Minds, Possible Worlds*, Cambridge, MA: Harvard University Press.
Burr, V. 2003, *Social Constructionism*, Hove: Routledge.
Butler, J. 2011, *Gender Trouble: Feminism and the Subversion of Identity*, Hoboken, NJ: Taylor & Francis.
Caetano, A. 2014, 'Defining Personal Reflexivity: A Critical Reading of Archer's Approach', *European Journal of Social Theory* 18(1): 60–75.
——— 2016, 'Coping with Life: A Typology of Personal Reflexivity', *Sociological Quarterly* 58(1): 32–50.
Casey, C. 1995, *Work, Self, and Society*, London: Routledge.
Cerulo, K. A. 1997, 'Identity Construction: New Issues, New Directions', *Annual Review of Sociology* 23: 385–409.
Charmaz, K. 2014, *Constructing Grounded Theory*, London: Sage.

Chasserio, S. and Legault, M.-J. 2009, 'Strategic Human Resources Management is Irrelevant When It Comes to Highly Skilled Professionals in the Canadian New Economy', *International Journal of Human Resource Management* 20(5): 1113–31.

——— 2010, 'Discretionary Power of Project Managers in Knowledge-Intensive Firms and Gender Issues', *Canadian Journal of Administrative Sciences/Revue Canadienne des Sciences de l'Administration* 27(3): 236–48.

Chopra, D. 2019, *Metahuman: Unleashing Your Infinite Potential*, London: Ebury.

Cicmil, S. 2006, 'Understanding Project Management Practice through Interpretative and Critical Research Perspectives', *Project Management Journal* 37(2): 27–37.

Clark, A. 2013, 'Whatever Next? Predictive Brains, Situated Agents, and the Future of Cognitive Science', *Behavioral and Brain Sciences* 36(3): 181–204.

Clarke, C. A., Brown, A. D. and Hailey, V. H. 2009, 'Working Identities? Antagonistic Discursive Resources and Managerial Identity', *Human Relations* 62(3): 323–52.

Clegg, S. 1975, *Power, Rule and Domination: A Critical and Empirical Understanding of Power in Sociological Theory and Organisational Life*, London: Routledge and Kegan Paul.

Clegg, S. and Courpasson, D. 2004, 'Political Hybrids: Tocquevillean Views on Project Organizations', *Journal of Management Studies* 41(4): 525–47.

Clegg, S. R., Skyttermoen, T. and Vaagaasar, A.-L. 2020, *Project Management: A Value Creation Approach*, Los Angeles: Sage.

Cohn, H. W. 2002, *Heidegger and the Roots of Existential Therapy*, London: Continuum.

Collinson, D. L. 2003, 'Identities and Insecurities: Selves at Work', *Organization* 10(3): 527–47.

Collinson, D. L. and Hearn, J. 1998, 'Men as Managers, Managers as Men: Critical Perspectives on Men, Masculinities and Managements', *Capital & Class* 22(2): 191–93.

Comte, A. 1830, *Cours de philosophie positive*, Paris: Bachelier.

Corlett, P. R. and Fletcher, P. C. 2015, 'Delusions and Prediction Error: Clarifying the Roles of Behavioural and Brain Responses', *Cognitive Neuropsychiatry* 20(2): 95–105.

Corlett, S., McInnes, P., Coupland, C. and Sheep, M. 2017, 'Exploring the Registers of Identity Research', *International Journal of Management Reviews* 19(3): 261–72.

Costas, J. and Fleming, P. 2009, 'Beyond Dis-Identification: A Discursive Approach to Self-Alienation in Contemporary Organizations', *Human Relations* 62(3): 353–78.

Crang, M. and Cook, I. 2007, *Doing Ethnographies*, London: Sage.

Czarniawska, B. 2007, *Shadowing: And Other Techniques for Doing Fieldwork in Modern Societies*, Malmö: Liber.

D'Alessandro, M., Radev, S., Voss, A. and Lombardi, L. 2020, 'A Bayesian Brain Model of Adaptive Behavior: An Application to the Wisconsin Card Sorting Task', *PeerJ* 8: e10316.

Deetz, S. A. 1994, 'The Micro-Politics of Identity Formation in the Workplace: The Case of a Knowledge Intensive Firm', *Human Studies* 17(1): 23–44.

Dispenza, J. 2012, *Breaking the Habit of Being Yourself*, Carlsbad, CA: Hay House.

Dostal, R. J. 1993, 'Time and Phenomenology in Husserl and Heidegger', in C. Guignon (ed.), *The Cambridge Companion to Heidegger*, Cambridge: Cambridge University Press.

Down, S. and Reveley, J. 2009, 'Between Narration and Interaction: Situating First-Line Supervisor Identity Work', *Human Relations* 62(3): 379–401.

Dreyfus, S. E. and Dreyfus, H. L. 1980, *A Five-Stage Model of the Mental Activities Involved in Directed Skill Acquisition*, Berkeley: University of Berkeley Operations Research Center.

Driver, M. 2013, 'The Lack of Power or the Power of Lack in Leadership as a Discursively Constructed Identity', *Organization Studies* 34(3): 407–22.

Drouin, N., Müller, R., Sankaran, S. and Vaagaasar, A.-L. 2021, 'Balancing Leadership in Projects: Role of the Socio-Cognitive Space', *Project Leadership and Society* 2: 100031.

Ellis, N. and Ybema, S. 2010, 'Marketing Identities: Shifting Circles of Identification in Inter-Organizational Relationships', *Organization Studies* 31(3): 279–305.

Ezzy, D. 2016, 'Theorizing Narrative Identity: Symbolic Interactionism and Hermeneutics', *Sociological Quarterly* 39(2): 239–52.

Fairclough, N. 1993, *Discourse and Social Change*, Oxford: Wiley.

——— 2013, *Critical Discourse Analysis: The Critical Study of Language*, London: Taylor & Francis.

Fetterman, D. M. 2010, *Ethnography: Step-by-Step*, Thousand Oaks, CA: Sage.

Fields, C., et al. 2018, 'Conscious Agent Networks: Formal Analysis and Application to Cognition', *Cognitive Systems Research* 47: 186–213.

Fletcher, A. J. 2016, 'Applying Critical Realism in Qualitative Research: Methodology Meets Method', *International Journal of Social Research Methodology* 20(2): 181–94.

Flyvbjerg, B. and Sampson, S. 2001, *Making Social Science Matter: Why Social Inquiry Fails and How It Can Succeed Again*, Cambridge: Cambridge University Press.

Foucault, M. 1980, *Power/Knowledge: Selected Interviews and Other Writings, 1972–1977*, New York: Pantheon.

Foucault, M. and Sheridan, A. 2002, *Archaeology of Knowledge*, London: Routledge.

French, E., Lloyd-Walker, B. and Crawford, L. 2013, 'Changing Times, Persistent Paradigms: Women and Men at Work in Projects', *Biannual International Research Network on Organising by Projects (IRNOP) Research Conference (11th)*.

Gabriel, Y. 2000, *Storytelling in Organizations: Facts, Fictions, Fantasies*, Oxford: Oxford University Press.

Gadamer, H. G. 1975, *Truth and Method*, New York: Seabury Press.

Gale, A. and Cartwright, S. 1995, 'Women in Project Management: Entry into a Male Domain? A Discussion on Gender and Organizational Culture – Part 1', *Leadership and Organization Development Journal* 16(2): 3–8.

Gibbs, P. and McRoy, I. 2006, 'Dwelling at Work: A Place Where Vocation and Identity Could Grow?', *Journal of Further and Higher Education* 30(3): 283–93.

Giddens, A. 2013, *Modernity and Self-Identity: Self and Society in the Late Modern Age*, Hoboken, NJ: Wiley.

Gill, M. J. 2013, 'Elite Identity and Status Anxiety: An Interpretive Phenomenological Analysis of Management Consultants', *Organization* 22(3): 306–25.

——— 2014, 'The Possibilities of Phenomenology for Organizational Research', *Organizational Research Methods* 17(2): 118–37.

——— 2015, 'A Phenomenology of Feeling: Examining the Experience of Emotion in Organizations', *Research on Emotions in Organizations* 11: 29–50.

Giorgi, S. and Palmisano, S. 2017, 'Sober Intoxication: Institutional Contradictions and Identity Work in the Everyday Life of Four Religious Communities in Italy', *Organization Studies* 38(6): 795–819.

Grant, D., Hardy, C., Oswick, C. and Putnam, L. 2004, *The SAGE Handbook of Organizational Discourse*, London: Sage.

Grey, C. 2005, *A Very Short, Fairly Interesting and Reasonably Cheap Book about Studying Organizations*, London: Sage.

Grotevant, H. D. 1987, 'Toward a Process Model of Identity Formation', *Journal of Adolescent Research* 2(3): 203–22.

Harnad, R. S. and Skinner, F. B. 1988, *The Selection of Behavior: The Operant Behaviorism of B. F. Skinner: Comments and Consequences*, Cambridge: Cambridge University Press.

Harvey, L. J. and Myers, M. D. 1995, 'Scholarship and Practice: The Contribution of Ethnographic Research Methods to Bridging the Gap', *Information Technology & People* 8(3): 13–27.

Haslam, A. 2004, *Psychology of Organisations*, London: Sage.

Haslam, A., Cornelissen, J. and Werner, M. 2017, 'Metatheories and Metaphors of Organizational Identity: Integrating Social Constructionist, Social Identity, and Social Actor Perspectives within a Social Interactionist Model', *International Journal of Management Reviews* 19(3): 318–36.

Heath, S. 1972, *The Nouveau Roman: A Study in the Practice of Writing*, London: Elek.

Heidegger, M. 1953, *Being and Time*, Albany, NY: State University of New York Press.

Heizmann, H. 2011, 'Knowledge Sharing in a Dispersed Network of HR Practice: Zooming in on Power/Knowledge Struggles', *Management Learning* 42(4): 379–93.

Herman, D. (ed.) 2003, *Narrative Theory and the Cognitive Sciences*, Chicago: University of Chicago Press.

Higgins, E. T. 1987, 'Self-Discrepancy: A Theory Relating Self and Affect', *Psychological Review* 94(3): 319–40.

Hoyer, P. and Steyaert, C. 2015, 'Narrative Identity Construction in Times of Career Change: Taking Note of Unconscious Desires', *Human Relations* 68(12): 1837–63.

Husserl, E. 1970, *The Crisis of European Sciences and Transcendental Phenomenology*, Evanston, IL: Northwestern University Press.

——— 1982, *Ideas Pertaining to a Pure Phenomenology and to a Phenomenological Philosophy*, Dordrecht: Kluwer.

Ibarra, H. 1999, 'Provisional Selves: Experimenting with Image and Identity in Professional Adaptation', *Administrative Science Quarterly* 44(4): 764–91.

Ibarra, H. and Barbulescu, R. 2010, 'Identity as Narrative: Prevalence, Effectiveness, and Consequences of Narrative Identity Work in Macro Work Role Transitions', *Academy of Management Journal* 35(1): 135–54.

Jung, C. G. 1933, *Modern Man in Search of a Soul*, New York: Houghton Mifflin Harcourt.

——— 1957, *The Undiscovered Self*, New York: Penguin.

——— 1959, *Aion: Research into the Phenomenology of the Self*, New York: Routledge.

——— 1966, *Collected Works of C.G. Jung: Two Essays in Analytical Psychology*, Princeton, NJ: Princeton University Press.

Kant, I. and Meiklejohn, J. M. D. 2018, *Critique of Pure Reason*, Mineola, NY: Dover.

Karreman, D. and Alvesson, M. 2001, 'Making Newsmakers: Conversational Identity at Work', *Organisation Studies* 22(1): 59–89.

Kaufman, J. M. and Johnson, C. 2004, 'Stigmatized Individuals and the Process of Identity', *Sociological Quarterly* 45(4): 807–33.

Knights, D. and Clarke, C. A. 2017, 'Pushing the Boundaries of Amnesia and Myopia: A Critical Review of Literature on Identity in Management and Organization Studies', *International Journal of Management Reviews* 19: 337–56.

Knights, D. and Willmott, H. 1989, 'Power and Subjectivity at Work: From Degradation to Subjugation in Social Relations', *Sociology* 23(4): 535–58.

Koveshnikov, A., Vaara, E. and Ernrooth, M. 2016, 'Stereotype-Based Managerial Identity Work in Multinational Corporations', *Organization Studies* 37(9): 1353–79.

Kuhn, T. 2006, 'A "Demented Work Ethic" and a "Lifestyle Firm": Discourse, Identity, and Workplace Time Commitments', *Organization Studies* 27(9): 1339–58.

Lacan, J. 2006, *Ecrits: The First Complete Edition in English*, New York: W.W. Norton.

Lacan, J. and Miller, J. A. 2018, *The Four Fundamental Concepts of Psycho-Analysis*, London: Taylor & Francis.

Lanza, R. 2009, *Biocentrism: How Life and Consciousness Are the Keys to Understanding the True Nature of the Universe*, Dallas: BenBella.

Leary, T. 1977, *Exo-Psychology: A Manual on the Use of the Human Nervous System According to the Instructions of the Manufacturers*, Los Angeles: Starseed/Peace Press.

Lindgren, M. and Packendorff, J. 2006, 'What's New in New Forms of Organizing? On the Construction of Gender in Project-Based Work', *Journal of Management Studies* 43(4): 841–66.

Lonergan, B. 1992, *Insight: A Study of Human Understanding*, Toronto: Lonergan Research Institute.

Love, P. E. and Edwards, D. J. 2005, 'Taking the Pulse of UK Construction Project Managers' Health: Influence of Job Demands, Job Control and Social Support on Psychological Wellbeing', *Engineering, Construction and Architectural Management* 12(1): 88–101.

Lum, G. 2003, 'Towards a Richer Conception of Vocational Preparation', *Journal of Philosophy of Education* 37(1): 1–15.

Marks, A. and O'Mahoney, J. 2014, 'Researching Identity: A Critical Realist Approach', in P. Edwards, J. O'Mahoney and S. Vincent (eds), *Studying Organizations Using Critical Realism: A Practical Guide*, Oxford: Oxford University Press.

May, T. and Perry, B. 2017, *Reflexivity: The Essential Guide*, London: Sage.

McAdams, D. P. 1993, *The Stories We Live By: Personal Myths and the Making of the Self*, New York: Guilford Press.

McHugh, P. 1971, 'On the Failure of Positivism', in J. Douglas, *Understanding Everyday Life: Toward the Reconstruction of Sociological Knowledge*, London: Routledge and Kegan Paul.

Miles, M. B. and Hubermann, M. A. 2014, *Qualitative Data Analysis: A Method Sourcebook*, Thousand Oaks, CA: Sage.

Mills, C. W. 1959, *The Sociological Imagination*, New York: Oxford University Press.

Miscenko, D. and Day, D. V. 2016, 'Identity and Identification at Work', *Organizational Psychology Review* 6(3): 215–47.

Müller, R., Vaagaasar, A. L., Nikolova, N., Sankaran, S. and Drouin, N. 2015, 'The Socio-Cognitive Space for Linking Horizontal and Vertical Leadership', in *Proceedings of the APROS/EGOS Conference 2015*, 9–11 December, Sydney, Australia.

Müller, M., Jedličková, L. and Halová, D. 2022, 'How Do Managers Make Sense of Their Crisis? Disrupted Relationships and Rediscovering Co-Existence', *Human Arenas*, https://doi.org/10.1007/s42087-022-00272-z.

Nagel, T. 1989, *The View from Nowhere*, New York: Oxford University Press.

Nietzsche, F. 1973, *Beyond Good and Evil*, London: Penguin Classics.

——— 2001, *The Gay Science*, Cambridge: Cambridge University Press.

——— 2018, *The Will to Power*, Vachendorf: Jovian Press.

O'Mahoney, J. 2011, 'Critical Realism and the Self', *Journal of Critical Realism* 10(1): 122–29.

Panksepp, J. 2005, *Affective Neuroscience: The Foundations of Human and Animal Emotions*, New York: Oxford University Press.

Parsons, T. and Turner, B. S. 1991, *The Social System*, London: Routledge.

Peterson, J. 1999, *Maps of Meaning: The Architecture of Belief*, New York: Routledge.

——— 2018, *12 Rules for Life: An Antidote to Chaos*, London: Penguin.

Polkinghorne, D. E. 2010, *Narrative Knowing and the Human Sciences*, Albany, NY: State University of New York Press.

Porpora, D. V. 1989, 'Four Concepts of Social Structure', *Journal for the Theory of Social Behaviour* 19(2): 195–211.

Potter, J. 2002, 'Two Kinds of Natural', *Discourse Studies* 4(4): 539–42.

Pratt, M. G., Rockmann, K. and Kaufmann, J. 2006, 'Constructing Professional Identity: The Role of Work and Identity Learning Cycles in the Customization of Identity among Medical Residents', *Academy of Management Journal* 49(2): 235–62.

Rolfe, B., Segal, S. and Cicmil, S. 2017, 'The Wisdom of Conversations: Existential Hermeneutic Phenomenology (EHP) for Project Managers', *International Journal of Project Management* 35(5): 739–48.

Sarbin, T. R. 1986, *Narrative Psychology: The Storied Nature of Human Conduct*, New York: Praeger.

Sartre, J.-P. 2018, *Being and Nothingness: An Essay in Phenomenological Ontology*, Abingdon: Routledge.

Schutz, A. 1945, 'On Multiple Realities', *Philosophy and Phenomenological Research* 5(4): 533–76.

——— 1967, *The Phenomenology of the Social World*, Evanston, IL: Northwestern University Press.

Sennett, R. 2011, *The Corrosion of Character: The Personal Consequences of Work in the New Capitalism*, New York: W. W. Norton.

Sewchurran, K. and Brown, I. 2011, 'Toward an Approach to Generate Forward-Looking Theories Using Systems Concepts', in M. Chiasson, O. Henfridsson, H. Karsten, J. I. DeGross (eds), *Researching the Future in Information Systems*, Berlin: Springer.

Sharp, D. 1991, *Jung Lexicon: A Primer of Terms & Concepts*, Toronto: Inner City Books.

Silverman, D. 2013, *A Very Short, Fairly Interesting and Reasonably Cheap Book about Qualitative Research*, London: Sage.

——— 2017, *Doing Qualitative Research*, London: Sage.

Smith, J. A., Flowers, P. and Larkin, M. 2009, *Interpretive Phenomenological Analysis: Theory, Method and Research*, London: Sage.

Smith, N. K. 2008, *Immanuel Kant's Critique of Pure Reason*, London: Macmillan.

Snow, D. and Anderson, L. 1987, 'Identity Work among the Homeless: The Verbal Construction and Avowal of Personal Identities', *American Journal of Sociology* 92(6): 1336–71.

Strauss, A. and Corbin, J. M. 1998, *Basics of Qualitative Research: Techniques and Procedures for Developing Grounded Theory*, Thousand Oaks, CA: Sage.

Sveningsson, S. and Alvesson, M. 2003, 'Managing Managerial Identities: Organisational Fragmentation, Discourse and Identity Struggle', *Human Relations* 56(10): 1163–93.

Tajfel, H. and Turnet, J. C. 1986, 'The Social Identity Theory of Intergroup Behaviour', in S. Worchel and W. G. Austin (eds), *Psychology of Intergroup Relations*, Chicago: Hall.

Tavory, I. and Timmermans, S. 2014, *Abductive Analysis: Theorizing Qualitative Research*, Chicago: University of Chicago Press.

Thomas, R. and Davies, A. 2005, 'Theorizing the Micro-Politics of Resistance: New Public Management and Managerial Identities in the UK Public Services', *Organization Studies* 26(5): 683–706.

Thornborrow, T. and Brown, A. D. 2009, '"Being Regimented": Aspiration, Discipline and Identity Work in the British Parachute Regiment', *Organization Studies* 30(4): 355–76.

Trethewey, A. 1999, 'Disciplined Bodies: Women's Embodied Identities at Work', *Organization Studies* 20(3): 423–50.

Van der Hoorn, B. and Whitty, S. J. 2019, 'The Five Modes of Comportment for Project Managing: Disclosing the Tacit in Project Work', *International Journal of Project Management* 37(3): 363–77.

Velmans, M. 1999, 'Intersubjective Science', *Journal of Consciousness Studies* 6(23): 299–306.

Vough, H. 2012, 'Not All Identifications Are Created Equal: Exploring Employee Accounts for Workgroup, Organizational, and Professional Identification', *Organization Science* 23(3): 778–800.

Waley, A. 2013, *The Way and Its Power: A Study of the Tao Tê Ching and Its Place in Chinese Thought*, Abingdon: Taylor & Francis.

Watson, T. J. 2008, 'Managing Identity: Identity Work, Personal Predicaments and Structural Circumstances', *Organization* 15(1): 121–43.

Watts, A. 1951, *The Wisdom of Insecurity: A Message for an Age of Anxiety*, New York: Pantheon.

Weber, M. 1968, *Economy and Society: An Outline of Interpretive Sociology*, New York: Bedminster Press.

Weedon, C. 1987, *Feminist Practice and Poststructuralist Theory*, Oxford: Blackwell.

Weick, K. E. 1995, *Sensemaking in Organisations*. Thousand Oaks, CA: Sage.

Wetherell, M., Taylor, S. and Yates, S. 2001, *Discourse as Data: A Guide for Analysis*, London: Sage.

Wilson, R. A. 2016, *Prometheus Rising*, Grand Junction, CO: Hilaritas Press.

Winkler, I. 2018, 'Identity Work and Emotions: A Review', *International Journal of Management Reviews* 20(1): 120–33.

Wittgenstein, L. 1968, *Philosophical Investigations*, Oxford: Blackwell.

Wright, C., Nyberg, D. and Grant, D. 2012, '"Hippies on the Third Floor": Climate Change, Narrative Identity and the Micro-Politics of Corporate Environmentalism', *Organization Studies* 33(11): 1451–75.

Ybema, S., Keenoy, T., Oswick, C., Beverungen, A., Ellis, N. and Sabelis, I. 2009, 'Articulating Identities', *Human Relations* 62(3): 299–322.

Index

www.ingramcontent.com/pod-product-compliance
Ingram Content Group UK Ltd.
Pitfield, Milton Keynes, MK11 3LW, UK
UKHW021825130926
8597IPUK00004B/13

9 781805 398042